GOOD COMPANY

'GOOD COMPANY,

*An anthropological study
of old people in groups*

DOROTHY JERROME

EDINBURGH UNIVERSITY PRESS

© Dorothy Jerrome, 1992

Edinburgh University Press
22 George Square, Edinburgh

Typeset in Linotron Baskerville
by Koinonia Ltd, Bury, and
printed in Great Britain by
The University Press, Cambridge

A CIP record for this book is available
from the British Library.

ISBN 0 7486 0374 3

Contents

Contents   vii

Tables and Figures

Acknowledgements

This book is the culmination of several years' work on sociability in old age. I am grateful to the Nuffield Foundation which made the first piece of research possible in 1980, and to the Economic and Social Research Council (Grant No. G01250005) which allowed me to consolidate my knowledge and develop new areas of interest in 1985/6. I acknowledge an intellectual debt to a number of social gerontologists - principally in Britain and North America - whose work stimulated me and offered legitimation for my own (then unfashionable) concerns. Their work has been referred to in the text.

There have been other sources of support. At annual conferences of the British Society of Gerontology I have come to feel part of a professional peer group. In a fragmented field whose adherents pursue their intellectual concerns in relative isolation, such meetings have been valuable in establishing affinities on the basis of shared subject interests and methodology. I am grateful to those conference participants, too numerous to mention, who have been receptive to my ideas about friendship and have helped to establish a climate of acceptance towards qualitative research on ageing. Reference to the professional peer group would be incomplete without mention of Professor Margot Jefferys whose support and encouragement as Project Officer of the Economic and Social Research Council Research Initiative on Ageing have been invaluable.

A third set of colleagues to whom I owe thanks are the numerous social workers and other practitioners at conferences and seminars who have individually assured me of the value of my ideas, asked for copies of papers, and pressed for dissemination of the research findings. Affirmative comments which have inspired me to produce this book ranged from that of the social worker in 1980 who told me with some emotion that in my material on friendship she had recognised herself, to an anxious German research worker (a nurse) in 1987 seeking guidance on the use of qualitative methods in what she felt was a totally uncharted area.

Thanks are also due to my students over the years. I include those in Adult Education classes who permitted me to share their concerns and acquire an understanding of what it means to be an ageing person in Britain. Some of them became informants in a formal sense in 1980. Another set of students have been those on professional courses – social workers, nurses, health visitors – who allowed me to test my ideas on them and were receptive to my suggestions.

The research could not have been accomplished without the help of the many older people whose experiences are documented here. To those people who generously gave their time, attention, energy and goodwill I am most grateful. Finally, I must thank Tony Becher, my best critic and greatest support, whose editorial skills were brought to bear to my great benefit on earlier drafts of this book.

Preface

The research which is reported in the following pages was conducted in 1985. My interest in the ageing process had developed much earlier. Since 1976 I had been teaching extra-mural classes for the University of Sussex in a part of the country known for its concentrations of retired people. My students were generally fit, active and reasonably affluent. As their needs and preoccupations became apparent, I was struck by several features. One was their sensitivity to the issue of age, and feeling of social distance from younger people as a result of the age gap. This distance was poignantly expressed by a woman of 80 who had joined a class on transitions from birth to death. Speaking of old age, she remarked sadly, 'You feel like a ghost; no one looks you in the eye'. In the protected environment of the classroom, interaction was intense and vibrant. One could imagine that the intensity with which these older people existed for each other at their weekly meetings was in sharp contrast to their social neglect at other times and to some extent compensated for it. Another feature which impressed me was the strength of attachment to friends and partners and sense of solidarity with members of the peer group. A persistent problem seemed to be that of replacing ties severed by retirement, ill-health, migration and death. Friends were relatively easy to make but to acquire a new heterosexual partner involved courtship procedures geared to youth, and cultural stereotypes weighed against the presentation of self in old age as attractive and marriageable. In my own family, a series of unsuccessful courtships by an elderly relative drew my attention in a powerful way to the operation of age norms which restrict the possibilities for intimacy in later life.

For women the problem seemed to be compounded by a shortage of potential partners. The circle of eligible spouses had contracted long before the onset of middle age but the need for a new partner was relatively recent, a product of bereavement or occasionally divorce. The requirement to replace a partner came at a time when they were least well equipped to satisfy it. The adjustment to singlehood in a couple-oriented society struck me as interesting and problematic. Equally intriguing were the strategies of those people who actively sought new partners. In both cases, the attitudes and support of friends appeared to be crucial.

As my interest developed, so did my commitment to educational work with older people and those concerned with their welfare. I became involved in pre- and post-retirement education and provided courses in social gerontology for student social workers and nurses, and other groups of professionals. As my knowledge of the field developed so did my awareness of the dearth of literature on life in retirement. Such material as there was offered a particular view which suffered from the limitations mentioned earlier. The literature on friendship, for instance, was largely restricted to the scope of networks and the social backgrounds of people in dyadic relationships. With the exception of the few studies which focused specifically on intimacy or confidant relationships, the concept of 'friend' was used uncritically. Even where it was carefully defined, the researcher's concept was imposed on respondents in the context of a formal interview situation which took little account of the range of subjective meanings attached to the term.

I began to feel that a sensitive and poorly-conceptualised issue such as friendship called for intensive methods of investigation rather than a social survey approach. A qualitative approach seemed the best way to discover the meanings attached to friendship and its role in the lives of older people. With help from the Nuffield Foundation in 1980 I was able to give expression to these convictions, and carried out research on the significance of friendship in later life. The results have appeared in a number of publications which are listed in the bibliography. The research was valuable in confirming the suggestion of American gerontologists that friends provide particular kinds of support in the ageing process and that old friends have special significance. My study produced evidence of some older women's capacity to make new friends and of others' failure to do so. I related this capacity to their ideas about themselves as ageing individuals (Jerrome 1981). It seemed that gender, social class and ideas about age were crucial variables though I was not able to do more than advance this as a hypothesis at the time (Jerrome 1983, 1984).

I concluded that friends play a part in the acceptance of physical ageing, in the management of transitions such as retirement and widowhood, and in coping with such age-related losses as youthful appearance, health and fitness, of home, kin and other friends. I found that friends played a role in caring for elderly relatives and other family-related activities such as counselling adult children with marital problems (Jerrome 1981). It seemed that between old friends there is a tendency to forget, or deny, the passage of time. Old friends, with a shared past, provide continuity. An old friend is cherished as someone who has known one in better times and can accept one on one's own terms, rather than in terms of negative stereotypes. But new friends also have a part to play in the construction of new lifestyles and identities. Values and attitudes which in contemporary terms are dated can be freely expressed with people whose life-span has given them comparable experiences and outlook. Between them, friends old and new provide a variety of services, support and company. But old friends contribute something unique to the acceptance of ageing and adjustment to changing circumstance.

Despite these insights, the research raised more questions than it answered. I had concentrated on women, and middle-class women at that. I now wanted to know about the expression of sociability in other groups: working-class women, and men. According to the literature, friend relationships vary by gender and social class. The next item on the research agenda, therefore, was a study of patterns of friendship in a broader section of the retired population. It is that research, funded by the Economic and Social Research Council in 1985, which is the subject of this book.

Several years have elapsed since completing the field-work and analysis of the material. In that time my thinking has developed, particularly in relation to social class and gender. Questions I would now want to ask cannot be answered within the framework I adopted then. I have tried to compensate for this in the final version of the analysis but not entirely successfully. If the study were to be conducted again I would approach it differently.

Dorothy Jerrome

ONE

Introduction

It is often thought that older people, who in Britain are not part of the work-force and whose links to the community have become attenuated, are socially disengaged. This book is about those elders, a significant minority, who are firmly embedded in networks of friends and associates. They share a lifestyle: they are joiners. Their time is taken up, to a large extent, with their various clubs and associations. In these pages I examine the behaviour of old people in groups. I view social processes in the elderly peer group through the lens of social anthropology. I focus on the conversations, routines and rituals of the everyday life of old people in the company of their peers. The assumption is that other people provide the social context for ageing, and that those people have ideas about ageing which influence the self-concept of ageing individuals and set limits on individual behaviour. Further, I suggest that the attitudes of people chosen as companions on the journey through time – friends and members of voluntary organisations – are especially significant. They are generally at the same stage of development, for people normally choose to associate with others most like themselves in terms of age, sex and other basic attributes: voluntary association occurs mainly between peers (Fry 1980). Peers in age have similar expectations based on a shared past, and – in contemporary western cultures – the same need for help in the interpretation of currently ill-defined rules of age-related behaviour. Together, peers can be observed setting standards for behaviour, monitoring each other's performance and judging those who deviate from collectively established norms.

My aim in showing the vital role played by members of the peer group in the ageing process has been to broaden the debate about old age. It is well known that western industrial societies are ageing. The age structure is changing, with a larger proportion of people being over the retirement age now than at the turn of the century. Within the retired population, the oldest old are increasing at the fastest rate of all. The common response to this demographic shift is alarm and despondency. Ageing societies are thought to face a future burdened by legions of frail and dependent old people, their frailty in direct proportion to their numbers in the popula-tion. But the picture has been exaggerated. The occasional lone voice of the historian or demographer can be heard warning against viewing the ageing of future cohorts of old people in the light of contemporary experience. A close study of the early years of successive birth cohorts and their lives in adulthood and old age prompts the conclusion that people are ageing differently; that talk of the growing burden of the elderly is based partly on ignorance of the ageing process. People are staying fit for longer (Jefferys 1987; Pifer 1987). Successive cohorts are socially more active and involved. Their community and friendship roles are more extensive (Pohjolainen 1987) and they are increasingly likely to be embedded in kinship networks as the rate of marriage and incidence of parenthood have increased (Timaeus 1986). Their educational standards continue to improve (Jones 1980, 1986). Their affluence and capacity for economic involvement has increased – as their opportunities for it have diminished (Thane 1987; Phillipson 1982). The decrements associated with extreme old age have not diminished and probably never will, but their onset comes at a progressively later age (Svanborg 1987). In some quarters the hope is expressed that eventually, by careful management of personal resources, they may be avoided altogether (Laslett 1984; Coni 1983). But there is no scientific evidence to support this optimistic view. What is clear, however, is that the legions of elderly people whose existence can be anticipated with certainty will, as far as we can tell, be healthier and more active, better off, better educated and socially more connected than equivalent cohorts today.

In spite of these advances, the ageing of society has been greeted as a negative phenomenon. The fact that more people are achieving great ages is regarded not as cause for celebration but for concern. The tendency to view long life as a social problem rests in part on the measurement of social worth in western industrial societies. Productivity, measured in terms of work performance in paid employment, is a major ingredient of status, and those whose productivity can be demonstrated are valued more highly than those who are apparently unproductive. A correlate of productivity – earning power and the capacity to consume – works the same way. Old age is problematic also as an experience remote from the youthful majority. It is kept remote by a variety of social and psychological mechanisms: institutional segregation, the existence of age boundaries in informal contexts such as friendship, and the denial of the possibility of ageing oneself.

The distancing occurs even among those who work with and study older people. Academic research on old age reflects the personal views of its perpetrators. The assumptions that old people are different are disguised behind highly sophisticated intellectual formulations but are there nonetheless. Theoretical assumptions in the literature betray the youthful orientation of the writers. The lives and needs of the old are perceived from a middle-aged point of view in which old age lacks social roles, resources and reference groups. In this presumed state of deprivation old people are vulnerable to disorientation and depression. There is an obligation on everyone else to make up for the loss of normative guidance and shrinkage of roles which afflicts the elderly population, to revalue old age and create roles which will restore the lost sense of purpose and meaning (Kuypers and Bengtson 1976). The view that old age is a time of rolelessness enjoyed widespread support in North America in the 1970s and continues to influence work on old age. The essence of the view is expressed in Rosow's memorable passage:

> The loss of role excludes the aged from significant social participation and devalues them. It deprives them of vital functions that underlie their sense of worth, their self-conceptions and self-esteem ... Because society does not specify an aged role, the lives of the elderly are socially unstructured ... They have no significant norms for restructuring their lives. There are no meaningful prescriptions for new goals and experience, no directions to salvation that occasionally accompany sin, loss or failure at younger ages ... Because they lack major responsibilities, society does not specify a role for the aged and their lives become socially unstructured. This is a gross discontinuity for which they are not socialised, and role loss deprives them of their very social identity. (Rosow 1976, pp 466–7)

In the generation of gerontologists writing in the mid-1970s the debate about roles focused on the possible emergence of subcultures of the aged with their own group consciousness. The emergence was dismissed as unlikely, on the evidence of an almost complete absence of formal, institutional provision by and for old people acting collectively in a political context. The writers' perspective was limited to what they could observe and measure, and what their particular views of old age told them would be worth pursuing. In the absence of an appropriate theoretical framework and methodology, no questions were asked about alternatives, and no evidence was produced. There was no incentive, therefore, to assume the existence of informally organised groupings of old people with their own roles and role expectations.

No longer is the concept of rolelessness, which had dominated gerontological research in North America for three decades, automatically applied to the later years of life (Dowd 1980). Indeed, the notion of old age being without social roles now seems nonsensical. Old people are encountered as family members, as neighbours, as consumers, as voters and so on. Moreover, the existence of social roles and age-specific norms of behaviour generated by the elderly peer group itself is widely suspected. But with rare exceptions their content remains a mystery.

Although ideas within the social sciences have moved on, the identification of issues and solutions to problems in old age is still restricted by limited and sometimes ageist perspectives. The negative orientation to old age still emerges in the intellectual concerns of gerontologists in Britain. In the currently fashionable 'catastrophic position' (Gutmann 1987) ageing is the tragic extension of active life. The old are victims of social forces which contribute to their dependent status. The literature is dominated by accounts of poverty and dependence. It focuses on issues of social policy and welfare, the provision of services, the maintenance of income levels, the solution to problems of poor housing, social isolation and physical frailty. The research problem is defined in terms of need; the data base is the needy. The 'silent majority' of elderly people who are independent and self-supporting are not featured, are not of interest and, if the literature is taken to reflect reality, hardly exist.

The methods used to acquire information are such that the subjective experience of ageing is subordinated to objective accounts provided by youthful researchers. The meaning of ageing as it is defined by participants is obscured. Very little contemporary research addresses the issues of ageing from the elderly person's point of view. Authors tend to be concerned with objective realities – those features which are easily measured. Social research on ageing is conducted within the conventional sociological research paradigm, with its emphasis on definitional rigour, hypothesis-testing and quantification. The over reliance on survey methods of investigation and statistical techniques in the analysis of data ignores the uniqueness of the individual ageing experience. It also offers a view of ageing which is static and ahistorical, ignoring as it does the expectations brought to the situation by elderly people whose experiences span many decades of change.

This book attempts to fill some of the gaps in our knowledge of the ageing process. It contributes to a view of old age which counters the common conception of the elderly as a burden. It offers a salutary reminder of the vigour and resilience of the majority who lead an independent existence. It offers an insight into what might be called 'normal ageing' as distinct from the pathological experience of the few in receipt of services, casualties of the welfare state. It goes beyond the majority of contemporary accounts in attending first to subjective experience. The analysis is guided by the meanings attached to relationships and events by the elderly partici-pants in the study.

This is a book about old women, and a few old men, though for the most part the issues are presented as those of old age as such. Gender has not often been addressed directly in studies of ageing. Early work, often arising from studies of the impact of retirement from paid work, reflected a masculine bias in ignoring women's experience. It would be easy to slip into the opposite framework of assumptions, given that the majority of retired people are women, and discuss ageing as an exclusively female experience.

Feminist consciousness demands attention to gender differences in age-ing. This involves taking account of the distinctiveness of experience for old men and women. It means acknowledging sexist bias in cultural construc-tions of ageing and in social gerontology itself. This book does not offer a feminist analysis but it goes some way towards identifying the different experiences of women and men in the context of peer relationships and sociability. It draws attention to some gerontologists' limited treatment of women.

The emphasis on peer relationships is also timely. Whereas at the turn of the century relatively few people survived to old age, one is more likely than ever before to age in the company of peers. In the late twentieth century successive cohorts move through time more or less intact until the retirement years, when deaths from a variety of age-related conditions begin to accelerate. Elderly peers provide a powerful reference group, a community of interest and supportive network. The possibility that elderly contemporaries might offer role models, socialisation experiences and social control in the manner of the adolescent peer group has been generally overlooked. Some gerontologists drew attention to the need for research on 'normal ageing' in general and the process of 'community formation' in the elderly peer group in particular, as early as the mid-1970s, but interest is just now beginning to develop.

The emerging interest in the lives of fit and active older people – those defined as 'young old' in the literature – over the last ten years or so, is part of an historical process. New life stages – childhood, adolescence, middle age, old age, extreme old age – are 'discovered' through a complex process. A new stage is experienced first in the lives of individuals and ultimately achieves public recognition through institutions designed to meet the special needs of the age group, the birth of a group of professionals who articulate its unique conditions and legislation to protect them (Hareven 1982). The emergence of new categories is influenced by the media. The advertising industry, working on behalf of commercial interests, takes a prominent part in the refinement of age categories. The identification and labelling of a new group such as 'teenagers' in the 1950s and 'mature individualists' (the 50-plus group) in the 1980s coincides with the discovery of a new market. An appropriate image is manufactured with a matching lifestyle to take advantage of the emergent purchasing power of a particular cohort.

The growth of academic research is part of the process identified by Hareven. In the last few years there has been a recognition of variation within what was previously labelled 'old age', an undifferentiated life stage following the middle years. A distinction is made between early and late stages of old age and social scientists are encouraged to give critical attention to the developmental needs associated with each stage. It is now legitimate to study the process by which a person becomes 'old' and is labelled 'old'. Most recently, theoretical interest has shifted from the refinement of age categories to the point of transition from one life phase to the next. Attention has been focused on the boundary situation and the strategies adopted by individuals in their attempt to avoid or hasten upgrading (Plath's (1982) age brinkmanship). The study of the way in which age roles are defined, learned and sustained – in a word, socially constructed – is legitimated by the allocation of public funds, perhaps the final step in the process of institutionalisation.

In Britain, the topic of ageing as a subject for academic study achieved a new legitimacy in the early 1980s with the Economic and Social Research Council's (ESRC) Research Initiative on Ageing. The birth of the initiative represented an acknowledgement by the controllers of social research funding of the fact of an ageing population. There had, of course, been a substantial amount of research work before that time. But it was invariably problem-oriented. Most had been commissioned by welfare agencies and carried out by contract researchers whose job it was to identify needs and draw out the implications for social policy. Even independent work in the universities had focused on needs and delivery of services. The ESRC initiative signalled social gerontology's coming of age in Britain. It indicated official recognition of the need for research which was not policy-oriented but designed to increase understanding of the ageing process in general. That is not to say that the research sponsored under the initiative was without implications for change and improvement in the lives of older people. But it sought initially to identify the underlying processes in the emergence of 'old age' as a social category. The aim was to show the variety of cultural and historical influences which make ageing as much a social as a biological phenomenon.

'Old age' as a social construct

Within social anthropology it is taken for granted that basic attributes such as age and gender acquire different meanings and that their significance in social life is culturally variable. But the notion that 'old age' and other age categories are social constructs challenges the popular view of differences based on chronological age, gender and other basic attributes as 'givens' of social existence.

A corollary of the cultural variability of ageing is that there is often a discrepancy between cultural definitions and subjective experience. In the culture in question, the emphasis on chronological age is in conflict with the inner feelings of the ageing individual. In this view the problem of reconciling the perceptions of other people, which are based on cultural stereotypes, with discrepant self-images is the main existential dilemma of ageing (de Beauvoir 1977). The relationship between social expectations and personal experience is problematic. Social scientists vary in their accounts of the accommodation between the two. In particular they differ in the degree of influence attributed to individuals over the process of definition. In one view, age roles are relatively fixed and immutable. Age expectations are experienced as social forces external to the individual. Conformity to them is ensured through a variety of social mechanisms, the 'prods' and 'breaks' which keep the individual to the predetermined path (Neugarten and Hagestad 1976). A fairly rigid programme of age roles regulates behaviour through the life-span, upheld by a system of socialisation and social control.

In another view, age roles are seen as products of negotiation between social actors. The actors operate within certain social and cultural limits but there is room for manoeuvre. Reality is constructed through interpersonal processes. Prevailing definitions of social reality reflect the interests of the more powerful in terms of political and personal resources. Their definitions become the basis for social action.

Up to a point the two views are not in conflict, but simply represent differences of theoretical emphasis. In the former the stress is on the social and cultural constraints to which the individual must adapt. In the latter the individual social actor is the starting point for analysis and the emphasis is on the negotiation of rules and roles. Attention is given to the mode of individual adaptation to cultural requirements and the modifications which can be achieved in interpersonal situations. This, the more phenomenological approach, has informed several recent studies in social gerontology, mainly in North America (Matthews 1979; Vesperi 1985; Evers 1983; Francis 1981, 1984; Keith-Ross 1977; Fry and Keith 1980; Myerhoff 1978; Hazan 1980).

The assumption in this book is that age roles are to a large extent the product of negotiation between acquaintances and intimates in a variety of settings. The negotiation takes place against a background of common assumptions about normal and proper ways of moving through the lifespan. Individuals in British culture are bombarded with images of age: in the media, in law and social policy (through their agents, the providers of social welfare and upholders of the law), in the workplace and in gatherings of strangers and intimates. The last of these – the significant others – play a crucial role in determining the way age is experienced.

Outline

The analysis draws on two sources of material. The first, which dominates the text, is ethnographic. On the basis of the research I offer a detailed description of the lives and concerns of a particular group of old people. The account of specific events and relationships in the lives of the research population is given in the belief that they reflect something of the lives of elderly people in general. I have identified features of old-age organisations and friendship networks in a particular town which I believe are shared by others. I would argue that the social processes outlined here are discernible in most gatherings of the elderly peer group. This statement is supported by the literature of social gerontology, the second source of material in the book. I have drawn on the work of a number of writers. The literature of friendship and social networks, of community formation or peer grouping, and of voluntary associations, has informed my thinking. Recent work on the biographical context of ageing, and on existential issues involved in the personal movement through time, has also influenced me.

I draw exclusively on the literature from the English-speaking West, notably North America. Enquiries revealed an absence of equivalent work in European languages (German, Dutch, French, Spanish, Scandinavian) where gerontology is informed by social science disciplines other than anthropology, and anthropologists are not inclined to look at old age. I make some reference to cross-cultural examples from social anthropology but generally restrict the comparative data to North America.

The rest of the book is arranged in eleven chapters. The following chapter establishes the context of the study. It sets out the theoretical issues which provide a framework for the analysis of participation in old people's clubs and associations. It provides a detailed account of the methods used in the research. It explains how social anthropologists work, focusing on the difference between anthropological and sociological procedures. The tasks of data collection and interpretation are given special attention. The chapter draws out the distinctive contribution made by anthropologists to the study of ageing.

The next two chapters introduce the reader to the social world of elderly joiners. Chapter Three identifies the research population, and shows that for the typical member, club-going is a way of life with enormous personal and social significance. There is a discussion of Seatown (the real name of the town has been changed to preserve the anonymity of informants) clubs and their activities. Special attention is paid to what goes on in the weekly meetings. Their ritual elements reveal major preoccupations and express important beliefs about identity and purpose: 'who we are and what we stand for'. The chapter ends with a review of the benefits of membership. These include social integration, a sense of security, practical and moral support, sociability and entertainment, a system of meaning and a context for ageing.

Chapter Four concentrates on age-specific organisations in a Seatown church. There is an analysis of the predominantly aged members of the women's fellowship and the equivalent men's group of the church. A detailed account of the official and unofficial activities of the women's group introduces a discussion of the benefits of membership. An explanation is sought for the continuing loyalty of the dwindling membership in the face of pressures which would erode it. The fellowship is viewed as an object of attachment and a source of prescriptions for behaviour. An analysis of the men's fellowship, which follows, underlines the importance of viewing these groups in the context of the social organisation and belief system of the church. The chapter accordingly ends with a brief account of the church as a context for ageing.

In Chapters Five to Eight the benefits of social participation are analysed in detail. Several themes are developed: the importance of friendship and sociability; the preoccupation with health and illness and their association with the ageing process; and the role of peers in the management of loss and change, of decline and death.

Chapter Five focuses on friendship in the setting of old people's clubs, for there it achieves most prominence. It starts with a review of the literature and considers the approaches to the study of friend relationships. It examines the significance of friendship through the life-span for men and women and focuses on the nature of sociability in retirement. The various functions of friendship – social integration, support, sociability, socialisation – are reviewed. Attention turns to the activities of friendship in the context of the old people's club. Conversation emerges as both a means of communication and a pastime. It is gender-specific in style and content. A comparison of official attitudes and personal beliefs about friendship reveals multiple meanings. Friendship turns out to be problematic. Difficulties surface in arguments about seating and in private misunderstandings between friends. The main source of conflict is the contrast in personal needs and organisational requirements.

In Chapter Six attention shifts to health issues and the role of the peer group in the management of health and illness. Friends and other members of the primary group play a role in socialisation to a variety of conditions associated with old age. Sickness is an ever-present possibility, even in this relatively healthy subgroup of the retired population. The preoccupation with health is examined with the help of case material, which is useful also in highlighting the role played by friends and peers in establishing the legitimacy of different responses to ill-health. They create norms of sickness behaviour and pass judgement about the rightness or wrongness of particular responses. Their stance indicates that health is a social, not just physical, phenomenon and has moral implications. I examine the range of individual responses to symptoms of ill-health and ask what factors influence the choice of personal strategy. The theme of the chapter, then, is the importance of perception, and the role of other people in the awareness of one's condition. Towards the end, it turns to more practical considerations: the role of friends in the provision of support during periods of ill-health. Discussion returns to the friendship literature and the puzzling suggestion that friendship and support are incompatible. The evidence offered here indicates, on the contrary, that caring for a sick friend is an obligation, particularly in long-term relationships. It suggests that the ideal type of friendship found in the literature rests on a misunderstanding of the ageing process and needs to be modified.

Chapter Seven is about dying and death – one's own and that of close associates. I consider responses to the death of a fellow member of an organisation or friendship network, notions of a good death, peer group norms for the expression of grief, and responses to the plight of the bereaved. Death is problematic in a culture where life and death are not treated as equal parts of the self. The rituals associated with death among these old people help to establish its meaning. Discussion centres on the peer group as a supportive setting for encounters with death. But not all older people, according to some anthropological studies, are open to the

subject of death. I seek an explanation for the different attitudes in personal circumstances and cohort differences.

Chapter Eight concentrates on beliefs about ageing. Age is used by
young and old alike to promote personal interests. But the vagueness
surrounding definitions of age leaves the old vulnerable to exploitation.
The process is observed in the age-mixed setting of the church. Both old
and young tread pathways through the course of life which are culturally
defined but which leave room for negotiation. The timing of transitions
from one age status to the next varies according to the individual capacity to
resist pressure or the urge to move on. The issue of elections to office in the
women's fellowship provides an illustration of what Plath has called age
brinkmanship. It also introduces a discussion of models of ageing. The
dominant model in the club and fellowship population must be understood
in its cultural context. It provides a standard for the evaluation of individual
performance. Being 'old' has moral implications: age, like health, emerges
as a moral category. Social participation in the world of voluntary associations is a strategy for successful ageing.

Chapter Nine broadens the discussion by viewing the culture of old-age
organisations in terms of the relations between the generations. It develops
the issue of age group solidarity. Despite moral distinctions within the
elderly peer group based on health and lifestyle, members are united by
their common interests in relation to younger cohorts and by a belief in
their own moral superiority. The moralistic stance of older generations is
perceived as a strategy to preserve their collective status in relation to youth
and their individual status in relation to negative changes through the life-
span. Peer group activities are thus a political phenomenon, part of the
struggle between the generations for the control of cultural resources. Age
group solidarity is perceived as a response to profound historical change
experienced uniquely by particular cohorts. Activities within old-age organisations are interpreted as a collective response to status loss and
intergenerational conflict. A different kind of explanation draws on recent
psychological research on psychosocial change. The issue is not so much
one of status as of the need for certainty. The elders defend the old moral
order to justify their existence and the lives they have led. Adjusting to social
change and to personal ageing simultaneously is a difficult developmental
task. It is aided by support from friends. The old values are defended
collectively.

However, collective resistance is itself under threat, for old-age organisations themselves appear to be in decline. The ageing and decline of
associations is the subject of Chapter Ten. Each cohort passes in step
through history, and within each cohort individuals make their unique
journeys through time. In the company of peers individual old people make
personal adjustments to change and the loss of important attachments. In
this chapter personal and social change are brought together. Various

explanations are considered for the state of general decline in old people's clubs and fellowships. A major problem is leadership. The model of ageing outlined in Chapter Eight, with its stress on activity and individual achievement, has a divisive effect within the peer group. Distinctions are made in terms of individual members' approximation to the ideal. As in groups of older people in other settings, health is a basis for distinction. Threats in the form of frail or confused members are contained through a variety of strategies. Club membership, in itself, offers a path to virtue since it demonstrates an active and coping stance; but leadership roles are the most valuable in this respect. An analysis of power and authority within the club reveals a personal strategy for ageing which makes retirement from office difficult. The chapter ends with a brief look at mechanisms for the transfer of authority.

In some clubs the issue of leadership has an added dimension. In the clubs run by charitable organisations authority resides in a permanent leadership of voluntary workers. Chapter Eleven looks at the interesting differences between these clubs and those run by old people for themselves. Although the workers are themselves retired and similar in many ways to the beneficiaries of their services, the clubs have a different ethos. Tensions between the organisers and members surface in arguments about seating, and in resistance to the official programme. In the analysis of these conflicts links are made between the ageing strategies of voluntary workers in clubs and those of other leaders.

The chapter discusses the practical applications of social research. In this case, identifying the different perspectives of participants can lead to an understanding of conflict and in consequence a clarification of aims and methods of intervention. The chapter ends by placing such an endeavour in context. Reference is made to a national organisation which draws social anthropologists, policy makers and practitioners in the field of health and social welfare together.

Chapter Twelve is a summing up which locates the study in the stream of gerontological theory and research. Attention is directed to the meaning of social participation in friendship networks and formal groupings of old people. Voluntary association in club and fellowship is the key to social integrity for this group of people. In the activities of old-age organisations we glimpse what Gutmann (1987) has called 'the strong face of ageing'. The possibility is raised that through skilful intervention their benefits might be enjoyed more widely.

The intended audience for the book is broad. It includes students of social gerontology, social anthropology, sociology and social psychology whose interests lie in the area of voluntary association, primary groups and social networks, methodology and interdisciplinary work on identity. Anthropologists in particular will benefit from reading the study. It is paradoxical that just as gerontologists have ignored an ethnographic and

anthropological approach to the study of ageing, so anthropologists have
been reluctant to study ageing itself, unless as part of the literature on age
sets. This study complements the increasing attention to children and
childhood which is gaining recognition in social anthropology as a category
worthy of study.

The study has relevance beyond the society in which it was located. There
is a high degree of comparability in the ageing process between the cultures
of North America and north-west Europe. Research located in the different
settings is of reciprocal interest, as my substantial use of American material
shows.

The book is also directed at the professional community, those who
come into contact with older people in the course of their work. Social
workers – paid and unpaid – who see in the supportive network a solution to
loneliness and dependency may find the evidence offered here a source of
hope and of ideas for intervention. Workers involved in the setting up or
running of old people's groups will discover useful criteria for the evaluation of their efforts. Healthcare workers, equally, will find the collective
definitions of health and ill-health, and the idea of social influences on
illness behaviour, of interest. Another group of professionals who might
find the analysis useful are clergy and layworkers concerned with the spiritual
aspects of ageing and the place of organised religion in older people's lives.
The aim is not to offer guidelines for intervention: the book is not practice-
oriented. But it might suggest a use for anthropological analysis to workers
in these fields. The material of social anthropology is useful and accessible if
professionals wish to supplement their conceptual armoury.

A third category of reader consists of policy makers and the controllers of
resources. The book provides an insight into the use of leisure in retirement. The benefits of leisure time spent in the company of peers might
usefully be noted by those planners and policy makers whose job it is to
adjudicate between competing claims for resources. The contributions of
friends and peers to well-being in old age tend to be devalued in favour of
those of relatives, particularly younger family members. Efforts are made to
sustain family ties across the generations at the expense of those outside the
family. On the evidence of this book one would argue that friends and peers
have a vital part to play in helping the elderly person to confront issues of
age and mortality.

TWO

The context

As a context for the present study, this chapter examines current thinking about the elderly peer group. It asks what gerontologists have had to say about old people's relationships with each other and shows that the research described in the following pages helps to fill a gap in the literature. The theoretical discussion is followed by an account of the methods used in the study. It includes the technical details of selecting a research setting, gaining access to it, and acquiring information. It explains how anthropologists work. Finally, I draw some crucial distinctions between anthropological and sociological procedures.

Insights in the literature

Over the last thirty years a body of literature has emerged to tell us something about peer relationships in old age, but only a small portion of it has addressed the issue directly. However, we can infer several things from studies conducted for other purposes. A variety of related topics – the primary group, personal networks, friendship, community formation, exchange relationships, voluntary associations, political activities, social support and psychological adjustment – have been the focus of research which contributes in some way to our knowledge of peer relationships. Diverse in origins and interests, this literature raises questions about who seeks association with peers – why and how? The task of drawing together the different lines of enquiry, pursued simultaneously over the last thirty years, is made easy by the fact that the literature is relatively sparse. Only a handful of names is associated with work in each of these areas.

A close reading of the literature produces a set of themes concerning the supposed need for activity, association, and intimacy. The dominant ideas and assumptions behind them reflect the disciplines of the research, and academic and popular perceptions of age fashionable at the time. They show interesting developments in the history of ideas about age.

The literature can be divided into dominant themes, expressed in a phrase or statement: social activity is a good thing; the response to loss; joiners: a special breed? leisure and lifestyles; a dynamic life stage; age and creativity; old people are like everyone else; and the issue of meaning.

Social activity is a good thing

Much of the early research in North America was influenced by the notion that activity was the key to successful adjustment to old age. The ideal according to advocates of the activity theory of ageing was to sustain a middle-aged lifestyle as far as possible, finding substitutes for disappearing roles and activities (Kuypers and Bengtson 1976). There were implications for mental health in the extent of social involvement the older person was able to sustain. A high degree produced high morale, a low degree made the old person vulnerable to depression and breakdown. High activity promoted life satisfaction because social roles and the support given by role partners could cushion the individual and act as shock-absorbers during periods of role change (Lemon, Bengtson and Peterson 1976). The person with high activity also had a larger repertoire of interactions and greater social life space, which made the readjustment process easier.

Throughout life, in this view, it is interaction with others which sustains the social self. Although self-conceptions are relatively stable by adulthood, they must be reaffirmed from time to time by the confirming responses of other people. Thus, the more one interacts with others or is exposed to the responses of others, even in adulthood, the greater the opportunity for reaffirming specific role-identities.

Proponents of the activity theory of ageing suggested that some types of activity were more valuable than others as sources of role support. Interpersonal activity in particular offered channels for acquiring role supports or reinforcements which sustain the self-concept; the more intimate the activity the more role supportive. They saw formal activity as geared to more general roles and therefore making less of a contribution to life satisfaction. Solitary activity was the least effective as a source of role support.

Although membership of voluntary organisations was, by implication, less rewarding than informal interaction, this kind of activity was nonetheless important. It was a sign of social involvement.

In the 1970s American gerontologists began to ask questions about voluntary organisations. The premise was that joining an association was a means of social integration and that it boosted morale. Both integration and morale were indicators of successful adjustment to old age. Sociologists investigated the rates of involvement in voluntary associations and personal variations in relation to other roles, health and the life course (Lowenthal and Robinson 1976; Creech and Babchuk 1985); subjective reasons for participation (Ward 1979; Brown 1974) and types of organisation (Babchuk et al. 1979; Cutler 1976).

Babchuk and Bates, for instance, offered a basis for classification in the distinction between expressive and instrumental goals. Expressive goals were immediately gratifying to the members. They included such things as comfort, relaxation and entertainment. Instrumental goals involved objectives beyond the organisation. They might include working to improve conditions in the neighbourhood or promoting members' interests in a national political context. Adopting a continuum based on this dichotomy, distinctions between different old-age organisations could be made. Subsequent work led to the observation that in North America the expressive organisations and those which combined expressive and instrumental goals were the most popular among elderly people (Babchuk et al. 1979).

Evidence was also provided of the quality of relationships within organisations (Jacoby 1966; Creech and Babchuk 1985). Members of expressive organisations were typically found to be engaged already in satisfying relationships. It was the presence of other members of their primary group which enhanced the attractiveness of the association and made participation emotionally rewarding.

There were studies of the use made of associations by welfare agencies as mechanisms for social change (Taietz 1976). A limited amount of comparative (cross-national) material was gathered on rates of associational participation (Barker and Barker 1963) and on the growth of age-homogeneous groups. Attention was given to the social characteristics – notably social class attributes – of those who would join such groups (Rose 1960, 1965; Trela 1976; Rosow 1967).

These studies had limited objectives. They set out to establish empirically the range and objectives of voluntary organisations. They were concerned with objective characteristics and measurable attributes in the membership. They paid little attention to interpersonal processes and broader issues such as the implications of membership for the process of ageing. They did little for our knowledge of the consequences of participation at either the personal or societal levels. But, on the premise that social activity was a good thing, they produced some information about the range of old-age organisations and the sort of people who join them. With other writers of the period they demonstrated an association between well-being and social participation.

The response to loss

Within the primary group of kin, friends and neighbours, friends – members of the peer group – assume importance at certain phases of life. One of them is the onset of old age. The loss of income and increase in leisure at retirement is likely to promote primary group ties with peers, who have similar life experiences, expectations and tastes. They have a similar need for companionship and support at a time of status loss and role change (Dono et al. 1979). The pattern observed within the primary group extends to more formal expressions of peer group interests such as voluntary organisations. An early study of old people's clubs confirmed the suggestion that peer grouping is a phenomenon of old age (Harris 1983). One would expect peer grouping to occur 'when the life experiences of successive cohorts are radically different, leading to the creation of distinctive age-related cultural styles ... It is also found at points of the life course characterised by transition between statuses and by normative confusion' (Harris 1983, p. 18). Peer grouping is a mechanism whereby deprived people

associate with others similarly deprived, hence reducing the sense of deprivation and exposure to people who might reinforce it.

Viewed in terms of the social exchanges which go on in encounters
between members of a western industrial society, it is often in the interests
of older people to restrict their interaction to people like themselves (Dowd
1980). The segregation of older groups is not necessarily an onerous
burden placed on the old by society. It is partly maintained by the old
themselves, as a strategy for minimising the costs of unequal exchange.
Associating with peers is a way of avoiding undermining talk with younger
people, talk which reinforces the elders' relative dependency and inferior
status. In any case, the old have little access to the opportunity structures of
mid-life, and are unlikely to meet potential exchange partners outside the
peer group.

The role of peers in a time of role loss and change, and their preference
for each other over younger people, is summed up in memorable terms by
Hochschild in her study of a retirement community of elderly widows:

> For old roles that are gone, new ones are available. If the world
> watches them less for being old, they watch one another more. Lack-
> ing responsibilities to the young, the old take on responsibilities
> towards one another. Moreover, in a society that raises an eyebrow at
> those who do not 'act their age', the subculture encourages the old to
> sing, to flirt, to joke. They talk about death in a way less common
> between old and young. They show one another how to be, and trade
> solutions to problems they have not faced before. (Hochschild 1973,
> p. 141)

Peer grouping takes different forms. It can be achieved through informal
networks and through formal associations. The choice is governed by previous experience and existing resources. For some old people with a history
of active participation in voluntary organisations it might be possible to
peer-group within existing sets of relationships. For others without such a
history of joining, and without extensive informal networks, joining clubs in
retirement might be a novel experience which meets the need for companionship and activity, for moral support and social status. Social class is a
major factor in the form peer grouping takes. Harris suggests that middle-
class women are more likely to rely on informal friendship networks. Working-class women find peer group support in formal settings such as old
people's clubs. Indeed, they are the main participants in old people's clubs,
which are age-homogeneous and established on the whole by old people
themselves. Retired working-class women are the most deprived and, with
the lowest rates of associational participation in earlier life, are the least able
to find a supportive peer group within their existing networks. Supporting
evidence of the predominance of working-class women in clubs for the
elderly is found in Abrams (1980), Unruh (1983) and Wenger (1984).

The organisations favoured by middle-class elderly people, who are less deprived, tend to be age-mixed, at least officially. The only officially age-specific associations attractive to them are those established by and for themselves for political purposes, such as the Gray Panthers in North America and the University of the Third Age in Europe, or those which can be seen as demonstrating skill and organising ability. It has been suggested that middle-class people wish to avoid identification with older people. They do so by continuing to operate in the heterogeneous clubs and associations of earlier adulthood (Harris 1983; Rosow 1967).

The argument is convincing. But the research designs of the earlier writers, and their field-work conducted in the 1960s did not produce the kind of evidence to justify pronouncements on the significance of peer group activities for ageing. However, drawing together the work on primary groups and on voluntary associations we might conclude that elderly people's needs for status and security are often met within the peer group.

We cannot ignore the fact that voluntary organisations exist in a particular social context. When considered in the context of the social system in which they operate, they can be seen to meet needs for status and autonomy. Membership of an organisation confers status, though not in the narrow sense – prestigious positions are not normally the object of competition. It offers meaningful activity in an area of choice. The Women's Institute, for instance, has been seen as anachronistic and fantasy-based, but during the 1970s, for nearly half a million women, it was a means of self-expression within a patriarchal social structure (Tomlinson 1979).

Joiners: a special breed?

The average member of the old-age organisation tends to be fit, and able to meet the financial obligations of association membership. She is socially active and always has been, though not necessarily in a formal setting. In the literature on voluntary associations in later life, membership is associated with high morale, or at least with a sense of relative well-being (Ward 1979; Pohjolainen 1987). It is often assumed that one causes the other; that participation improves morale. But both are likely to be the product of other factors – good health and an adequate income. Elderly members of voluntary associations are already distinguished from non-members in respect of their superior physical and material circumstances, and it is difficult to say whether their sense of well-being is a cause or consequence of membership.

A survey of the limited literature on old-age organisations in Britain indicates that this kind of social participation is very much a minority interest. It is difficult to establish the exact scope of involvement. Official statistics are of little use, for the range of leisure activities surveyed is limited and retired people are not treated as a separate category. A useful source of information is the Age Concern Research Department survey material, which offers details of age and rate of affiliation of different types of organisation, together with social class and regional variations (Abrams 1978, 1980). From this we learn that Hove, a town on the south coast of England, had a mere 11 per cent of its very elderly population (75 plus) attending old people's clubs. The percentage of 'young old' who participate – around 15 per cent – is slightly higher. Of the surviving 25 per cent of the over-85s cohort, only 14 per cent belong to old people's clubs. These figures are broadly similar to those produced by other studies (Townsend 1963; White 1965; Hearnden and Fujishin 1974) and close to the national average.

When membership of other kinds of organisations (religious or political) are included, the proportions of old people active in this way increase. Nationally, about 25 per cent of retired people pursue leisure activities in formal settings, including attendance at church services, sports and social clubs (White 1965; Townsend 1963; Hearnden and Fujishin 1974).

Research so far has been largely statistical, concentrating on the linking of variables such as age, social class, region and gender, with voluntary association. From this literature it seems that participation in formal organisations varies by age and region, by gender, social class and residence patterns, the crucial distinction being between living alone and living with others. Women are particularly likely to join clubs for the elderly, and church groups, while men favour sports and social clubs, as well as supporting church-based organisations.

Churches attract the highest number of elderly adherents of all types of voluntary association. The popularity of religious organisations, especially among women, is a feature of elderly people's use of leisure in North America, too (Babchuk et al. 1979). The reasons for this are subject to speculation; explanations are not offered and indeed lie beyond the scope of this type of research.

Generally, apart from the women's guilds which are by definition exclusive, organisations contain both men and women. In the church there are exclusive subgroupings and in rare instances old people's clubs are segregated by gender (Hearnden and Fujishin 1974). Overall, very few men appear to join old people's clubs. The main reason for the low rates of attendance by men might be demographic (Abrams 1978). Members join on widowhood and relatively few men are widowers. In Abrams' national survey, women made up 70 per cent of the sample of club-goers, a reflection of the fact that women outnumber men by 2 to 1 in this age group. However, when participation is considered in terms of attendance at meetings rather than simply membership, women outnumber men even more. While the percentage of joiners among men and women is similar, women are more frequent attenders. Again, the reasons are not sought.

On other dimensions – according to the literature – voluntary associations enjoy an equally high degree of homogeneity. A major variable is social class. Evidence from community studies suggests that clubs and

Table 2.1 Leisure of the elderly and social class, by age, sex and household. (Source: M. Abrams, B.S.G. Annual Conference, Aberdeen, 1980.) Percentage in each group who belong to named organisations and attend its meetings at least once a month.

	Clubs Elderly	Sports Clubs	Social Clubs	Church Groups	Church Attendance	Political Parties	Trades Unions	Other Clubs
Women, 65–74								
MIDDLE CLASS								
living alone	11	11	7	18	35	2	2	8
not living alone	5	4	13	9	36	1	0	15
WORKING CLASS								
living alone	19	0	8	13	30	0	0	12
not living alone	8	1	10	8	20	0	0	4
Men, 65–74								
Middle class	3	12	17	12	27	1	0	9
Working class	5	5	10	5	12	2	1	9
Men and Women all ages (i.e. inclusive 75+)								
Middle class	7	4	9	13	30	2	–	10
Working class	13	2	9	9	19	1	–	7

voluntary groups are, almost without exception, class-based groupings (Tomlinson 1979). Membership is based upon members' conception of social comfort, and the basis of such comfort is usually homogeneity.

By this argument, focusing on common interests, the few examples of cross-class leisure groupings, including women's groups like the women's institutes and townswomen's guilds, are difficult to explain. In such cases the basis for homogeneity would appear to be shared interests which override social class. We might speculate that these have something to do with age or lifestyle, as independent variables.

Leisure and lifestyles

Some writers focus on the individual use of leisure as a means of self-expression. A lifestyle is individually selected to supply the challenge and security necessary at all ages (Gordon, Gaitz and Scott 1976). The limited literature on leisure and lifestyles offers some valuable clues to the nature of voluntary association in old age. The concept of lifestyle is useful in differentiating between older people. Indeed it might be more meaningful as a basis for social differentiation than social class (Taylor and Ford 1981). Most people's lives have a focus, a dominant concern, something which occupies their thoughts and activities. They typically dispose of their leisure time in a certain way. A lifestyle has several components: structure, content and meaning. The structure consists of social roles associated with that activity; content refers to the activity itself: helping people, involvement in family affairs, being with other people. Meaning consists of a set of attributions by which the participants themselves refer to the activity and describe its significance in their lives. A range of lifestyles is discernible in old age, though there has been little attempt to study them systematically. Taylor and Ford (1981), in a useful synthesis of the literature, identified ten distinct orientations towards life. They can be summed up in a word or phrase: taking life easy (someone who feels he or she has earned a rest and fills the time without doing anything in particular); gregarious (someone who is very sociable, spending as much of the time with other people as possible and avoiding being alone); solitary (someone who describes him or herself as a solitary person, a loner, and spends most of the time doing things alone); spouse-centred (someone who shares everything with the spouse, they have similar interests and when they are together they do not need any other company); invalid (someone who feels unwell a lot of the time and is prevented by ill-health from doing a lot of things he or she would like to do); altruist (spends most of the time doing things for other people and feels this is the best way to spend time); hobbyist (has a serious hobby or interest which takes up a lot of time); family-centred (someone who spends as much time with his or her family as possible and prefers being with them to doing anything else); work-centred (someone who describes him or herself as a doer because he or she is busy doing a job most of the time. Such a person does not often sit doing nothing and feels the time should be spent doing something useful); and a full life (someone who lives a full life, is an active person involved in a large number of outside interests and activities).

At first glance a number of these categories seem interesting and relevant to the lives of old people who join associations and have active friendship networks. We might expect elements of gregariousness, altruism, work-centredness and the full life to crop up frequently. It seems likely that members of voluntary organisations share a lifestyle which is distinguished from those of other old people. The concept of lifestyle, with its three components of structure, content and meaning might provide a most useful framework for understanding what this particular group of older people do with their time, and how they set about it and why it occupies their thoughts and energies in the way it does. The value of the concept is marred for many social gerontologists by methodological difficulties in the study of its components. Apparently a common response is that while the topic is fascinating and probably necessary, it is 'utterly unresearchable' (Taylor and Ford 1981). Taylor and Ford's pioneering work belongs in the realm of qualitative research and sophisticated conceptual analysis, an impossible challenge to some of the more conventional social scientists.

A dynamic life stage

From the evidence offered by Harris in his sociological analysis of peer grouping (1983) we might infer that joining an old people's club is a developmental phenomenon. It seems to occur at a certain stage in the life of working-class woman, for whom joining an association is a new departure prompted by an acute sense of relative deprivation. With no tradition of joining organisations or of taking collective action, this is a form of association with peers called for by the need to share experiences and cope with the vicissitudes of age. The literature of developmental psychology supports this view. It confirms the picture of change across the life-span, though the focus here is on personal development rather than social circumstances.

The importance of peers in accomplishing the social and developmental tasks associated with old age is made clear in studies of friendship and social networks (Lowenthal and Robinson 1976; Francis 1981, 1984; Hess 1972; Rosow 1975), of day centres (Myerhoff 1978; Hazan 1980) and of retirement homes (Keith 1977; Hochschild 1973; Gubrium 1975; Hockey 1983). These provide evidence that peer relationships meet important needs for old people. Together, peers deal with issues of identity and continuity, with isolation and marginality, with the need to create new social roles, with loss and impending death.

The literature which focuses upon change and adaptation has often identified gender differences in the adaptation to this new life stage. It has sought to explain the dominance of older women in group activities. Some writers have interpreted the assertiveness and buoyancy of women, compared with the more subdued and passive stance of older men, in a developmental framework (Gutmann 1977, 1987) or in terms of role changes and social opportunities (Myerhoff 1978). Others, like Townsend (1963) offer no explanation at all but simply note the difference in energy and vitality. In the psychological view, the dominance of older women reflects a powerful psychological development being given public expression. The emergent energies of women are breaking into public light. The men's psychological development works in the opposite direction. Their competitive and achievement-oriented drives are satisfied earlier in life, and they respond now to the demands of the senses for a different kind of pleasure: companionship, sensuality, eating and drinking with friends, a quiet life.

From this we might infer that the interpersonal needs of older men and women converge. But there are important limitations in Gutmann's analysis. Gutmann bases his observations on a cross-sectional enquiry. He infers life-span changes from comparisons between groups of old and young informants. He is unable to take account of individual biography and indeed his object is to identify broad trends and psychological characteristics within age groups.

The existing friendship literature, similarly, is weakened by an ahistorical approach (Matthews 1986; Armstrong 1988). It is based largely on cross-sectional data, thus ignoring the biographical dimension which gives particular friendships their contemporary character. But there are other limitations. Early studies in particular were concerned with objective characteristics; how many friends existed in the typical network; the similarities between friends. The emphasis on numbers and social characteristics produced general statements about objective features but ignored the variability of friend relationships and their place in the individual life-span. Further, most studies rest on a questionable premise about the significance of friendship in the ageing process. Friendship is approached as a source of support and aid to psychological well-being in later life. This limitation needs to be considered in some detail for it has in the past ·drawn our attention to some aspects of older people's friendship and not others. It has obscured the meaning that sociable relationships have for the actors – old people themselves.

Ageing and creativity

As we have seen, much early research on peer relationships was conducted to establish the preconditions for high morale or mental health in old age (Matthews 1986). The early work on friendship came out of this tradition. The early studies examined the number of friends and their availability in relation to other members of the social network, on the premise that friends were good for morale. Implicit in the research on psychological well-being was the assumption that the old are more likely than other people to be unwell. They are conceptualised not as social actors but as passive and needy. On the basis of her own study of friendship and the work of fellow anthropologists, Matthews argues that the old *are* actors. They endow their worlds with meaning, they make choices; they engage in purposeful behaviour. The metaphor of a career (Myerhoff and Simic 1978) conveys well the dynamic response of older people to the exigencies of their life stage.

The newer conceptualisation of older people as psychologically healthy, as creative and as purposeful provokes different questions about the relationship between friendship and ageing. It focuses attention on the dynamic quality of friend relationships, the transactions achieved by friends and their role in individual trajectories (Matthews 1983, 1986). It looks for parallel activities in friendship at all ages. It asks how far friends individually maximise their interests and collectively establish ways of viewing the world.

Old people are like everyone else

When old people get together in groups they behave much like anyone else (Hochschild 1973). Provided they have certain things in common, a sense of solidarity and a shared interest in making things work, they will develop social systems which promote harmony and contain conflict. The work of Jennie Keith (1977, 1980a, 1982) has been valuable in drawing out the factors which promote or inhibit positive relationships in the elderly peer group. She distinguishes between background factors, present at the beginning of the process of community formation, and emergent factors which develop over time. Background characteristics include such features as social and cultural homogeneity of the individuals, the size of the collectivity and leadership skills. Shared symbols, a degree of interdependence and a sense of threat from outside are among the emergent factors which help to turn a collection of individuals into a community. The outcome is a pattern of organisation which could be recognised anywhere. Like all communities Les Floralies, an old people's home in Paris, contains 'friendship, sexual ties, fictive kinship, distinctive norms about sex and death, internally focused conflicts, resistance to outside status ranking; reciprocity of goods and services; support for the ill or handicapped; autonomous definitions of roles and formal activities.' (Keith 1980a, p. 188.)

Working in the 1970s, Keith and a number of other anthropologists – Hazan, Gubrium, Hochschild, Myerhoff – were using qualitative research techniques to reveal for the first time the subjective reality of life in an old people's home or day centre. But such settings involve only a small minority of old people. Keith pointed out the need to extend detailed anthropological work on ageing to the vast majority of old people who existed beyond the segregated residential and day-care setting. On these people the data we had then were predominantly quantitative: how many and what kinds of contacts old people had with what categories of individuals. There was a need to know the significance to old people of different types of ties to peers and others. Keith indicated that peer grouping was an important principle about which we needed to know more, particularly at the level of meaning. It was important to understand the significance such arrangements have for participants, and the identities and roles they manage to negotiate for themselves.

The issue of meaning

Recent anthropological and psychological research has moved in the direction indicated by Keith. The focus has shifted to the meanings attached to experience, though less in terms of social roles than more fundamental philosophical issues concerning age identities and the individual movement through time. Old people are seen to be preoccupied with issues of time and mortality (Myerhoff 1978, 1984; Hazan 1980, 1984; Coleman 1988; Hockey 1983; Vesperi 1985). Their lives have a dynamic quality and they engage with each other in a creative way. Their preoccupation with time is often expressed through peer group activities and rituals. In gatherings of old people, we see the collective resolution of existential problems. To cope with personal discontinuity and cultural change they reconceptualise their experience (Hazan 1980). The individual is submerged in the collectivity, change is suspended and made manageable. The limited and unpredictable future of each individual is set against a background of social continuity and a sense of time rolling on (Hockey 1983).

This more recent work, concentrating on the insiders' view, has broadened our knowledge of the quality of life in old age and old people's view of the world and their place in it. It also provides a much richer account of peer relationships. Starting from the standpoint of the social actor, and focusing on qualitative issues, the work has raised different questions from those which inspired the earlier research. Work in the 1960s and early 1970s, conducted within a more conventional sociological framework, took certain issues as given and sought information which confirmed initial assumptions and prejudices. The cultural obsession with morale and adjustment, the value attached to activity and social engagement, the tendency to view old age through youthful eyes, produced a set of research questions and answers which, while useful in themselves, said little about the subjective experience of ageing.

It is the emphasis on subjectivity and reliance on old people's own categories of experience which distinguishes the anthropological approach. But the study of ageing has only recently been enriched in this way. In North America, social anthropologists at first accommodated themselves to current preoccupations in gerontology. Given the prevailing views about social connectedness and disengagement they took 'social role' as a point of departure and sought to illuminate the social vacuum of retirement which had been identified by sociologists. Vesperi (1985) notes the curious sterility which consequently characterises much early anthropological work on ageing. She herself chose to deal with issues closer to conventional anthropological concerns, concentrating not on social role but on systems of meaning. In doing so she aligned herself with a new wave of anthropological gerontologists like Myerhoff and Simic, Fry and Kertzer, Keith and Francis.

Though it could not ignore social roles, my research, too, was to be concerned with meaning: the meanings attached to events and relationships by elderly men and women from a variety of backgrounds. In particular, I aimed to examine the meaning of friendship and voluntary association in old age. I intended to view the participants in the study as social actors and provide an account of the systems of meaning they had elaborated. In addition, I sought to uncover underlying structures and processes which are not immediately apparent to even the most sophisticated members of a social group. The social construction of old age was one such process. The way in which these objectives were made operational – transformed into issues which could be investigated empirically – and how I actually set about pursuing them is complex. The technical details of selecting a research setting, of gaining access to it, the difficulties encountered in acquiring information and what I did with it when it had been obtained, occupy the remainder of the chapter.

Methodological issues

As an anthropologist I considered a small-scale intensive study to be the best way of understanding the significance of friendship and group ties in the lives of older people. To achieve these goals I felt it important to enter into the social worlds of my informants, sharing their lives as far as possible. I believed informal interaction to be crucial in the social construction of old age. Everyday conversation would be a vital source of information about the content of relationships and the meanings attached to age (Dowd 1980; Francis 1981, 1984). Like Vesperi (1985) I aimed to examine the social construction of old age where it unfolds, 'in the interstices of daily living, in the commonplaces of conversation and the "informal formalities" of social interaction' (p. 48).

But in defining the goals of the research and in selecting appropriate field techniques I faced the dilemma which confronts the advocate of qualitative methods in a field dominated by the scientific research paradigm. While the balance has changed somewhat since the early 1980s, when in Britain an anthropological approach had to be defended at length in order to achieve publication in academic journals of gerontology (Jerrome 1981), one still faces the problem summarised succinctly by Vesperi of knowing what sort of an entrée to make and how to model one's enquiry to achieve credibility among fellow gerontologists.

Social anthropologists tend not to combine an account of their field-work experience and the analysis of data in the same text (Yates 1985). It is even less common to give an account of the intellectual processes through which the data are converted from social phenomena observed and experienced in the field to units of analysis on the printed page (Bohannan 1981). This chapter dwells on both aspects of methodology. It does so in deference to those readers who require such information as essential background knowledge for an appreciation of social research. Self-consciousness over methodological issues is much more a feature of sociological than anthropological research. Within social gerontology, the dominance of the sociological approach – with its emphasis on hypothesis-testing and quantification – suggests that a discussion of the particular methodology of this study might be welcome.

It seemed clear at the start of the study that at least three basic techniques for data collection would be involved: participant observation, for the insider's view and to produce questions and theoretical propositions; interviewing, to check information and confirm or invalidate hypotheses; and observation – of physical and social contact, of spacing, of verbal communication and so on (Pelto and Pelto 1978). The three techniques of participant observation, interviewing and observation – conducted over a lengthy period – would allow me to compare what people thought and did with what they said, checking both against what others said about them. This variety of sources would be important in eliminating the bias which can be introduced by over-reliance on a single method of acquiring qualitative information. One needs to employ a variety of methods to check the validity of the statements of key informants (Fennell 1981; Keith 1980b). Broadly speaking, I expected my research activity to correspond to what had been described in an early, unrefined definition as participant observation:

> some amount of genuinely social interaction in the field with the subjects of the study, some direct observations of relevant events, some formal and a great deal of informal interviewing, some systematic counting, some collection of documents and artifacts, and open-endedness in the direction the study takes. (McCall and Simmons 1969)

As a technique of investigation, participant observation appears to the uninitiated as at once both attractive and difficult, if not dangerous. Yet, as a means of gaining an insight into qualitative aspects of ageing it is highly appropriate. No-one has done more than Jennie Keith to establish the credibility of participant observation in gerontological research. Her observations provide a useful justification for the approach adopted here.

Participant observation *involves active participation as a means of observing the setting under study*. There are many degrees of participation but the central feature is the observer's personal involvement in the research setting as a means to understanding it (Keith 1980b). As a technique it is deceptively simple. Most people tend to think of it as total immersion in the lives of a research population, in a role chosen to provide the maximum amount of access, recording information indiscriminately and presenting a holistic view of the social situation under study. In fact, there can be several stages of which only the first resembles the popular stereotype. From full participation in a newly acquired role, the participant observer goes on to focus on specific issues. These issues generate hypotheses which, in the third phase, can be tested by means of the research instruments familiar in other kinds of social scientific research: questionaires, card sorts, and network profiles. The analysis can also take a conventional form with the coding of categories and the use of computer software.

Despite these similarities participant observation is distinguished from more quantitative approaches in crucial ways. The differences – in intensity, in personal involvement, in the adoption of the social actors' perspective – are what makes it highly appropriate for the study of ageing. Participant observation is valuable in four different ways. First, it is useful in filling in gaps in our knowledge of the quality of life of older people, about the mutual influence of the old and various cultural contexts, and about old people's views of the world. It is the best technique for the unseen areas (Bohannan 1981), those corners of experience which are not perceptible by more objective measures, which are private and unarticulated. Through participant observation it is possible to discover both measures and questions for topics like the meaning of friendship and kinship, preparation for death, the structure of the daily routine and the salience of age in social interaction. These are all issues about which little is known and little can be learnt through conventional techniques.

The second value of participant observation is that it illuminates those issues which are too sensitive for direct questioning. Old age is itself a sensitive topic for many people and in many contexts. Direct questions may be inappropriate on account of both the topic and the attributes of the questioner. Many a research worker has felt handicapped by his or her youth and found the use of such words as old or even age inhibiting to respondents. For some groups of elderly women, for instance, such words are taboo (Jerrome 1984).

Thirdly, some people are, in any case, unable to respond to questions. Short-term memory loss, idealisation and cultural pressures to confirm a particular view make individual reports unreliable. Keith gives the example of old people who describe their peers as depressing and boring, consistent with negative cultural stereotypes, but are observed 'in active, powerful, warm, interesting interaction with age mates'. Another by now familiar example is the contradiction between the protestations of independence and actual levels of interaction observed in single-room occupancy hotels in inner city areas (Sokolovsky 1980; Eckert 1980; Stephens 1976).

Finally, there are collective and emergent realities which require observation. The dynamics of age-homogeneous and age-mixed gatherings cannot be captured accurately through the aggregate of individual reports. This observation, like the others, stems directly from Keith's own work in a retirement community. It is also most relevant to the concerns of the present study.

The choice of participant observation, then, was amply justified by the objectives of the research. I next sought research settings which would provide the social mix and age range I needed while allowing for the intense involvement of anthropological field-work. Voluntary associations struck me as suitably bounded units which met these requirements. I selected a church community near my home with various age-specific societies and a working-class old people's club which met under its auspices. Through the latter organisation I became involved in a network of old people's clubs. This combination allowed me to explore the issue of peer grouping and the relationship between friendship and ageing.

The achievement of my research objectives came only after early doubts about the range and quality of my material. I had gained access to the church fairly rapidly, initially through the minister who introduced me to senior officers. I also made use of the church newsletter to advertise my presence and justify the demands I planned to make on old people's time and energy. The text of the article was carefully phrased to be informative without being boring or confusing, or patronising, to be inviting without being imposing, friendly without being presumptuous. It included autobiographical details and a brief description of my earlier research; its outcomes and relevance for the people whom I hoped would help me in the new project. The article described the proposed investigation in what I hoped were non-threatening terms. It listed the benefits of participation, both to the church and to the individuals within. It invited people to contact me if they wished to take part, and expressed the hope that they would want to help me if I contacted them first. It offered assurances of confidentiality.

Disappointingly, with rare exceptions people did not offer themselves; they had to be approached. All the initiatives were mine. I endeavoured to work my passage, as it were, balancing requests for help with offers of involvement in various church activities. I gave talks to the women's organisations, I made my car available for the church outing, I helped to wash up, and once drove a lunch club cook to the market to collect meat. I took part in the church quiz and in a drama workshop. The people most obligated helped me in return but others were not influenced by their example. When my offers of help were accepted with alacrity I began to feel that I was being used (a salutary experience, for a social researcher!) and that my investment was heavier than the returns justified.

My initial contacts with the club population were also somewhat unsatisfactory. I found the process of getting to know people, and entering their social world, very slow. Perhaps this was inevitable, given the fragmented nature of people's lives in urban areas, and a spell of extremely harsh weather which coincided with the start of my field-work (in January 1985), keeping my potential informants indoors and out of sight. Even when fully involved in the clubs I found it difficult to gain access to people's homes in order to interview them. This was possibly because I had become identified as a member of particular information networks and therefore liable to gossip. A different possibility was that, despite the similarity in gender between myself and the majority of the club members, differences of age and social class reduced their confidence and inclination to talk freely. My continued presence in the club community over eight months might have inhibited the kinds of confidences which (I am told) are shared with one-off interviewers who are total strangers and never to be seen again. My field methods, in themselves, raised difficulties by their informal nature. In a culture where the concept of research is familiar and the role of 'social researcher' clearly defined, activities which do not fit into the survey research mould – with its emphasis on questionnaires and formal interviewing – are difficult to classify and so arouse suspicion. In similar circumstances anthropologists have been obliged to adopt formal methods in order to achieve credibility (Holy 1984).

As a study of private lives, therefore, I began to feel that my project had limitations. At the organisational level, too, it initially seemed to be handicapped. Many club officials would not permit me direct access to the most basic information. Membership lists were waved under my nose and concealed again, despite assurances that the information required was merely statistical and would not involve any intrusion into members' privacy. To an extent this problem was resolved by those club leaders who kindly compiled the statistics for me after finding out what I wanted. The risk run by anthropologists engaged in this kind of research, of being identified by one set of informants with another set, hampered my access to decision-making processes, too. In one club I was denied the opportunity to observe a committee meeting in progress after the members had debated my request and decided that 'the committee meeting was for members of the committee only'. By that time I had been assimilated into the category of ordinary member, and my exclusion was sociologically significant. As such incidents suggest, entering the social world of informants is done at a price. In becoming identified with one category one is denied access to others. But participant observation nonetheless offers first-hand experience of the situation under study. I was eventually able to put the incident in the context of the general ambivalence towards committee work and the need of the leaders to preserve a social and moral distance between themselves and the rest, summed up in the belief that 'a few of us are looking after the rest of you'. The difficulty involved in crossing the boundary between ordinary members and committee members was, as I eventually discovered, related to the significance of leadership work as evidence of successful ageing. Just as I had learnt in an earlier study that becoming a friend is the best way of understanding the meanings attached to friendship (Jerrome 1981), so participating as an ordinary member in club activities taught me much about the dynamics of power and authority in club culture.

In the same way, early mistakes which seemed disastrous at the time yielded dividends. The tendency in research involving participant observation to break social rules on immediate entry to the field of study – almost inevitable given the researcher's initial state of ignorance – is a crucial learning experience and yields valuable material (Holy 1984). Indeed, whereas in sociological research field-work relationships *produce* data, in anthropological research the relationships between researcher and informants *are* data (Yates 1985; Crick 1982). Rather than *using* a research instrument the participant observer becomes the research instrument (Keith 1980b). In this approach the distinction between observer and observed is less pronounced and less critical for the production of knowledge. Discussions of subjectivity and bias through personal involvement have very little place. In anthropological research the core problem is not validity but interpretation. For sociologists, methodology is external and technical and related to the possibility of objective knowledge. For social anthropologists, methodology is the internal apprehension of relationships and their transformation through sets of cultural meanings. The goal of field-work is to gain an insight into the construction of meaning by the people under study. This can be achieved only by participating in the process of meaning construction. The important skill in field-work therefore is not to become integrated but to be able to reflect on the experience. What is of significance is competence of introspection (Holy 1984).

This view of methodology differs from that of sociologists, even those at the 'soft' end of the spectrum who place a similar emphasis on the production of ethnography through the use of qualitative research methods. Participant observation – a principal source of ethnographic data – is regarded by social anthropologists as a process internal to the researcher rather than an external set of techniques for the recognition of data and the production of authentic accounts.

Access to the clubs, as I have said, was not easy. I experienced difficulties in the church for different reasons. In addition to the problem of access mentioned earlier, I was not sure how to interpret the unusually bland and conflict-free existence of the group. Norms are more easily perceptible in the breach. In the church, where principles of harmony and conciliation are strong, violations were rare. It was difficult to find clear-cut principles of social differentiation, in the official absence of all hierarchies – sexual, political, spiritual or age – and social boundaries. Conflict did exist in several areas of activity, as I eventually discovered. There were disputes over the use of resources (room allocation), over the tendency of some individuals to ignore the values of democracy and communal ownership, and over the burden of committee work which fell on disproportionately few shoulders. But conflict was minimised by frequent reference to Christian principles. Resentment and irritability caused by pressures of work during the committee cycle, when four evenings a week could be spent at church meetings, surfaced in individual remarks like, 'Oh, is *that* where I am tonight?' in response to the announcement that the meeting of the X committee would begin. The potential confusion was minimised by ritual to mark the change of role between one committee meeting and the next. Thus the opening prayer at the meeting of the Finance Committee expressed gratitude for God's care which extended over everything, although some activities – like the business of the meeting – were not spiritual. More important than ritual acknowledgement of role changes were the frequent references to the Work, or Vision, and the rightness of age-related responsibilities in the context of a church career. Conflict was itself devalued in the use of such expressions as 'naughty', for those who violated the rules; X was 'a blighter' for wishing to deprive others of their democratic rights; the keen disagreement over the issue of tea at a women's meeting was dismissed as a 'cafuffle' and so on.

The majority of church members would at first talk only about the commonplace. They were unwilling to submit themselves to personal scrutiny or to be unchristian in referring critically to others. Such remarks as, '*Mrs J* is very good, but as for a *nameless* lady …!' involved me in detective work which was both frustrating and time-consuming.

It is sometimes assumed that anthropological research in familiar settings confers special advantages, not simply of access but of understanding born of shared cultural experience. Aguilar (1981) offers three arguments in favour of insider research. First, the research worker is able to blend into situations and is therefore less likely to alter them. Secondly, she is better able to read non-verbal indications of subjective states like suspicion, confidence and embarrassment and so she is able to adapt her behaviour more effectively to sustain the flow of information. Finally, her ability to read behavioural cues allows her to gauge the trustworthiness of verbal responses.

But the very fact of the research means that one remains an outsider: true insider status is impossible to achieve (Sarsby 1984; Aguilar 1981). A scientific perspective and professional ideology have been absorbed and carried into the field. In addition, the structural complexity of British society – differences of class, age, ethnicity and so on – makes the insider relatively outside the research population. This marginal status provides the opportunity to retain some of the assets of insider status while minimising some of its liabilities: over-familiarity and loss of curiosity. The danger to be avoided is that of assuming one understands the other person's experience intuitively while occupying a quite different structural position.

The anthropological assumption that things are never what they seem, and that in addition to what people say or do there is always something else going on, takes on a fine irony in anthropological research 'at home'. As a member of the culture under study I had to be doubly careful to check my own assumptions. There was the danger that my own attitudes to age, a product of social conditioning, would interfere with my perception of what was happening and my interpretation of the material, and thereby influence social processes in ways I did not appreciate. My awareness of the danger was heightened by the extensive literature on ageism (for example, Itzin 1986; Ward 1979; Butler 1969) and by personal experiences 'in the field'. One never-to-be-forgotten verbal exchange took place before a meeting of the women's fellowship. Grace (78) was telling a small group about her current piece of home improvement. She had had a rush to get to the meeting because of the need to finish papering her bedroom walls. 'I had to get on and finish it. After all you don't know how long you've got before ...'. At this point her friend Bettie interrupted with a related remark, and I silently anticipated what was coming, 'you can't climb the ladder'. The actual conclusion of the sentence was chastening: 'before the paste goes dry'. This private exposure of ageist assumptions was an important lesson in the need to be fully aware of my own attitudes before attempting to study other people's.

In some ways, the similarity between researcher and subjects was an advantage. It is easier to become integrated into a voluntary association which is primarily expressive in orientation when one shares significant social characteristics with the members. Similar in age, gender, social class and family circumstances to members of the younger women's organisation in church, I found it easy to gain acceptance and enter into the experience of membership. Such ease of access has been noted by other researchers who resemble their informants in crucial ways (Finch 1984).

After a number of compromises I achieved in the end an adequate range of informants and material, in both church and clubs. During the eight months of full-time field-work (January to August 1985) I studied in depth nine old people's clubs and three age-graded organisations in the church community. As I have said, my methods included participant observation, unstructured interviewing and the use of documentary evidence. This latter consisted of church and club newsletters, minutes of meetings, annual reports, personal letters and newspapers and popular literature favoured by club members for private and public reading. I attended approximately forty old people's club meetings and the same number of business, devotional and social meetings in the church. I went on three coach trips and a church outing.

I got to know approximately one hundred and seventy people, ranging in age from late 30s to mid-90s, of whom the majority were in their 70s and 80s. I have detailed information on fifty-five of them. My informants fell into three categories: club and society members, voluntary workers in clubs run by charitable organisations, and professional people in regular contact with elderly people (a coach driver, the minister, social workers). People in the first category were by far the most numerous. They included my principal informants, with whom I had repeated personal contact, made visits, went on club outings, and whose relatives and friends I interacted with. The rest of this group were old people with whom I had regular but less intimate contact. They provided a substantial amount of case material.

Between September 1985 and March 1986 I had only sporadic contact with my informants but still acquired some useful new information and additional insights into the culture of old-age organisations. The final three months of full-time research – April 1986 to July 1986 – were set aside for processing the results of the study. This meant analysing my copious field-notes, interview material and documentary evidence and writing it up. Before the writing could begin I had to classify my field-notes according to my original interests and new categories based on unanticipated discoveries in the field.

In the nature of anthropological research, new and interesting issues had emerged which I had not foreseen in the absence of intimate acquaintance with the world of old-age organisations as it is experienced by participants. After eight months of involvement in clubs and friendship networks important new themes stood out (Jerrome 1986). They concerned models of ageing, the allocation of leadership roles, the place of ritual in the social construction of old age, and the ageing of organisations themselves. There were several stages in the analysis of my material. I outline them here in some detail in order to dispel some of the mystery which surrounds the intellectual processes involved in translating field-notes based on observed phenomena abstracted from the flow of events into a final analysis, procedures which are often not entirely clear to anthropologists themselves (Pelto and Pelto 1978). The question of how data are recognised in the field and turned into intellectual artifacts has been dealt with by a number of writers (for example, Crick 1982; Holy 1984; Yates 1985). Social anthropology does have an apparatus for legitimating its claims to knowledge. There are rules for the production of knowledge, and the production of authentic anthropological work must be bound by them. Contrary to the belief that social anthropology is atheoretical or mindlessly empirical, it is in fact deeply influenced by trends in European thought (Salmond 1982) – in my case the hermeneutic model.

My material consisted of informants' statements, expressed beliefs, discernible attitudes and values; formal and informal interactions – verbal and physical, from conversation and joking to making tea and choosing seats – as I had observed and experienced them; poems, sayings, prayers and other verbal and physical rituals which I had heard or witnessed and in which I had taken part; and my interpretation of these phenomena, and explanations sought from or volunteered by informants. This material, recorded chronologically in note form in a number of notebooks, was typed up as soon after it had been collected as possible. At the end of the field-work period the mass of typed notes needed to be analysed. The analysis of extended open-ended interview material poses problems, though such interviews produce texts that can be coded thematically through a type of content analysis (Clark and Anderson 1967; Keith 1980b). The hundreds of pages of field-notes recorded throughout participant observation research are more problematic. They must be indexed and cross-referenced so that patterns can be discovered. Various writers have indicated how this might be done. Whyte (1955) describes an indexing system. Spradley (1980) offers a system for making a cultural inventory from field-notes. Keith (1980b) refers to software packages available for microcomputers to deal with the task of indexing and creation of subfiles in narrative texts.

In my own case, the analysis was conducted in three stages. In the first I coded my field-notes in terms of a number of categories. The categories included such issues as 'age characteristics of members', 'age references in conversation', 'values', 'death'. They had emerged through a close reading of my completed notes in May 1986. There were forty-one categories altogether. I then made three copies of the original set of typed field-notes. In the second stage I rearranged the notes into these forty-one categories. I combined some which overlapped, such as 'seating arrangements' and 'social networks'; and 'assumptions about friendships' with 'activities of friendship'. This reduced the original forty-one categories to twenty-one. In the third phase I grouped the twenty-one categories into broader topics, such as 'benefits of membership', 'health and illness', and summarised each one with cross-references to my notes. At the same time I drew out the theoretical implications and links with the literature of social gerontology. The broader topics provide the basis for the chapters of this book.

In trying to condense social experience into identifiable trends and regularities I might have given my findings a coherence they do not possess. This is a theoretical problem in all empirical social science research. It is tempting to impose order on the chaos of everyday life. But the connections made in the following pages do not, I am sure, distort the social reality of my informants. Nor do they conflict with major insights existing in the literature.

THREE

The social world of elderly joiners

This chapter is about old people's clubs, one of the types of organisation chosen as a setting for the study. We see them first in the broader context of old-age organisations. The range of clubs and associations for retired people in Seatown is wide. 'Pensioners' clubs' as they are popularly known, are to be distinguished from those for which former occupation is a basis for membership. These include clubs for retired nurses and members of particular trade unions. Pensioners' clubs also exclude organisations based on specific intellectual or cultural interests such as the University of the Third Age. A fourth group have as their aim the promotion of physical well-being through the provision of meals: lunch clubs are normally run by voluntary or statutory welfare agencies, including charitable and religious organisations. There are numerous other associations which attract predominantly old people, though age is not a criterion of membership. Among them are women's organisations (the Women's Institute, Townswomen's Guild, Mothers' Union), special interest groups based on sports or hobbies (horticultural societies, bowls clubs, 'fur and feathers' clubs) and church-based or religious organisations.

In addition to these age-specific groupings are heterogeneous organisations like working men's clubs, churches and political parties which have their share of elderly participants. Older people do not necessarily participate in the same way as other members, however. There is relatively little mixing, elders occupy a peripheral place and there are noticeable subgroupings based on age. During the day, the bar in the working men's club is the province largely of the old. In the church, fellowships of age mates from the youngest to the very old gather together to pursue their common interests.

There are about forty pensioners' clubs in Seatown. Some have been operating for more than thirty years. The majority were founded more recently. They vary in size from nearly two hundred and fifty members to less than thirty, though most have between sixty and ninety with a weekly attendance of about fifty. In terms of organisational links the clubs fall into four categories. The largest includes those which are affiliated to the National Federation of Retirement Pensioners' Associations. In the next largest group are independent clubs. The two remaining categories consist of those clubs which are organised by charitable bodies such as the Red Cross and Age Concern and those which are affiliated to age-mixed umbrella organisations – churches and community associations.

The environmental setting varies from church hall (the most popular) to community centre, local authority old people's home and public house. With the exception of Age Concern clubs (run by the local branch of a large national charity), the role structure of the clubs is broadly similar, varying only in the degree of formality and number of office holders. The conventional range of officers consists of chairman and vice-chairman, secretary, treasurer and social secretary. In the larger clubs there is also a registrar, responsible for enrolments and attendance registers. Most of the other jobs involve financial transactions: selling second-hand books and clothing, food items, the pensioners' magazine, bingo and raffle tickets, tickets for tea and biscuits. Other members of the committee make the refreshments, call the bingo numbers, and provide musical accompaniment on piano or accordion where necessary. In the smaller clubs functions are combined so that executive committees are small. All the main offices may be undertaken by the chairman or a husband and wife team.

The clubs are generally self-financing and self-supporting. In all apart from the Age Concern clubs and one or two which benefit from occasional donations from business interests or subsidies from sponsoring organisations (church or community associations), weekly costs are balanced by income. With minor variations from club to club, the weekly income is produced by sales of second-hand goods, of refreshments, bingo and raffle tickets, proceeds from the weekly bring-and-buy sale, profits from the sale of foodstuffs bought at wholesale prices (and in one club from the resale of egg boxes to egg retailers in the local market), from silver and copper collections (the benevolent or 'sick fund', the general collection) and contributions to a thrift or savings club. Weekly expenditure on refreshments, bingo prizes (a few pence each), flowers for sick members, birthday cards and gifts, is more than covered by the income. The balance is saved for extraordinary expenditure – the occasional concert party, periodic celebrations and so on. In some clubs members play bingo for nothing but the prizes are donated – a house plant, a bar of soap, some sugar lumps in a polystyrene cup, a bunch of flowers.

Beyond the weekly income the club collects other sums. There is the annual members' subscription, at least one bring-and-buy sale a year; special raffles, the interest on members' savings, occasional donations, and the interest on contributions towards outings and the club holiday. This income is used to pay the rental charges on the hall. It also meets the cost of outings and the Christmas party, and of special raffle prizes and extra treats on club outings. Both income and expenditure are on a small scale. The sale of raffle tickets on the coach, for instance, is set against the coach parking fee. The items in the weekly income and expenditure are given in pounds and pence. Financial management in even the largest club is on the scale of a modest single-person-household economy. Annual balances are substantial – running to hundreds of pounds – but the weekly balance of a few pounds and pence produces murmurs of appreciation, applause if it reaches double figures.

Organisational goals are broadly similar, expressive rather than instru-mental. Clubs exist to provide company, practical and moral support in illness and adversity, an interest in life, a number of treats, and a respite from less desirable associates such as difficult family members. The benefit most frequently cited by organisers and appearing, indeed, to be the club's *raison d'être*, is the opportunity for friendship and social involvement through conversation and shared activities. Leaders see the club holidays and day trips as the highlights of club activity. They provide an intensity of interaction unrivalled in the normal day-to-day experience of members, most of whom live alone. So vital is the service provided by the clubs that the belief, 'We *never* close', is deeply rooted in club mythology.

The Federation clubs have an additional goal, more instrumental in nature. It involves promoting the interests of retired people both nationally (through a system of financial contributions to political struggles fought at national level) and locally through mounting campaigns on specific issues. However, the Federation clubs in the study tend to be ambivalent towards these political activities, claiming that member subscriptions to the national association are too high. They claim that the battle for an improved standard of living has been fought and won. They assert that members are not particularly interested in the work of the Federation or in attending regional meetings. One of the strongest branches, on the point of leaving the Federation, had in previous years sent many delegates to regional meetings. But their chairman, highly committed to the political goals of the organisation, had hired a coach and made an outing out of it. With her death the instrumental goal of political achievement beyond the confines of the club finally gave way to the expressive goal of entertainment.

Differences in title express the conflict in orientation. The Good Com-panions Club, as its members call it, becomes the Prospect Place branch, in the records of the Federation. The difference in outlook and aims between different levels of the Federation emerged clearly in a district committee meeting debate on recruitment. A club leader lamented that there were too many clubs competing for a few good entertainers. Her cry was greeted with astonishment by the politically-oriented regional organiser. For her there could never be too many clubs in support of a political movement. The Federation clubs share a framework, a constitution and a set of objectives defined nationally. But their members and executive committees are gener-ally more interested in entertainment than politics.

While similar to Federation clubs in organisational aims and outlook, other pensioners' clubs are autonomous. Independent, self-financing and self-supporting, they collaborate only to fill the coach for the annual sum-mer holiday. The clubs are run largely as personal projects by leaders with entrepreneurial leanings and a social conscience. Leaders talk about 'my

Table 3.1 Club memberships of five women friends

	Silver Lining	Sunday Club	St Brelade's	St Anthony's	New Place	Good Companions	Pit Crescent	St Thomas's	Red Cross	Good Shepherd	Residents' Assocn O.P.C.	Stamford Rd Lunch Club	Current Total
Laura		✓									✓	✓	3
Nellie	✓	✓								✓			3
Jean	✓	✓	✓	✓	(✓)	(✓)	(✓)						4
Edna	✓	✓	✓	✓	(✓)	(✓)	(✓)						4
Bessie	✓	✓			✓				✓	✓			5

(✓) = formerly

club' and 'my members'. For members too the club is a source of pride and a focus for loyalty. There is competition between clubs, manifest in the gossip and rumour about the inferior practices of rivals. Leaders say darkly, 'We hear a lot!'

We pass·round a box (for contributions for tea): Mrs S makes you pay in advance!'

'You don't get *any* tea up there!'

X club is going to be shut by the council, unsuitable premises!'

'Other clubs get financial support (from the Social Services Department, local business etc.): mine doesn't.'

'My trips are better than their trips, we have a raffle on the coach.'

Such issues provide a basis for comparison, and invidious distinctions are drawn. There is much talk about clubs over tea as members exchange views about recent meetings attended or missed, about proposed visits and outings, about the relative costs and benefits attached to membership of particular organisations. The leaders have their own information network but also rely on general gossip for their knowledge of what is going on.

While the clubs are autonomous at the organisational level they are linked by visiting pianists, concert parties and other entertainers. Some of these people are on the executive committees of their own clubs. There is also a substantial overlap in membership; people who go to clubs at all tend to belong to several. Multiple membership, frequently of as many as four or five clubs, is normal. Club-going is a way of life, hence the indigenous expression, 'in the clubs'; 'she's, like, *in* the clubs'. This describes someone's involvement in a system or circuit (see Figure 3.1).

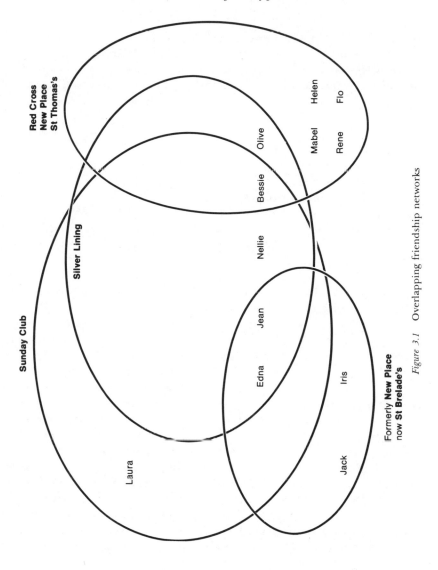

Figure 3.1 Overlapping friendship networks

The world of the clubs

If clubland implies a geographical area, 'clubworld' is a social phenomenon, a bounded unit with its own system of relationships, values and
interests. Social networks in the club population are close-knit. Their
character is a product of plural membership, of movement into and out of
organisations. Friends belong to additional clubs and invite each other on
their club outings and holidays. The example of a group of friends at the
Sunday Club is typical (see Table 3.1). The five women belong to ten clubs
between them. Adding the clubs which they have joined and left previously,
they have direct knowledge of twelve. Through other friends in their
networks they have indirect knowledge of many more.

In each club they belong to a different friendship network, acknowledged by outsiders as 'Your gang'.

The overlap in membership has several implications. On entering a club,
a prospective member will invariably recognise some of the people present,
and will probably know some well enough to talk to. Members have access to
information about other clubs and people. A further consequence is the
tendency for members to get caught up in interpersonal conflicts starting in
one club and spreading beyond it.

Information spreads rapidly and over considerable distances. Paths of
information are frequently marked by material exchanges. In club meetings
items can be seen changing hands, to the accompaniment of enquiries
about health, news of recent deaths, assessments of recent events and
information about forthcoming ones. Items such as women's magazines,
local newspapers, church magazines and newsletters follow regular paths,
reinforcing relationships among members of the distribution network. As
in some classical trading systems, material items are vital in the promotion
of non-material exchanges (Malinowski 1922). Viewed in this way as a social
rather than material transaction, the lending and borrowing of books and
magazines is a vital part of the club communication system. People who
have no particular interest in the content of the literature involved and
apparently no reason to disseminate it become involved as a social strategy.
Such was the case of a woman who undertook to deliver copies of the *Warcry*
to various people though she herself was not a Salvationist. The absence of
one of these 'customers' at a meeting where she had been expected led to
questions about whether she had received her copy through a friend of the
distributor, as arranged. This sparked off an investigation leading to her
discovery at home in a state of physical collapse. The following case illustrates the role of material items in sustaining relationships.

> Her magazines are very important to Miss A, who lives alone in a
> council flat. She has the *Christian Herald* (two copies), the *Weekly News*,
> the *People's Friend* and *Woman's Weekly*. She is fit and active and goes out
> a lot, always taking a magazine with her. If it is fine she goes out most

afternoons and finds a comfortable place to read – the pier, the local park. On Sundays, the only difficult time of the week, she lies on her bed and reads the *Christian Herald*. Miss A has two friends with whom she goes to church, and a sister in the town. On different days she goes to a women's fellowship, a lunch club and pensioners' club. She is rather shy and does not talk much at her Thursday club but sits next to the woman who sells the second-hand books. She likes 'the book lady' very much and has started giving her the spare copy of the *Christian Herald* which Miss A used to collect for a neighbour who has since died. Her own copy she passes on to Mrs B who used to work on the same factory bench. Miss A began giving her copy of the *Christian Herald* to Mrs B soon after her husband died. She also gives Mrs B the *Weekly News* and the *People's Friend*. Miss A does not, in fact, ever see Mrs B. Miss A's sister drops the papers in to Mrs B since she lives nearby. Miss A sometimes bumps into Mrs B when out shopping but otherwise they have no direct contact. Miss A passes her copy of *Woman's Weekly* on to her sister first, who passes it on to Mrs B and a neighbour after that.

In Miss A's case, magazines are a substitute for direct contact with people she wants to keep as part of her network but whom she rarely sees. Items are lent with the object of establishing friendly relations or to strengthen failing ones. So long as the loan is retained the lines of communication are kept open and the recipient is under an obligation to respond to friendly overtures. The return of the item closes the transaction and the recipient is under no further obligation. There are striking parallels here with the pattern of material exchanges in very different societies. In marriage trans- actions in a Nigerian society a token amount, the value of a small coin, is left outstanding to preserve the sense of obligation in the man's family towards the woman's. The obligation is discharged in a series of ongoing acts of reciprocal help (Jerrome 1973).

In one instance, a set of *Woman's Weekly* library books was deliberately used to keep the lines of communication open between a core member of a network and a woman on the periphery who seemed on the point of withdrawing altogether. So long as the magazines were not returned plans could be made collectively for their retrieval, involving visits to the woman's home and a chance to monitor her health and general behaviour. While the magazines were outstanding there were many anxious conferences in twos and threes. People in overlapping networks were consulted for news of the deviant and their evaluation of her state of mind. The eventual return of the loan (through a third party) meant that there was no basis for the relation- ship and it ended, to the regret of the core member and the obvious satisfaction of the other.

The core member, Grace, is an intelligent, shrewd and politically astute woman, typical of club members in many ways. Club-going marks the boundaries of her social world. Beyond her daughter's family and domestic organisation, her main interests are clubs and their members. The cognitive map of the average club-goer is similar. Its landmarks are clubs, people, health, diet and personal issues such as housing. Grace has extensive knowledge of clubs and their personnel, and displays a remarkable memory for personal detail. She knows the day, time and place of all the local meetings, their social composition and the addresses of their key officials. Her impressive memory and other intellectual skills displayed in relation to club life underline the point that the expression of intelligence is culturally determined.

The typical club member is an astute judge of the quality of club life and the success of its leadership. She samples clubs and judges them according to personal criteria. Her movement from club to club and membership of several is less a sign of social deprivation (as some organisers are inclined to see it) than a rational exercise of consumer choice. Contrary to the stereotypical view held by club officials of the club-goers as passive, dependent and undiscriminating, she is independent and critical.

The typical member is seen by the leadership as an elderly widow, living alone and potentially lonely. The official view is consistent with popular stereotypes including those of old people who strenuously avoid such gatherings. Pensioners' clubs are seen as catering for the dispossessed – the elderly, the widowed, people who have low status by virtue of their age, marital standing and social class. The club population is thought to consist of people with few resources for more pleasurable and less stigmatised activity, with no experience of voluntary associations before retirement and inadequate social networks. As we have seen, this picture is confirmed in some of the literature on old people's clubs (Harris 1975, 1983). Such organisations are marginal and set their members further apart from the main stream of age-heterogeneous living. Occasionally members of clubs set up by charities to cater for the old and lonely describe the pain of finally acknowledging that they belong to the stigmatised category, the shock of identification with those lonely old people, the feeling of disbelief that they had 'come to this'.

People do generally give the need for social contact as the reason for their participation. Their sense of relative isolation is a product of bereavement. The loss of a spouse or sibling creates an intolerable gap in their lives. But in relation to similarly bereaved non-joiners – the majority of the retired population – they are well connected, an elite in terms of morale, health, social contact and positive outlook on life. It is true that the reasons given for joining an old people's club are somewhere to go, something to do, somewhere to meet people and pass the time. These stated reasons confirm the leaders' perceptions of their members as lonely, isolated and in need of support. Membership is indeed a strategy for dealing with loneliness and the lack of activity. But members start from a position of relative advantage.

The truly isolated and stereotypically disadvantaged old person – lonely, depressed, lacking in confidence – who most needs the expressive outlet afforded by social participation of this kind is least likely to enjoy it.

Members of the age-graded organisations I studied already belong to social networks, often active, extensive and close-knit. Access to the association is itself gained through these contacts. This is even the case in the one Age Concern club in my sample set up specifically for the lonely and unattached. The very few people in the club population who belong to one club only are an exception. Even they, with smaller and more loose-knit networks, entered the club world originally through an older relative, a neighbour or someone known in a service capacity such as a friendly hairdresser. The following examples give some idea of the circumstances in which people join:

> Mrs W moved to Brighton on the death of her husband twenty years ago, to be near her older sister. She had looked for a local Women's Institute to join, but couldn't find one. So she went to the local old people's club with her sister and brother-in-law. The club dwindled in members and closed, but a friend of Mrs W's sister who was vice-chairman of St Anthony's – another club in the neighbourhood – suggested they join. Both the sister and the friend are dead now. Mrs W is quite friendly with two other people on her table, Mr and Mrs G who joined ten years ago. Mrs G had come along first, at the invitation of her husband's sister who was a member. Everyone said, 'Bring your husband'; so she did. The husband's sister, whom Mrs W got to know through the Gs, and visited from time to time, is also dead. Mrs W is trying to persuade some of her neighbours to give the club a try.

> Maisie, aged 77, social secretary and pianist of the Stamford Road club, joined seventeen years ago on the invitation of a retired friend, and an uncle who had played the piano before her. When the friend died Maisie took over her job as social secretary. She belongs to no other clubs.

> The day after her retirement, Rose fell into conversation with an elderly couple in a cafe. They invited her to join their club and she did, fifteen years ago. There she discovered people she already knew, such as the chairman's wife, president of her townswomen's guild. She became friendly with other members too, and through one of them joined the Good Companions Club.

> Mrs K in her 80s loves 'the clubs' and couldn't do without them. She includes in this term a number of different types of organisation – pensioners' clubs, a lunch club and a women's devotional group. She joined the Thursday afternoon Stamford Road Pensioners' Club twenty years ago at the suggestion of her lodger, a man she subsequently married. When he died three years ago she was desolate,

and her health began to fail. She joined the Wednesday lunch club for unattached people, run by members of her church. One of the organisers was an old friend, a woman of her own age whom she had first met in the women's fellowship. At the lunch club she shared a table with old Mr A whom she had known years before when he had a bedsitting room on the sea front. He was now living nearby, with the same landlady. Mrs K began to accompany him to St Anthony's Old People's Club after lunch on Wednesday. To fill the gap which still remained, Mrs K revived her membership of the Tuesday women's fellowship and joined the Good Companions on Fridays at the suggestion of two old friends from the Thursday afternoon Stamford Road Club. There she met a woman who shared her love of dancing and suggested she joined a dance club on a Monday afternoon. She goes there when she feels fit, with a friend from Stamford Road.

The typical member is widowed and in her 70s. She has joined on the death of her husband or, in some cases, together with him on his retirement. There are some unattached men and married couples. A disproportionate number of them hold office. But in general the clubs are female-dominated. The ratio of men to women at meetings ranges in the nine clubs I studied from 1:10 to 1:30. Indeed, where the chairman (as she is universally called) is female, as is the case in most clubs, members may be addressed collectively as 'ladies'. The few men are socially invisible.

Gender

The predominance of women and its effect on club culture raises a question about the salience of gender. The designation of the clubs as 'old people's clubs' implies that they are open to everyone. The popular assumption is that male members are limited by their numbers in the population. But their representation at meetings does not reflect demographic patterns exactly: proportionately fewer male members actually attend meetings.

The reason for the gender imbalance emerges when we consider what goes on at meetings, and in particular the expressive orientation of club culture. The club exists to promote social intercourse among its members. The social interaction it affords is highly·valued. In some cases it provides a respite from conflict-ridden family relationships. It offers a breathing space for elderly siblings – generally pairs of sisters – in claustrophobic relationships, for mothers whose daughters are too demanding or controlling. Through conversation, joking, gift-exchange and shared activities such as card-playing and bingo, women's needs for intimacy and companionship are met. Their identity of interest and outlook is affirmed. The busy talk which is a feature of meetings goes on unabated over the tea and often *sotto voce* through the games session which follows.

The special qualities of women's talk, in particular the therapeutic and socialising functions which have been noted by several writers (for example,

Johnson and Aries 1983; D. Jones 1980) help to explain the predominance of women in the clubs. In the choice of friends and voluntary associates like is drawn to like. The ease of communication which arises from shared experience is assisted by shared linguistic forms: women and men inhabit different speech communities (Spender 1980, Lakoff 1975). To some extent then the gender imbalance can be related to the different social worlds inhabited by men and women.

Clubs are female-dominated though what this means in terms of culture is not clear. In terms of gender there is a theoretical issue to address. It concerns the preponderance of women and degree of female solidarity. In the club population there is little consciousness of gender issues. Sexual politics in this world of old women take the form of ambivalent remarks and lewd jokes. Humorous references to men and sexual activity express both desire and contempt, though in a practical sense men are of little importance in the lives of the majority of the women. The absence of men in meetings of the peer group does not appear to be a matter either for regret or satisfaction, though there is some concern to protect individual friendship groups from encroachment by male members. Participation in club life is as much an expression of friendship with other women as coming to terms with – or even celebrating – the absence of men. But occasional comments by the women suggest that the activities currently enjoyed with female friends would be abandoned in favour of the partner's company if he were alive. The relationship between friendship and marriage is developed in a subsequent chapter.

The programme

The programme reflects the cultural uniformity of the clubworld. The membership is almost without exception white, Christian and British. The majority originate in the south of England and belong to the same subjective category in ethnic terms.

The typical meeting starts with a hymn and a prayer. In the more religious clubs – those whose affiliation to the church extends beyond the hire of the church hall – this part is referred to as 'devotions'. The hymn may be chosen from the Pensioners' Song Book published by the National Federation or be a regular favourite. The opening prayer expresses concern for the club and its members, especially the sick and those who have organised the meeting, and anticipates a happy afternoon. In a minority of clubs the devotional element is replaced by a similar ritual activity. The hymn is replaced by the club's signature tune followed by the Lord's Prayer. Gabbled or muttered with little ceremony, the rendering of the Lord's Prayer, sometimes in the incongruous setting of the upstairs room of a public house, seems to have little religious significance. It is important as a customary practice.

Next comes the announcement of deaths (if any), followed by birthdays.

At the news of a death a brief silence is kept in the dead member's memory and details of the funeral are given. The atmosphere changes instantly with the birthday item. Birthdays are celebrated with cards, a small gift such as a bar of chocolate or soap, a kiss and the birthday song. The very old are sometimes given money, in recognition of their achievement. The words of the song vary from the conventional 'Happy birthday to you' to the more moralistic kind quoted at the beginning of Chapter Eight. After the birthday announcements comes the 'sick news', with up-to-date information about absentees. Condolences are extended to the sick and congratulations are offered to returning members, welcomed back with a round of applause.

'The business' comes next, starting with the minutes of the previous meeting. The style is formal and business-like with a recurrence of conventional phrases: 'Your kind attention is requested while the secretary reads the minutes ... ' 'May I have your approval for the minutes ... ' The minutes themselves follow a conventional form and are highly repetitive from week to week. Phrases such as 'Tea was served with willing helpers' are used week in, week out, year after year. A forest of hands signifies the wish to propose and second the minutes. The competition to be recorded in the minute-book ends in triumph for the successful members and resignation or laughter for the rest.

Business announcements include items of particular interest to retired people in an urban area in the south-east of England: a special offer of home security devices for pensioners by a local businessman; a similar offer from Woolworths department store of cheap photographs for bus passes; and so on. The treasurer gives information about donations (if any) and money is collected for particular purposes in boxes passed from hand to hand. In some clubs such collections are made at the door on entry to or exit from the meeting. The social secretary makes reference to forthcoming outings, inviting a show of hands in favour of possible alternatives, urging payment for those already planned, and giving the latest information about the proposed club holiday.

The first part of the meeting ends with refreshments, invariably tea and two biscuits. Arrangements vary from club to club for the payment and distribution of tea. In some a ticket is purchased at the beginning, in others a collection is made during the meeting. In one club each member receives at the beginning, on payment of ten pence, a saucer, two biscuits and a raffle ticket, and sits with this collection on her knee until it is joined eventually by a cup full of tea. The twenty minutes or more spent on consuming refreshments is the noisiest part of the meeting. It is the main opportunity for informal interaction and is welcomed as an opportunity to talk to friends. In a meeting at St Brelade's, a club where the seats are arranged to maximise eye contact, every one of the eighty or so members present was involved in conversation. All were observed to be either talking or listening: no-one was isolated. In other clubs the pattern of interaction is the same.

The second half of the meeting is spent on entertainment of some kind. The majority of clubs play bingo, either occasionally or every week. If only occasionally it is interspersed with card games, quizzes, dancing and musical or dramatic performances by members. The wealthier clubs invite outside entertainers, most of whom offer a revue-style programme consisting of sketches, dancing, jokes and singalongs (in which the audience is invited to participate).

Bingo is taken seriously as a game demanding concentration (Dixey and Talbot 1982). The silence is broken only by the voice of the caller, normally the chairman but occasionally another committee member. In the larger clubs the prizes are relatively high – one pound for a full house – which might account for the intensity of play. In most the financial rewards of the game are low. The regular announcement that bingo 'will be played for Big Money' always brings a laugh, but a win is a source of great pleasure. One of my informants brightened at the recollection of a win four weeks previously, 'the first for years'. The pleasure is shared by friends, whose noisy response when 'our table' wins suggests a sense of collective achievement.

Card-playing is a more individual affair, though different groups of players have their own particular style of play. These differences reflect the motives of the players and the significance the game has for them personally and for the group. Cards are played either as a pastime or to demonstrate skill. In the former situation the game is less important than the conversation which accompanies it. In the latter the priorities are the other way round: the game is satisfying as an end in itself. Among those who play to demonstrate skill the game is given an extra dimension with financial stakes. However small, their pursuit generates an intensity and excitement missing in the cards-as-pastime groups. Viewed by the other group as people who take cards too seriously, they see themselves as skillful and dashing. Their approach to cards has a *risqué* element which the less sophisticated might find off-putting. Rose, for instance, told with relish of the good time she and Flo had had on Sunday. They had almost got thrown out for their noise. Furthermore, 'we frightened off a little old lady who had come to visit: *we* play for money!'

Apart from the bingo and card-playing clubs are those whose entertainment takes musical or dramatic form. The performance is given either by paid entertainers or club members on a 'do-it-yourself' basis. 'Do-it-yourself' afternoons take much the same form from week to week with the same group of individuals offering their usual pieces. A typical example comes from the Stamford Road Club. First the pianist, Maisie, played a selection of Rogers and Hammerstein film music, in an arrangement for piano. Next there were solos from Violet, who sang popular and sentimental songs dating from the pre-war years such as 'Little Old Lady' and 'She Was Too

Young'. One of the men read some jokes from a joke book, again with reference to age. (There was the one about the old man in the cinema who was scrabbling about on the floor looking for a toffee. Hadn't he got another one? 'Yes, but that one's got my tooth in it!' and one about the 18-year-old and her elderly husband who got into difficulties on their wedding night: 'She'd never been told and he'd forgotten!') Next, Doris shared with everyone a touching incident observed on a recent outing. It involved a mentally handicapped woman made comfortable in the boot of her parents' car so that she could enjoy a performance of the band. The father and mother seemed to adore her and the whole family was very happy. With emotion Dorothy concluded, 'It taught us (Dorothy, and her friend, the mentally handicapped woman, her parents) what we had to be thankful for … the care being taken of her … I hope that her parents will live long to care for her'. This beautiful if slightly obscure message was greeted with applause. The next item was musical. Harold sang some old favourites – 'Bless this House', 'Sussex by the Sea' and 'Old Father Thames'. That was followed by a quiz in which members were invited to think of as many words as they could, beginning with cat- and mat-. The afternoon ended with 'Just a Song at Twilight', another popular song associated with their youth, led by Harold with a chorus which everyone sang.

Visiting concert parties offer sketches and nostalgic accounts of the Old Days when life was better. 'Do you remember …' may be a rhetorical question but the audience responds with murmurs and private reminiscences. Another regular feature of both do-it-yourself afternoons and visits by guest performers is the reading of extracts from *The Friendship Book* by Francis Gay. *The Friendship Book* is an annual publication, consisting of wise sayings, apothegms, texts, prayers and stories with a moral, one for each day of the year. It belongs to the genre of Patience Strong and the Readers' Digest, its tone semi-religious, moralistic, sentimental and somewhat trite. Its popularity as a source of public reading is unrivalled, and it is a popular gift for private consumption, to be found in homes where there are no other books.

Like Doris's story of the mentally handicapped woman, many extracts reflect the theme of coping with adversity. The message of acceptance, stoicism and hope is conveyed by popular expressions such as, 'We have a lot to be thankful for', 'Count your blessings', 'Every cloud has a silver lining'. Other themes which emerge from the readings are interdependence and reciprocity as a basis for relationships, the importance of caring and concern for others, and the principle of just deserts. The virtues of tact and conciliation, of modesty and humility and of trust, are constantly upheld.

The final twenty minutes of the meeting are spent drawing the winning raffle tickets and singing the closing hymn or club song.The raffle goes on as long as there are still prizes to be won. Before the closing rituals, the chairman utters the usual words: 'Thank you for all the gifts on the table and for any help you give to the club in any way – Thanks for coming and making this a successful afternoon ... Now let us end in the usual way'. The usual ending is typically a hymn, or old wartime song adopted as the club's own: 'God be with you till we meet again', 'Now is the hour when we must say goodbye', 'You are my sunshine', 'Be sincere in everything you do'. The singing is in many cases rounded off with Auld Lang Syne, hands linked where seating permits.

An exception to this pattern is provided by the Age Concern Sunday Club which closes its meetings with a reading from *The Friendship Book* and a prayer. A typical ending of this club meeting is worth quoting in full, since it raises important questions which will occupy us for the remainder of the chapter. At the end of the meeting in question the organiser, Miss C, made the usual remarks:

'Well, we've had a lovely time'.

(This was greeted with the usual applause.)

'We'd like to welcome our new members, hope to see you again'.

(Applause)

'Thanks to our helpers'.

(Applause)

(She then read from *The Friendship Book* about a handless man struggling to overcome his handicap. There was again applause which Miss C interrupted):

'Here's a message for us all. Our members are handicapped in various ways, and lonely too. But they come and have a happy time and share friendship. And that's what it's all about'.

The members signified their agreement by applauding Miss C. After a short prayer, largely repeating these sentiments, the meeting was over. The choice of words from *The Friendship Book* is significant. Set alongside observation of club members' behaviour and conversation it provides a clue to their ideas about living with age. The phrase, 'That's what it's all about', is a popular one in the language of the clubs. It signifies a definition of the situation, in this case by the organiser whose view is expressed ritualistically every Sunday and affirmed collectively by the members. Other repetitive phrases and responses to them serve a similar purpose. Their use brings us to a consideration of the meanings attached to various parts of the programme and its significance for members individually and collectively.

Peer group rituals

The remark, 'That's what it's all about', is used regularly to affirm the shared values of friendship and sociability, of struggle and of coming to terms with adversity. The recurrent activities and statements which make up the programme form a predictable sequence with symbolic significance. Through the phrases and expressions which are repeated over many years, through the songs and readings, and the dramatic performances, certain values are collectively expressed and sustained. The messages are sometimes vague as in Doris's story, and contradictory. But their vagueness allows the listeners to attribute their own meanings, based on personal experience. In the same way, the choice of songs is significant. Certain songs are repeated constantly. Their appropriation by members lends a more profound significance to the words than was originally intended (Hockey 1983) and gives them immediate personal relevance.

Through them members express doubts and uncertainties experienced collectively by virtue of their membership of a particular cohort and generation, and individually by virtue of their personal circumstances. The recurrence of songs like 'Old Father Thames' and 'There'll Always be an England' can be interpreted as a statement about the nature of time. Despite individual ageing, the things members stand for persist unchanged. The permanence of institutional arrangements and cultural patterns is in contrast to the uncertainty and loneliness of the personal journey into the unknown future. The knowledge that the uncharted passage towards extreme old age and death brings with it the possibility of disrupted relationships and abandoned lifestyles adds poignancy to the old songs, 'We'll Meet Again, Don't know where, Don't know when'; and 'I'll Walk Beside You'; and to the club songs, 'God be With You 'til We Meet Again', and 'Now is the Hour when we Must Say Goodbye'. In the prayers which start meetings and the intensity of involvement and enjoyment which follows, there is a sense of time left to live, of a present orientation which is in contrast to the future orientation of youth.

The shared activities which occupy club-goers during their meetings can thus be interpreted as rituals, in the sense of a series of patterned acts having symbolic significance, a significance related to the wider social situation of the participants. The most striking rituals are those expressing allegiance to the age group. Most of the singing – of hymns, of birthday and greeting and parting songs, and of popular songs dating from earlier periods – are of this type. They symbolise unity and solidarity, continuity of past and present, and the members' location in time. This is apparent in the seasonal rituals of Christmas and Easter. In the VE Day celebrations the old war songs are rendered with serious faces, all word-perfect. Through them and the accompanying reminiscences the war experience stays alive and with it the value of patriotism. The performance underlines the cultural distinctiveness of this generation and the value of its bequest to succeeding ones. It takes place in a context of diminished social status and of difficult age relations. The birthday songs, the sick news and welcoming back of healthy members express the value of a long life, and of resistance to illness and adversity. There are also rituals of friendship – the collection from the kitchen, distribution and consumption of cups of tea, the informal hugs and handshakes and the welcoming clap for new members. All express acceptance and solidarity in a world of attenuated social ties and exclusion from significant areas of social life.

It is suggested in the literature that social status is one of a number of areas of ambiguity in retirement. On departure from the work-force the basis of social assessment shifts. Status is no longer achieved but assigned on the basis of age. Previous identities become meaningless. Cultural prescriptions – rules for behaviour – are vague or lacking (Rosow 1967). Myerhoff (1984) puts it bleakly: 'Retirement and funerals are crude markers for the stark beginning and end of old age; in between there is a universe of differentiation that remains a cultural wasteland for each to calculate or navigate alone ...' (p. 312). Myerhoff talks about the difficulty of discontinuity in cultural conditioning. There occurs a reversal of expectations from active and assertive to passive and serene. Elderly people are seen, in the anthropological literature, as being in a state of liminality: in limbo between the fixed and regulated states of mid-life and extreme old age (Myerhoff 1984, Keith 1982). Like adolescents, they are on the threshold of a new, undefined experience.

In the circumstances the peer group assumes significance. Members of a single cohort, with common expectations based on a shared past, are a source of moral and practical support. One of the most important functions of the peer group is to engage in collective rituals which dramatise and ameliorate their situation (Hockey 1983; Myerhoff 1984). By its repetitive character ritual provides a message of pattern and predictability. There are some groups of elderly people in particular whose social invisibility calls for symbolic and ritual elaboration. The circumstances of elderly ethnic minorities, of groups who have lost their natural offspring to carry on their stories and traditions, of people without natural heirs and witnesses to validate their claims to have led worthy lives, generate ritual in old age. The sharp need expressed by elderly Jews in Venice, California to dramatise and ritually display their own version of themselves, eloquently described by Myerhoff (1978) is to some extent mirrored in the experiences of elderly British people in their clubs and fellowships. Faced with the erosion of traditional values (authority, patriotism, duty, family life) they seek constantly to affirm their belief in tradition, through symbolic displays.

In this perspective, the weekly meetings of club and fellowship are what Myerhoff calls 'definitional ceremonies', ritualised performances that 'provide arenas for garnering honour and prestige, for enacting and displaying one's own interpretation of oneself, against the play of accident, chaos and negative interpretations that may be offered up by history and outsiders' (p. 320). The recurrent themes and phrases, the prescribed responses and modes of participation, provide security, a sense of personal location in time, a link between the individual and the collective. The intensity of emotional involvement, particularly apparent during the ritual singing and entertainment, heightens feelings of solidarity and gives sensory experience of continuing existence and vitality.

The ritual process identified in this chapter is not, it appears, an isolated or untypical phenomenon. Over forty years ago, investigators for the mass observation unit witnessed very similar words, gestures and sentiments. The parallels between club activities in the mid-1980s and those of the 1940s are striking. The following is part of an account of an afternoon meeting in the London area attended by nearly 200 people, mainly women:

> After tea, a talk entitled 'How I became a Pauper'. The audience was amused by the title, inattentive during an account of the origins of the Poor Law, but finally listening intently and applauding and laughing at revelations of workhouse procedure in the 1890s ... At the end of the talk the lady chairman, who appeared to have been much moved by it, rose, and coming to the front of the stage, held out her arms to the audience and said:
>
> 'Friends! Today they are offering us all sorts of charity. Well, we don't want their charity! We want them to give us enough to get the things we need for ourselves. That's the real reason for these meetings. To organise ourselves into a fighting brotherhood and sisterhood, to get these things. That's what we want, a decent pension, not charity.'
>
> There was a burst of prolonged applause, and then the meeting closed with the draw for cinema tickets and the singing of Auld Lang Syne. People did not seem very anxious to go, and there was much lingering before the final good-byes were said. (Beveridge and Wells 1949)

Benefits of membership

In addition to their function as definitional rituals the clubs are an important source of social integration. Members are incorporated into a fixed and unchanging routine. The remarkable regularity and predictability of club life contributes to personal security. As the magazine incident quoted earlier suggests, the club provides a system of informal support, both moral and practical, for those who want it. Support is offered formally, too, in the system of 'sick visiting', in the cards and flowers sent to people suffering ill-health, and in the 'sick-news'. Personal security is also enhanced in other ways. The existence of sick members continues to be acknowledged in their absence through a seating rule by which people become identified with particular seats. Seats are occupied for many years and preserved in a person's absence. Attachment to one's seat is strong enough to withstand pressure to move. In a club whose attendance had shrunk from 130 to 40 over the years, an elderly couple continued to sit at the back of the hall near the serving-hatch, where one of them had once helped to make the teas, despite the gradual disappearance of the rows in front of them.

Viewed as a context for ageing, the peer group is seen to confer significant advantages on its members. Together, members work out appropriate ways of behaving in what is, in some senses, a normative vacuum. The stories, readings and poems offered as statements of belief about ageing give guidance on how to evaluate experience. Individual responses to ill-health, bereavement and other age-related problems are compared and assessed in terms of collective standards. Models of successful ageing are reflected in the ritual celebration of birthdays, in the detailed and lengthy sick news, the welcome extended to members returning after illness and the approval bestowed on the widow or widower who copes well with bereavement. Members are socialised into new roles and given a chance to get used to them in a supportive setting. Some actively seek confirmation of their new identities, like Michael, who was forced to find an alternative to his earlier professional self-image and is now keen to show press-cuttings about his voluntary work to anyone who will look at them; and Ruth, smiling bravely through her troubles, keen to tell how she is a source of inspiration to others.

Association with peers – formal or informal – brings with it a range of benefits: an opportunity for self-expression, a sense of security, a supportive network, a chance to confront some of the ambiguities and losses of ageing. For members of the club-going population, the club provides both challenge and security, lifelong needs which in retirement are met through the cultivation of a particular lifestyle. The goals of the old people's clubs in the study are overwhelmingly expressive. They exist to gratify the needs for friendship and support, stimulation and self-expression, for personal autonomy and meaningful integration (Gordon, Gaitz and Scott 1976). Even in the Federation clubs instrumental goals are subordinated to expressive ones to retain the commitment of members and the viability of the club. The social processes identified in this chapter will be developed in the chapters which follow. First, though, in contrast to the world of clubs, we turn to the Christian fellowships which operate in the age-mixed setting of the church.

FOUR

Fellowships of the aged

Two of the age-graded organisations studied in depth were Christian fellowships, meeting under the auspices of a Methodist church. The fellowships
resemble the clubs in several ways, the main one being the age of the
members: they are in practice, though not officially, age-graded. Their
members have similar attitudes and values, and activities to some extent
overlap. But there are differences. The fellowships are predominantly middle
class in membership, and have instrumental as well as expressive goals
arising from their location within the church. As members of 'the church
family' – eighteen affiliated societies and formal groupings – the fellowships
make a vital contribution to the strength and viability of the parent organisation. Individually, the members have rights and responsibilities not
shared by adherents to age-segregated associations. The ageing experience
is set in the context of an age-mixed organisation with an ideology of
fellowship and of lifelong service. The significance of the fellowships in the
lives of the members, particularly as they age, cannot be isolated from the
religious and specifically Christian context in which they operate.

The women's fellowship

The thirty-six current members of the women's fellowship (WF) include
some who have come regularly to the Tuesday afternoon meetings for forty
years. Five others who joined at the same time do not attend and probably
never will again, for they have since moved away or become incapacitated;
but officially no-one leaves except through death. Names remain on the
register until attendance in person is technically impossible. Of the thirty-
six women enrolled, therefore, thirty-one attend regularly, producing an
average meeting of twenty-two people. Among regular attenders the length
of membership varies from fifty years to a few months, though there are
relatively few newcomers.

More than half the current members have been in the fellowship for
fifteen years or more. These figures relate to first attendance for it is
common for members to leave and rejoin as their circumstances change.
Such events as re-entry into the labour force in mid-life, and widowhood in
old age, prompt these moves. The never-married women, by contrast, tend
to show more continuity in their affiliations. Half of the members (eighteen) are widowed. The rest are evenly divided between married (ten) and
never married (eight) members. The ages of regular attenders range from
late 40s to upper 80s but the majority are in their 70s and above. The WF is

Table 4.1 Membership of the women's fellowship

Length of membership (years)	Numbers	Circumstances
0–4	7	
5–9	8	joined as widows or
10–19	3	retirees
20–29	9	
30–39	6	joined as young
40+	3	mothers
	36	

thus made up of elderly women and is known in the church as an old women's meeting. That is also the view which the members have of them-selves, expressed with sadness and regret. As in the clubs, change is asso-ciated with decline; a turnover of members occurs largely through death, and the rapid decline in numbers over the last fifteen years – from eighty-seven to thirty-six – occupies the thoughts of members a good deal.

Like members of pensioners' clubs, the women's fellowship members tend to belong to a variety of other societies and associations. Half a dozen women attend three other fellowships in the neighbourhood; seven are part of the lunch clubs network, either as workers or diners. About a dozen with more catholic tastes belong to pensioners' associations. A minority are heavily involved in various kinds of church work and, while not belonging to other formal organisations, sit on a variety of church committees. The result is a pattern of overlapping memberships similar to that of the pensioners' clubs and integrated with it to some extent through the activities of the substantial number of women who belong to both types of organisation. The following examples illustrate the pattern of multiple membership, the circumstances in which women join, and the extent of their commitment.

Gertie, Winnie, Joyce, Peggy and Molly are five friends all in their mid-70s. Until Winnie moved away recently they all lived in adjoining houses or adjacent streets near the church. They have known each other since the mid-1940s, and all but Winnie still live in the same houses. Their children were playmates and grew up together, and they are closely in touch with each other's family affairs. Within the group they align and realign for different purposes – to go on holiday, to do particular jobs in their various societies, to join clubs. They have other close friends outside the group but the intensity of interaction within it marks them out in church and in the women's meeting. They sit together in church and in the fellowship, where they are known as 'that little group' or 'the five'.

Winnie, who lived in Church Terrace, left her own church when the minister refused to christen her baby because the godparents had not been confirmed. The local church was much more welcoming so she became involved and has remained so. She joined the fellowship in 1953 when her younger son went to school.

Molly, a neighbour of Winnie, joined the church in similar circumstances, feeling abandoned by her own. So did her friend Joyce who
also lived in Church Terrace. She joined the fellowship in 1948 when
her daughter was eight. Peggy, whose garden backed on to Molly's,
joined the following year, in 1949, when her second daughter was a
baby. Peggy took the baby, too: in those days there was a woman to
look after the children of fellowship members.

Molly, 72, was widowed about thirty years ago. She is quite involved in
the church, currently occupying the minor office of door steward. In
the women's fellowship she shares the job of registrar with her friend
Winnie, but her best friends are Peggy and Joyce. Joyce suffers from ill-
health and can't do as much as the others. But with Peggy, Molly goes
to the Silver Lining Club where they help to make the teas. They used
to make things for the stall too, but that got too much. They go on
club holidays together. Like Peggy, Molly works for one morning a
week in a local charity shop. She used to help with the church lunch
club (Peggy still does) and make teas for the fellowship, and help with
the 'sick visiting'. But that, too, became a struggle. Life isn't as much
fun as when her husband was alive. If he were still alive she wouldn't
be doing 'all this'. She would be at home with him, enjoying herself.
Between them, the members of this little group have links with several
associations. Their relationships are multifaceted, involving activities based
on neighbourhood, church, fellowship and clubs. The strength of their
friendships, which have withstood Winnie's move to a purpose-built flat a
mile away, rests on the shared experiences which extend forty years into the
past. Some of the other friendships in the fellowship are of even longer
standing. Several of the women in their 80s knew each other as adolescents
and young adults, and their links include the dimension of kinship, a
product of marriage between church families.

Benefits of membership

Both the men's and women's fellowships are religious organisations, the
content of their meetings largely devotional. The 'devotions' consist of
hymns, prayers, and an address on a religious or moral theme. A collecting
plate or bag is passed round for financial contributions which are used for
charitable purposes, to cover costs and swell the sum which is paid annually
to the church. The disposal of this sum is interesting, for it reveals conflicts
of interest in the members and differences of opinion as to the goals of the
organisation. In the women's fellowship, the instrumental goals of the
organisation – to do good works – are in conflict with the expressive
orientation of some of the members who would rather have an occasional
outing and regular cups of tea.

Despite the formal setting a series of informal exchanges goes on. Indeed,
the structure and process of the women's meeting bears resemblance to

that of the secular old people's club. The setting, too, is similar: a cluster of wooden chairs arranged in rows in the middle of a large church hall brightened by sun light. The visual focus is a splendid blue velvet cloth draped over the front table. It is embroidered with the fellowship's initials in gold.

The weekly meeting has changed little in style or content over many years. Members arrive early and take up their usual seats in the three rows of chairs, or elsewhere if they have a particular responsibility – for taking the register, for collecting contributions to the Christmas savings club, for running the stall, for putting out hymn books or (occasionally) making tea, or for officiating from the front. These offices involve nearly half of the members and before they slip quickly into their seats at the start of the meeting there is movement and talk. On the way from one position to another, from the registrars' table to the savings club, to the stall and to their seats, members chat about a variety of personal topics: Irene is going daily to the nurse as a result of her fall last week; Bea was kept away from church on Sunday by the rain; Mary won't be coming to the club on Wednesday as she still has influenza; her friend Nora probably won't get there either as she's expecting a delivery of coal. Such issues are a matter of general interest, too, as the formal announcements about 'sick folk' show. There is talk of visits from the respective families of members ('It's good to see them but nice when they go') and of new additions in the form of grandsons-in-law and great grandchildren; of the church committee work in which several are involved, and of forthcoming events such as the AGM, the women's service and the anniversary tea. The formal part of the meeting starts with a hymn and prayers. Then there are the notices. These range from birthday announcements and health bulletins to publicity about events which might interest members such as a talk by the local crime prevention officer on home security. After another hymn members either settle down for the address, normally given by an outside speaker, or prepare to entertain each other.

The addresses are generally on a religious or moral theme but sometimes deal with such topics as the theatre, childhood in history, missionary work or holidays, the latter illustrated by slides. The do-it-yourself afternoons, as in the clubs, involve solo performances and readings with an emphasis on *The Friendship Book*.

A typical session, in March 1985, started with a conundrum, and a reading from *The Friendship Book*. Next there was a solo with members joining in the chorus and another reading and a recitation. A member told a story with moral implications on the theme of redemption. The next item, known as 'surprise packages', involved the purchase of small parcels brought in by members on a 'lucky dip' principle, which raised six pounds for fellowship funds. The afternoon ended with tea and biscuits to fill the remaining time.

The fellowship is an object of strong attachment (Troll and Smith 1976). These women attend out of loyalty to the leaders, out of habit, of a sense of devoutness, of religious duty fulfilled. Fellowship in the sense of spiritual solidarity is sought, rather than friendship. They come for company, to pass the time, and in memory of past glories, of the days when the meeting was one hundred strong and supported a large and famous choir. Attendance is an opportunity for self-expression, and the demonstration of skills acquired in earlier years. The economic activity of buying and selling which goes on at each meeting, the recycling of old and the marketing of new, often home-made, produce not only demonstrates continuity in skill but is intrinsically enjoyable, a variation on the shopping and window-shopping which for women can be a leisure activity shared with friends. In the same way, the singing of hymns, for some members the most pleasurable part of the afternoon, is both a source of enjoyment and a means of recalling, if not demonstrating, previous heights of musical achievement.

The fellowship is an object of loyalty and positive sentiment. It provides an opportunity for focusing thoughts around a particular theme, though the bland responses to some of the more challenging outside speakers suggest that thoughts are not, perhaps, centred on the content of their message. On one occasion, for instance, a speaker from a church known for its fundamentalist position on religious and social issues delivered a passionate talk on some of the evils of modern living. She spoke with emotion of her horror at encountering 'creatures – animals with long hair – who must have been men' – at a festival of creative living when she was mayoress of the town and obliged to attend such events. Her powerful delivery, with the use of emotive words and phrases ('a black cloud of evil hanging over me', 'animals') was greeted with the customary round of applause. There were murmurs of 'very nice' as the speaker sat down, and one member was heard to say, as she leant towards her neighbour, that what with Mrs X and the soloist it had been an exceptionally nice afternoon. The moral stance of people of this generation, particularly towards the young, is an interesting phenomenon which will be explored fully in a later chapter. For the present it is important to note that participation in such events, at whatever level, enhances self-respect and confirms members' identities as thinking, concerned, morally superior individuals. They come away from such talks feeling emotionally aroused if not intellectually stimulated, especially by a vigorous performance.

Disagreement with points raised in the meeting (and on the occasion just described there *were* members who confided privately that they felt the speaker had gone too far in her condemnation of alternative beliefs) does not generate argument or even tension. A consensus exists about the expression of disapproval or negative emotions. It is summed up in the comment of a woman who was often irritated by the chatting of the women in front of her, and of the way the business of the fellowship was conducted, but who would not intervene in either case: 'You mustn't show what you feel, must you?'

The meetings are harmonious. There is nothing abrasive or confrontational about them. The norm of passivity and a non-critical stance prevails to keep conflict to a minimum. Such differences of opinion as do come to the surface are devalued by the use of such descriptions as 'cafuffle'. They are set in the broader context of Christian values, with their emphasis on harmony, conciliation and cooperation. It is the lack of challenge which makes the fellowship such a satisfactory context for social intercourse. The content of the talks, described as 'very nice' at best and, 'well ... different' at worst is less important than the sense of communion generated by the weekly coming together. The routine aspects of the meeting and the social contact it affords produce a sense of security. The general atmosphere of warmth and friendliness, and the predictability of the proceedings, account for the non-critical stance towards narrow-minded, even bigoted offerings which do not correspond to the views of the listeners. Unacceptable views are tuned out or accepted in the name of tolerance, to preserve enjoyment of the occasion. The object of the address is not, it appears, to clarify the thoughts of the listeners or to challenge them into taking issue. Such an outcome would detract from a major benefit of membership.

The most striking feature of the fellowship is its gentle and relaxing quality. It is peaceful, an oasis in a busy life. Summed up in the expression of 'it's nice to sit down for an hour', a number of women in the fellowship find the enforced repose of the weekly meetings relaxing and reviving. Grace (78), for instance, is always on the go. She attends church and another meeting and helps at the lunch club. Her best friend lives in the same street and they visit regularly. When not engaged in social activities Grace is busy at home. She normally has an interior decorating project on the go, and applies herself energetically, for 'you don't know how long you've got before the paste goes hard'. When she sits down there are the hidden-word puzzles to get on with 'to keep my brain ticking'. Grace – in the face of her self-imposed busyness – feels comfortable in a situation of other-imposed silence and spiritual reflection. The meetings have a timeless quality in sharp contrast to the time-stressed daily routine. It might be the case that women like Grace, and there are many of them in the fellowship, manufacture pastimes to avoid feeling alone. They cannot relax at home – but in the consensual and socially homogeneous setting of the Tuesday meeting, they can.

The stillness which descends after the initial flurry of exchanges – of greetings and news, of goods and money – combines several elements. It encapsulates the silent women, giving them a sense of invulnerability which contrasts with (and compensates for) the vulnerability of life outside the fellowship and the community of the church which incorporates it. In prayer the members dwell upon the nature of old age, its frailties and dependencies, the sense of time left to live rather than time since birth. But this linear concept of time, expressed in the notion of a personal journey, uncertain but irreversible, is set against another more hopeful concept in which time is cyclical. In its routine and predictable aspects the fellowship reflects the cyclical dimension of time, expressed in ritual performance. Their repetitive nature gives them a timeless quality which contrasts with the progression through time marked by irreversible personal changes in the lives of participants. The recurrence of annual ceremonials marking the yearly cycle – such as the opening service in September, the Christmas party and Easter celebrations, the Mother's Day service, the Women's Anniversary and Women's World Day of Prayer – convey beliefs about the nature of time.

The final meeting of the annual cycle held in July is particularly noteworthy in this respect. It is held in the church, rather than the church hall. The content of the service is as formal as the setting. Taken from a book, which the officiating clergyman and members of the congregation read alternately and together, it is devoid of spontaneity. Apart from the notices announced at the start, including the date of the first meeting in September, there is no acknowledgement of time or place. There are no references to endings or beginnings. The final part of the service – the ritual consumption of sacred food and wine known as taking communion – affirms the fellowship of participants and their involvement in a process which transcends time.

The significance of age and gender

Members of the women's fellowship are conscious of their age. As in the clubs, reference to age is made in deliveries from the platform or top table, and in the banter which punctuates the more serious parts of the programme. Contained within the activities and passages selected for presentation to the members are fundamental beliefs and prescriptions for behaviour. A model of successful ageing is contained, for instance, in the following lines, entitled 'A Happy Old Age':

> A little more tired at the close of day,
> A little less anxious to have our own way.
> A little less care for gain or gold
> A little more zest for the days of old.
> A broader view and a saner mind;
> A little more love for all mankind.
> A little more love for the friends of youth,
> A little more zeal for established truth.
> A little more charity in our views,
> A little less thirst for the latest news.
> A little more leisure to sit and dream;
> A little more real the things unseen.
> (*The Friendship Book*, by Francis Gay, 16 May 1984)

This ideal view of old age, presented to the women's fellowship at their afternoon meeting, sees the old as repositories of virtue: less demanding, materialistic and narrow-minded, more loving, charitable and socially committed. But they are also increasingly detached and other-worldly.

The subject of age emerges from time to time in conversation, as on the occasion of the acting president's 70th birthday. There was singing and a celebratory cup of tea. The conversation was also punctuated by humorous references to age. Invited to say something about my talk, planned for the following week, I started by saying that it was rather serious. The response was laughter and the comment 'Yes, we're old!' (in other words, we can't cope with serious material).

Violet announced an event which members could read about in the church newsletter: 'If you can [i.e. will] read it (please) ...'. This remark was greeted with mock indignation: 'Ooh!' [are you suggesting we can't read?].

In private conversation members comment on certain people's ability to cope with ill-health, and evaluate their approach to the ageing experience as either good or bad, successful or unsuccessful, in terms of collective standards. These standards are shared with club-goers, but modified to some extent by the framework of beliefs provided by the church. For fellowship members, ageing takes place within the setting of the church. A combination of instrumental and expressive goals contributes to a distinctive view of ageing among church members. In the women's fellowship members are encouraged to view their lives in the context of the whole group, made up of people of all ages, each making a vital contribution to the achievement of its goals. The old contribute to the socialisation of the young, ensuring their incorporation in the life of the church.

'There must be people here who have sown seeds', remarked a popular speaker and retired Sunday school superintendent, referring to the seed of Christian thought. This was an invitation to WF members to think back, to put current experience in the positive context of constructive involvement between the generations. The old women in front of him could think of themselves as having introduced the younger people – their children, or Sunday school class – both to Christian values and to acceptable standards in general. The emphasis was on continuity, again involving the cyclical dimension of time. The theme of the talk on this occasion was growth, life, regeneration in nature and society.

The concept of creation and the value of creativity, central to the belief system of the Christian community, features prominently in fellowship thinking, particularly among the women. For them, gender to some extent mitigates the effects of age. Those events in the church calendar which have a gender reference normally focus upon women: the Women's Anniversary, the Mother's Day service, the Women's World Day of Prayer. In these, womanhood is associated with creativity, with life and regeneration, with nurturance and warmth. The theme song of the Women's World Day of

Prayer 1984 was sung in both the women's organisations in the church during the field-work period in 1985.

> She that trusts in me, from her deepest heart
> Shall rivers of living water flow forth.
> She that trusts in me, from her deepest heart
> Shall rivers of life flow forth.

On other occasions women are told that their prayer is going to move the world, for nothing else will and the need is desperate.

For the old men no such compensations exist. Yet, like the women, they are acutely conscious of their relative age. The two fellowships in the church – one belonging to the oldest women, the other to the old men – have much in common. Not least is the sense of decline which pervades meetings. For the women, personal deterioration and collective replacement by younger generations can be set in the context of regeneration, of life-giving and life-preserving forces which in the belief system of the church are essentially feminine qualities.

In other ways, too, the older women's lives reflect the contradiction in Christian thought and practice: the subordinate and humble role of women and their vital contribution to the strength and continuity of the church. These two sides reveal themselves in the public and private faces of the older women. In public they are a sad, dwindling and marginal group. They are passive and unassertive. At formal gatherings of the fellowship, the official values are clearly enforced: family and fellowship, spiritual growth and creativity, service, self sacrifice, modesty, humility and acceptance. At a meeting in March, for instance, the opening item was a reading chosen and delivered by the acting president, from *The Friendship Book*, 15 May 1984, on the theme of the simple life. Its focus was the war years and the merits of austerity. Its message ended with the need to be thankful for small mercies. Next the acting president read Martha's prayer, a piece about ordinary people and humdrum activities. The visiting speaker picked up the theme. Her somewhat rambling talk, punctuated by texts and apothegms, was well received. She spoke of dandelions, weeds whose roots were difficult to eradicate but must be removed, like the gossip, criticism and indifference which are the weeds of the church. She urged the women to be themselves but to be humble. It was the humble who were called, not the clever, for everyone has talents like Martha, the homemaker, and cleverness is a handicap. Her final message was that 'since God had given us two ears and only one mouth we should listen much and speak little.' The message of acceptance, of non-assertiveness and of forbearance corresponded well with the experience of the women, confirming the value of their customary skills and modes of interaction.

In private, however, the women behave with the vigour and independence associated with older women (Myerhoff 1978; Gutmann 1987). They have their own priorities and act upon them, while appearing to conform to masculine requirements. Although the WF, like other church organisations, is governed by a constitution and formally organised, the women's conduct of affairs indicates a lack of regard for formality and bureaucratic procedures. The relatively large number of office holders – there are fifteen named posts – can be seen as a way of involving as many women as possible in the collective effort rather than a means of discriminating between the more and less important. The tendency to go their own way was highlighted in the annual committee meeting which followed the AGM.

Notification of the meeting had been given by word of mouth or on scraps of paper torn from a large sheet, containing a simple handwritten message. The committee assembled and proceeded to work its way through an agenda, relaxed and in high spirits. There were frequent interruptions, digressions and changes of subject. Communication between both ends of the long trestle table was occasionally lost. The minutes secretary abandoned her task half-way through and several members admitted some confusion at the end as to what had been agreed. However, there was no real disquiet at this state of affairs and people went their separate ways cheerfully. Apart from a member who confessed afterwards to feeling ashamed that an outsider should witness what she regarded as a chaotic and disorderly meeting, the committee felt that its objects had been achieved. It had been businesslike (if non-legalistic). Members had gone through the motions of a committee meeting, leaving fellowship affairs much as they were, enjoying each other's company, and getting home in time for the expected telephone call or the favourite television programme or tea. The deliberate violation of committee procedures evident in satirical remarks and humorous asides made this a mockery of formal procedures.

The men's fellowship

The old men take the formal procedures much more seriously. The language of their own annual general meeting was that of business and officialdom. They referred to 'the governor' and 'the boss, and 'will you show, gentlemen?' when it came to a vote. Such terms reflect the members' occupational experience, familiarity with committee procedures, and respect for them, all largely absent in the women's group.

The men's fellowship resembles the women's in age distribution, in the pattern of recruitment and in the decline in numbers in recent years. Of the fourteen members, ten are in their 70s and 80s, two are in their 60s, one is 55 and 'the baby' of the group is a disabled man in his mid-30s. Most have been members for many years. The oldest joined over sixty years ago when a much larger organisation – the Preston Brotherhood – existed in its place. The brotherhood had nearly 200 members. The fellowship itself has been much larger in the past, having declined dramatically from twenty-eight to fourteen in the last fifteen years. At first glance this is a society of widowers, for a substantial number are unattached (six widowed, two never married). But nearly half the men still have wives. The pattern of their organisational affiliations is rather different from the women's. None belong to old people's clubs, though one is active in a horticultural society, several belong to profess- ional associations and a number go to a men's billiard group at a neighbour- ing church. Most of the fourteen members belong to Stamford Road Methodist Church and hold, or have held, a range of offices and serve on a variety of committees. Within the group there are ties of friendship. The group as a whole engages in sociable activities, focusing on billiards, which occupies the seven or eight men who care to stay an hour or so after the meeting. In both men's and women's organisations members are as likely to join alone as with a friend. Unlike the clubs, fellowships have some instru- mental goals and identification with their aims is a sufficient basis for membership.

The men's fellowship meets one evening a week in a small room off the church hall. It is barely large enough to contain a circle of chairs, a piano and a small table for the speaker and secretary. There are fewer offices than in the women's meeting – only a secretary, a treasurer and a pianist. The conduct of the meeting is formal, with a fixed order of events. It includes hymns and prayers, punctuated by news of the sick, and notices. The main item is an address or bible study. The meetings end with refreshments and conversation, followed by a game of snooker in the adjacent hall. Unlike the women, the men have a formal printed 'syllabus' for the whole year. On the front cover it bears the fellowship motto: 'the fullness of the Christian life cannot be known except in fellowship – fellowship with God and fellowship with one another.' The men describe the fellowship as a great meeting, the highlight of the week, a wonderful experience which they would like to share.

The relationships within the group are those of friendship, involving emotional intimacy, companionship and mutual support. Members share a fund of memories – of better times, of humorous experiences – which are recounted periodically, reinforcing the solidarity of the group. They tell, for instance, of the strength and vigour of the old Preston Brotherhood, when the men took their young families on weekly PSAs (pleasant Sunday after- noons) with cricket and tea. A more recent and personal subject for remi- niscence is the night the tea was grey. The two brothers whose job it was to make the evening refreshments had boiled the ancient teapot without includ- ing the tea. The usual refreshing brew was a dreadful mixture which has become part of the folklore of the group. The friendship experiences of these men, and of the few who enjoy the shared recreation of old people's clubs, bring to mind Gutmann's observations about older men. As men age, according to Gutmann, they are compensated for their loss of drive by the development of other appetites and capacities. Their earlier preoccupations give way to 'milder passions'. They develop a capacity for communion rather than agency, for collaboration rather than competition, for receptivity rather than productivity. The newer interest in expressive interpersonal activity takes over and energises limbs and sense organs that have been abandoned. Older men are 'freed up to discover new pleasures of the sort that have little to do with either combat or production' (Gutmann 1987, p 103).

A sociological explanation of friendship patterns in the fellowship might focus on marital status. The relatively large number of widowed and never-married men (eight out of fourteen) raises the possibility that intimacy with each other replaces spousal intimacy. This possibility is explored in the following chapter.

In short, the meeting provides a high degree of emotional, intellectual and spiritual satisfaction. Beyond the meeting, the group has a presence in the church, pursuing the fellowship goals of purposeful collective action. In the language of adherents the men's fellowship is 'a source of hope and fellowship'. It meets needs at different levels. It provides an opportunity for purposeful action beyond the group itself – 'mission' – and for sociable interaction within the moral community of peers – a game of snooker. Participation extends experience on two dimensions: meaning and belonging (Gerard 1985). Membership of this community provides an integrated system of beliefs and a chance to express them through ritual participation. But more than simply a devotional group the fellowship is a set of friends growing old together.

The men's meeting, as much as the women's, is felt to be part of a larger collective endeavour, involving purposeful action. Its members are, like some of the women, actively involved in the instrumental activities of the church. These include projects designed to strengthen the financial base of the church, and to extend its work in the local community. The fundamental beliefs and dominant values of elderly men and women in the fellowships reflect the Christian ideology of the organisation to which they belong. Christian beliefs, in conjunction with the beliefs of secular society, provide a framework for the ageing experience. In the rest of the chapter we consider the church as a context for ageing.

An integrated community

Stamford Road Methodist Church has 123 adult members and a youth wing or junior church of about 40 children. The majority of members are middle aged and older, and women outnumber men by 2 to 1. Combining members and adherents (those affiliated through church organisations), people in their 60s and above account for over half, and one-sixth are in their 80s and older. Three-quarters of the total are women.

The gender imbalance is pronounced in the 40s, where divorce largely accounts for women on their own, and the 60s, where their ranks are swelled by the never-married and the newly-widowed. Widowhood and women's greater life expectancy lie behind the preponderance of very old women. More fundamental reasons for the imbalance in sex and age in

Good Company

Table 4.2 Age and gender distribution of church members and adherents, 1985

Age	Members		Adherents		Total
	Men	Women	Men	Women	
18+	1				1
20+	5	7			12
30+	6	7	1	3	17
40+	2	8	5	12	27
50+	9	10	4	6	29
60+	2	11	1	7	21
70+	11	18	1	7	37
80+	3	23	1	5	32
Total	39	84	13	40	176

church membership lie in social and cultural developments in British society through the course of the last sixty years, changes which we return to in Chapter Ten.

A number of overlapping social networks based on kinship, locality, cohort, membership of church associations and adherence to a set of values create a cohesive and close-knit unit with historical depth and permanence. The existence of multi-generational and inter-married families has produced an extensive kinship network. There are nine two-generation families, seven of three generations and seven of four or more generations, the upper and lower levels absent through death or detachment. Twelve families are linked by marriage one, two or three generations back. Some of them are now almost extinct through low rates of marriage and the tendency for younger generations to move away or reduce their involvement in the church.

The As and the Bs, for instance, intermarried in the 1950s. The Bs are also linked to the Js by marriage. One very elderly A remains and so does an elderly never-married B, a middle-aged B and her husband. The B children are not practising Christians and are bringing up their own children outside the church. The Cs and Ds and the Ks and Ls also became linked by marriage in the 1950s, a glorious time in the history of the church when the legendary youth club was one hundred strong and spilt over from the pews on the left. Several of today's middle-aged couples met in the youth club during that time. The younger Cs and Ds, Ks and Ls have also moved away, though their parents remain. One of the Cs had married an H a generation earlier, and another of the Hs had married a G. The Fs and Es intermarried in the 1920s and 1930s. The links established by these families currently involve no more than twenty people, mostly in their 50s and 70s. But friends of relatives and relatives of friends ensure that each is embedded in an extensive and close-knit network. Apart from these intermarried families and others of more than one generation, there are four pairs of elderly sisters and two sets of elderly brothers.

Members are linked also by physical contiguity. Most live within a mile of the church in houses which they own. The majority of the older people, particularly the women – who tend not to own or drive cars – live in Edwardian terraced houses within yards of the church. Some moved in as children when the area was first developed round the turn of the century. Other old people and most of the younger ones live in a 1930s residential area half a mile (about one kilometre) away. The size of the older contingent was reduced substantially a few years ago when the only bus travelling along Stamford Road was withdrawn. A few of the more affluent people have moved slightly further afield to more modern, semi-detached houses and purpose-built flats. Some have left the area altogether but continue to travel back once or twice a week.

Members of the church regard themselves as a family, in principle and in practice. Like the ideal family, the congregation is mixed in age and its constituent parts are bound in a special relationship of cooperation, positive intervention, conciliation, the sharing of resources and mutual enjoyment. One of the main committees, consisting of representatives from the eighteen affiliated organisations, is known as the Family Committee. Each constituent unit of the church family is required to contribute to the church's income and undertake a range of tasks. The failure to participate adequately (the scouts for instance, proved unreliable in taking their turn at the monthly coffee mornings) earns criticism as failing to recognise the privileges and responsibilities of family membership. Intervention in internal affairs is justified in the same way. The notion of a church family is expressed in the annual pastimes – the church quiz and the church picnic. At a christening service, when the birth of a baby is formally acknowledged, the infant is ritually carried up and down the aisles in full view of the congregation to 'meet its new family'.

The imagery of the family is used to express and confirm unity, obedience and security. The Mother's Day service, for instance, invokes parallels between God's family, the Holy family and the human family of the church. The address on this occasion focuses on the home as the seat of affection and source of support, haven in a harsh world, microcosm of the Christian community. At the Women's Anniversary service, similarly, the Holy Family is presented as the model for the earthly one. At Easter, the imagery of the family is used to describe the loneliness of God at the loss of his only son and, by implication, the waywardness of his earthly offspring. A second unifying principle is that of fellowship. All acts of worship or business or convivial occasions in the church are ritual gatherings of believers. They meet 'in fellowship'; in a climate of spiritual communion and solidarity. Other central values include growth and creativity – in nature and in the family, of the self and the life of the church. Loyalty, commitment and perseverance are also esteemed. They are the antithesis of self-interest, a principle which is inimical to the caring roles which members are encouraged to adopt both inside the church and outside it. The emphasis on service to the community is reflected in the committee structure and the allocation of resources – time, energy and money – to projects of a charitable nature.

A crucial value is that of conciliation, which is reflected in the conduct of interpersonal affairs and can be translated into a set of personal standards: modesty, humility, non-assertiveness, discipline, self-control and tolerance. There should be no conflict in the church, or indeed any assertive behaviour likely to undermine the community. Conflict is discussed and breaches are minimised in the use of diminutive terms: 'niggles' to describe criticism of the committee structure; 'cafuffle' – vigorous disagreement over the solution to the perennial problem of tea in the women's fellowship; and 'naughty' to describe a committee member who unilaterally acted in breach of the constitution. Assertive people are criticised as 'strong minded'. Criticism is classed with gossip and indifference as evils to be avoided. The norm of passivity and a non-critical stance reduces the likelihood of confrontations and preserves the highly consensual style of discourse.

Participants in church affairs identify three sets of inter-related activities: spiritual, financial and social. The church resembles both a business and a community association with a budget and array of affiliated organisations. It is also a spiritual entity, an organisation which offers an integrated system of beliefs and a means of expressing them in ritual performance. Its orientation is thus both instrumental and expressive. To achieve the ultimate goal – the extension of God's kingdom on earth – the church seeks to promote its presence in the community by enlarging its membership and expanding its material resources. It must maintain its viability in relation to equivalent units (other churches in the local Methodist circuit) by recruiting and socialising younger generations (Jerrome 1989). Expressive goals include spiritual and emotional gratification, summed up in the concept of fellowship. The activities of fellowship are intrinsically rewarding. The intensity of individual involvement varies. But for all participants the church offers a sense of belonging, a meaning for existence and a framework in which to interpret experience. Everyone has a part to play in advancing the aims of the church. Officially neither age, gender nor any other ascribed characteristic is a barrier to participation. There is an expectation that everyone will behave appropriately: take on tasks when they are the best qualified or there is no one else to do them; and if necessary give them up in the interests of effective management. Any member qualifies for office, for the Methodist church is a democratic organisation with a marked absence of hierarchy.

A church career

Age is not a criterion of worth, nor is it officially a basis for action and association outside the youth movements. But there is an understanding of church work in terms of shifts in personal time. The pattern of involvement of different age groups and through the life-span of particular people suggests that activity is age-specific. People progress from infancy to old age through a number of stages. The church begins with inclusion on the Cradle Roll. The final stage is initiated by death and terminated when references to the departed cease. The stages of the typical church career are most clearly discernible from the lives of the oldest members and their ancestors who, it would appear from church records, have trodden the same path before them. Records of office holders in the 1950s, for instance, indicate kinship ties with current incumbents. The younger people's paths are slightly different, unsurprising in view of changes in employment patterns and gender roles. In addition to cohort differences, factors such as gender, marital status, education, health and family responsibilities make a difference. At each point in the church career some members leave and others join.

The church career starts with membership of the Sunday school and boys' or girls' brigade. The brigades are for many the gateway to church membership, administration and senior leadership roles. An alternative route used to be through the youth club, which in the decades after the war was responsible for the introduction of several new members through courtship and marriage into church families. Those young people went on to membership of the appropriate church organisation: the Young Wives' Group (now called Feminine Focus), the men's fellowship. They ran the brigades and taught in the Sunday school. Junior church work, variously described as 'wonderful service' and 'hard labour' is highly esteemed. Sunday school teaching can span several decades of adult life and when it does the individual is publicly honoured as a major contributor to the socialisation of the young and hence the continuity of the church. Membership of the various church organisations, similarly, can extend from early adulthood to old age. Elderly men and women continue to support the brigades, the men wearing their badges and the women watching daughters and granddaughters engage in familiar displays.

Through leadership in the organisations and involvement in low level church work (for instance, standing at the door on a Sunday morning to welcome attenders and distribute hymn books, the work of the door stewards) a church member becomes visible and liable for more and more committee work. Engagement in minor church work in early middle age (or even earlier, if a young person can be persuaded to take it on) is a rite of passage for church managers. The role of society or vestry steward – one of the senior posts – is regarded as interesting and challenging, 'running the show', a link between minister and members. These days it may be taken on relatively early. Three of the six stewards in 1986 were in their 30s; the others ranged in age from 50 to 73. More experienced members take on jobs which involve representing the church at district meetings. By the time old age is reached, a man will have held most offices in the church, some several times. He continues to serve on committees, and attend church and social functions. Those old men who have been active in church affairs occupy the role of elder statesmen. They sponsor younger people into minor office and groom them for heavier responsibilities. Most of the members of the men's fellowship have held strategic roles on church committees. Several continue to do so. Others undertake different tasks: playing the piano, editing the church newsletter, organising the door rota, addressing the women's fellowship.

An old woman is less likely to have been involved in committee work. She continues her pastoral work (visiting the sick), helps deliver the church newsletter and attends meetings of her organisation. Collectively, the older women have been displaced by the younger women who take on such jobs as repairing hymn books. The two groups cooperate for special acts of worship – the Mother's Day service, the Women's World Day of Prayer – and for domestic activities such as the provision of refreshments at church social events. Involvement in charitable activities both inside and outside the church is a feature of women's lives from early middle age onwards. Most of the younger women have full- or part-time jobs and dependent children. Their limited disposable time is occupied with the pursuit of leisure activities through the church – drama, singing – and outside. In middle age, part-time employment is either extended or complemented by voluntary work, in a range of national charities. Middle-aged women (40s, 50s, 60s) are active in church organisations and involved in minor office. The never- or formerly-married are more actively involved and more likely to occupy senior roles than their counterparts with dependents. The younger men's time is taken up with paid employment which limits the opportunity for church work, though they take part in committee work and patronise or help to run their children's organisations.

Upon death, the elderly church members join the communion of saints. Thanks are offered in prayer for their fellowship, service and salvation. They are remembered not only in prayer but in legend, in reminiscence among friends and peers and in the use of their (sometimes substantial) legacies. Some elderly people are more likely than others to qualify for this treatment. An important criterion seems to be success in the performance of age roles; the extent to which old people behave as expected and in such a way as to advance collective interests.

Membership of an age-mixed grouping with a history extending over several generations provides a distinctive experience of ageing. People at different points hold reciprocal expectations which influence the ageing experience. Older generations provide role models for their successors, despite historical and cultural developments which create a unique setting for successive cohorts. Involved in a system of interlocking roles and over-lapping networks, the old person in the church enjoys the security of a highly integrated existence. For some old people the church is the extent of their social world. Apart from relations with family and neighbours they are part of no networks unrelated to the church. Family members are often, indeed, similarly involved, if not in the same church then in a similar one. The oldest men and women in the church fall particularly within this group, their horizons narrowing with age. Another, larger group, includes some very old but also some retired women and men in their 70s. Their networks extend beyond the church to clubs and fellowships outside. They undertake voluntary work for other agencies and have friends with different affiliations. Men and women in their 60s may be heavily involved in church work but, again, belong to other organisations and often extensive friendship and occupational networks. The amount of life space occupied by the church in early middle age – the 40s – rivals that in extreme old age. For the very old, and for those younger people most heavily involved in church management, the church is the main source of social activity. It is their principal social world (Unruh 1983). Unlike most of the social worlds identified by Unruh as age-mixed, the church accords the old status as principal actors. They are not peripheral, not tourists or spectators, but crucially involved in helping to promote the interests of the organisation.

FIVE

Friendship

In the church, demands are made and met in the name of fellowship, a vital Christian concept implying spiritual solidarity, universal goodwill and tolerance. In this somewhat impersonal setting, personal needs for friendship and intimacy do not always find expression. But within the church, as in the clubs, informal ties of friendship and looser sociable relations with other members of the peer group are vital in the management of day-to-day living. In this chapter we take a closer look at friendship, particularly in the context of the old people's club where it is part of the official ideology and the principal organisational goal.

Friendship is highly valued in the club population. 'Count your age in friends not years' runs the Silver Lining Club birthday song. Its triumphant climax reflects the importance of sociability in principle and in practice. The existence of friends is a measure of social success, important at all ages but in later years a sign also of continuing vitality and social involvement. Friends are distinguished from other members of the older person's informal network in important ways. Friends are chosen on the basis of shared interests. The ideal (best friend) relationship is characterised by intimacy and dependability, by reciprocity and mutual support, by its dyadic (one-to-one) quality and long-term character. Interaction between friends is primarily expressive: it involves emotional support, mutual visiting, shared social activities and small reciprocal acts of assistance which are mutually enjoyable. Friendship is characterised by a high degree of personal involvement.

Friendship, in British culture, is a voluntary, informal, personal and private relationship. The behaviour appropriate between friends is not culturally prescribed but subject to negotiation. It lacks institutional supports and controls, and is liable to break down. In a society which values sociability, but provides few mechanisms for making friends and managing conflict in informal relationships, the formation and persistence of friendship is problematic. Despite these interesting features, friendship has received little direct attention in either sociology or social anthropology and our understanding of its social significance remains limited.

What evidence there is suggests that the western definition of friendship is anthropologically atypical. Friendship in the West is a luxury which cannot be afforded in many structural situations. Where the whole of social life is channelled through particular institutions such as kinship and where conduct is closely regulated by a series of cultural rules, personal choice is restricted and there is no room for informal, voluntary and private relationships between status equals. With regard to choice of associates and conduct of sociable relations, this society is peculiar in its relative permissiveness.

In societies with rigid hierarchies and rules of kinship, friendship takes a particular form, though the same qualities of affection, reciprocity and mutuality are present. Friendships in these societies tend to be more formal and ritualised, and do not necessarily involve freedom of choice. Friends may be chosen for one at birth, they may be preordained by dates of birth, and ceremonial friendships may be used to cement alliances or accommodate strangers. The contractual nature and ceremonial trappings of friendship are explained partly by its value to individuals. On the personal side, affection, reciprocity and equality are possible only in friendship because of the restrictions, formalities and essential conflicts of interest which surround relationships between spouses, in-laws and kin (Wolf 1966; Brain 1976). It provides emotional release from the strains and pressures of role-playing. The benefits are social as well as personal. In particularistic societies, institutionalised friendship supports the social structure at its interstitial points, for example between kin groups, (Eisenstadt 1956). In a modern, universalistic society, friendship is neither institutionalised nor ritualised, but personal (in the sense that one person has the right to expect only what the other chooses to give) and private. It is possible that friendship, no longer institutionalised, provides the individual with a refuge from the glare of public life and its burden of institutional obligations (Paine 1970). In fragmented, plural societies based neither on kin groups nor on corporate structures, where relationships are particularistic and security and stability are not provided by the state, coalitions of friends are the basic form of social organisation. They organise production and protection as well as providing affection, companionship and the other rewards of friendship (Boissevain 1974).

In the sociological literature on urban industrial society such references as there have been to friendship are rooted in a broad concern with the nature and strength of primary group ties. The character of interpersonal relationships, and of primary relationships in particular, has long been of interest to sociologists. The classical writers – Tonnies, Durkheim and others – maintained that the process of industrialisation undermined community (defined as a degree of intimacy and moral commitment). The decline-of-community thesis, taken up and elaborated by other more recent writers, identified a change in the quality of personal relationships. The importance of the primary group as a unit of identification and action was thought to be reduced. A number of writers have since demonstrated the strength and persistence of primary group ties, including friendship, despite the existence of state welfare provision, increasing choice in the selection of roles and relationships and a high rate of social mobility (Allan 1979;

Cantor 1979; Fischer 1977; Litwak and Szelenyi 1969; Verbrugge 1977; Dono et al. 1979).

A greater emphasis on friendship is found in the American literature of social psychology. In a theoretical essay, Hess (1972) offers a useful framework for the analysis. She identifies four possible types of connection between friendship and other roles: fusion, substitution, complementarity and competition. In focusing on the relationship between roles, Hess resembles earlier writers who sought to establish the significance of a non-kin relationship in a social world polarised around work and family. But whereas Paine (1970) speculates that it is a refuge from the strains of role playing in other institutional spheres, Hess sees it as a substitute for those roles when retirement or bereavement remove them. Friendship thus assumes special importance at times of relative rolelessness. It serves as a means of social integration and, where the individual is in a state of transition to a new pattern of existence, assists in the process of socialisation. The role of friendship in socialisation has been noted in relation to both old age (Bankoff 1981; Hess 1972; Jerrome 1981; Huyck 1974; Lowenthal and Haven 1968; Rosow 1975) and youth. (Indeed, the psychological literature of friendship, and other personal relationships, and the social skills needed for their practice, is extensive.)

In Hess's analysis we are offered a more phenomenological view of friendship. Friends are important in the construction of reality. Dialogue with friends is a source of concepts and categories describing the world: in common with friends one attaches certain meanings to events and relationships, a process which has implications for all areas of social life. Social roles are learnt and reinforced and social boundaries are maintained. The work of Lupton and Wilson on the City of London (1959), Guttsman on British political elites (1963) and Cohen on freemasonry (1971, 1974) shows that friendship is often a vital ingredient in economic and political relationships, the cement which binds together people with interests to conserve. Thus the theoretical significance of friendship might be seen to lie in its capacity to express and promote common interests. In choice of friends and in the activities and rituals of friendship, status distinctions are expressed and reaffirmed. These processes are observed in studies as varied as Littlejohn's account of community relations in a Yorkshire village (1963), Packard's analysis of class behaviour in North America (1959) and the much earlier, theoretical analysis of class relations in North America offered by Veblen (1899).

The broader implications of friendship can only be inferred, though, for the focus of this group of studies is largely social stratification, social integration and control. With the exception of Cohen's (1971) study and Boissevain's (1974) anthropological analysis of the structure of sociability, the interest in friendship tends to be peripheral, if indeed it exists at all. We do not, in fact, know very much about the content of this relationship, about its personal meaning or its significance for society as a whole. With one or two exceptions (for example, Allan 1979; Brain 1976; Pahl 1971; Boissevain 1974) theoretical developments in the study of friendship have not taken place. Commenting on the poverty of this situation, Beth Hess (1979) notes:

> How strange that there is no large corpus called the 'sociology of friendship'! Here, surely, is the quintessential social relationship: voluntary, mutual, enjoyed for its own sake, always in danger of dissolution, dependent upon, and illustrative of, all levels of social analysis (personality, social system, culture). But, with few exceptions such as George Simmel, sociologists have been enamoured of other phenomena: power, stratification, social phenomena of immense importance to men. Perhaps friendship has been too insignificant, or too unstructured, ephemeral and emotionally tinged to be pinned down to 'hard' data analysis.

The private, informal and transitory nature of friendship in western cultures, its lack of structure and predictability, have made it less amenable to study by conventional methods than other social relationships. This fact, combined with a view of friendship as depending more upon idiosyncracies of personality than upon regularities of social structure, and as providing only a secondary and potentially tenuous source of solidarity and integration, has made it of only minor interest to sociologists. This view has been echoed by others (Acker, Barry and Esseveld 1981; Smith 1977; Seiden and Bart 1975) who point out that friendship, women's friendship in particular, is outside the world sociology knows. Ignorance of its real nature is coupled with a lack of interest because female-female relationships are considered irrelevant to the social structure. Sociologists tend, therefore, to rely on popular and misleading stereotypes. According to writers of this persuasion, what is needed is a closer examination of the process of friendship formation and maintenance, concentrating on the content of relationships rather than range and frequency of contact. There are other limitations in the friendship literature. Much of it tends to ignore subjective accounts of friendship in old age. It rests on enquiries which are limited in scope and depth, informed by the researchers' own definitions and assumptions about the nature of this relationship and its meaning in people's lives. The earlier studies suffered from constraints in the form of a priori definitions (friends were by definition non-kin, intimate, the same age), limited scope (to relationships which were local, or active, or 'best') and numerically restricted (descriptions would be sought of 'the five people you like best, see most often' and so on). More recently the survey approach has been abandoned in favour of a more intensive and exploratory style of investigation. Recent work reflects an interest in allowing the older adult to define friendship and identify his or her friends. To the newer subjective accounts have been added the insights from cross-cultural research accumulating

since the late 1960s on the theme of friendship (Armstrong 1988). Methodological difficulties have brought to light the special requirements of
studies of informal networks in Britain, too (Willmott 1987).

A special relationship

The most striking characteristic of friendship to emerge from recent studies
is its variability. Lacking in social supports and external control the content
of each relationship is unique. The relevance of specific behaviour between
the partners is determined by them alone: what others think of it is not
relevant. Another feature is the notion of equivalence – of contributions
and benefits. But the private and negotiable character of the relationship
gives scope for variation in the pattern of exchanges. The exchanges do not
always, it seems, have to be equal. Asymmetry arises through the partners'
different perceptions and the absence of objective, externally imposed criteria
(Paine 1974; Matthews 1986). Friendship, located in the private and personal
domain, affords a greater measure of autonomy than all other relationships.

Despite the high degree of individual variation some generalisations are
possible. I have commented on the general significance of friendship in
different types of society – industrial and non-industrial, class-based and
kinship society, urban and rural and so on. Something can also be said
about the significance of friendship for men and women at different ages,
about individual changes with age and about social class. The experience of
friendship varies across the life-span. As circumstances change, roles
change in significance. Young unmarried people often have close and
active friendships which provide companionship and emotional support. A
new parent, particularly a working-class young mother, may allow some of
her friendships to wither away as her new commitments based on home and
family take up her time and energy (Gavron 1966). So might an older,
unmarried woman who takes on responsibility for an elderly relative (Equal
Opportunities Commission 1980). People with active and satisfying work
relationships, or a professional job which is demanding and leaves little
time for extra activities, may also have attenuated friendship roles.

Comparing life after retirement with earlier stages, new needs and possibilities become apparent. The activities of friendship in later life include, as
in earlier years, mutual help and support, emotional intimacy and the joint
pursuit of shared interests. As with younger people friendship for older men
and women is valuable as a way of passing the time, as a source of companionship and help, and as an opportunity to give and receive affection and
intimate attention. The difference between later life and earlier years is that
friendship may be the *only* role which involves these activities. Informal
roles assume special significance at times when other roles are diminished,
through retirement, for instance, or bereavement (Rosow 1967, 1970 and
1975; Lowenthal and Robinson 1976; Hess 1972; Jerrome 1981; Blau 1973).

At periods of intensive role learning and role loss, friends function as a valued resource for the individual. Friendship serves also as an important mechanism of societal integration (Hess 1972). At this time the presence of intimates is important (Rosow 1967, 1970; Lowenthal and Haven 1968; Lowenthal and Robinson 1976). Intimacy acts as a buffer against age-related losses. Friends play a vital role in the process of socialisation to old age. They impart instrumental knowledge, provide an opportunity for role rehearsal and set controls on behaviour. Ageing people look to friends for direct aid, in the form of behaviour cues and sanctions, and indirect aid which consists of support and permissiveness in trial-and-error learning, validation of self, and ritual observance of achievements. Friends 'provide protective insulation in managing confrontation with the wider society' (Hess 1972).

Intimate exchanges with peers are more rewarding than those across age boundaries. In all age groups not only are there common interests and resources which can be enjoyed most in their own company; peers confirm favourable self-concepts and help sustain personal defences against the deskilling which can occur between old and young. The choice of peers as friends is a product of choice not constraint, a way of avoiding talk which undermines confidence and underlines the status differential between older and younger people (Dowd 1980). Talking about their friendships, old people say they feel supported, cared about, able to talk things through with someone who is available to them for this purpose. The values placed on friendship in old age – confirmation of self, sharing, trust, intimacy – seem to extend across cultures, as studies in Britain, North American and Germany show (Wenger 1987).

The opportunity and capacity to make friends in later life has been related to the structural factors of age, gender and class. Other variables are marital status and household composition. The literature on friendship has presented it as a more middle-class than a working-class phenomenon (Allan 1977; Gavron 1966; Harris 1983; Blau 1961). The view of friendship as class-specific has sometimes been a matter of definition. An overemphasis on particular activities (reciprocal visiting for instance) and a tendency to define friendship and kinship as mutually exclusive, has restricted the range of people to whom this relationship might apply. A recognition of the diversity of content and possibility of conducting friendship with selected people from a range of social categories (cousins and sisters as well as unrelated people) was ruled out in the earlier accounts. A more phenomenological approach recognises this diversity.

Gender emerges in the literature as a crucial variable in the pattern and meaning of friendship (Hess 1979; Powers and Bultena 1976). One of the benefits enjoyed by older women is the opportunity to use the skills for which they have been trained since birth (Myerhoff 1978). Girls are encouraged to direct their energies towards cultivating and sustaining relation-ships. The different bases for status and self-esteem in men and women give women an advantage in retirement, when people rather than things, and the maintenance of relationships become the focus of activity. This is a time of life when expressive activities – 'women's work' – are valued. Retirement offers little scope for the pursuit of instrumental goals and the use of conventional masculine skills. Men's and women's relationships have different characteristics, which develop in childhood. Girls' friendships tend to be intimate, involving self-disclosure. The best friend and confidante is an important figure. Boys' friendships tend to be less intense and are less frequently dyadic. In adulthood, the patterns persist. In married life a man's most intimate friend is generally his spouse rather than 'mates', fellow club or team members. Women go on having intimate ties with other women, who can be relied on for advice, sympathy and moral support. Their relationships are more meaningful. In a study of middle-aged, middle-class couples Hess (1972) found that women are twice as likely as the men to talk about personal problems and feelings with friends.

In later life these sex differences are still apparent. Men tend to have more frequent social contacts, a smaller proportion with intimate friends, more with family and less close friends. As far as friendship is concerned, women have the more stable, long-lived and intense relationships (Powers and Bultena 1976). Old women are, according to the literature, better at making and sustaining intimate friendships than old men. Men are less likely to replace lost friends. An elderly woman may find her relationships disrupted by bereavement (if it occurs early) but they are resumed when the friends themselves become widowed (Blau 1961). The main emotional investments of older men tend to be in their wives – if they have them. Asked who his best friend is, the elderly man will generally name his wife. A married woman, on the other hand, is just as likely to name another woman (Lowenthal and Haven 1968). The dependency needs of old men are met in marriage and widowerhood brings great isolation and loneliness (Blau 1973). Widows, on the other hand, have higher morale because, it is suggested, they are more likely to have confidantes.

In short, the main differences in the friendships of men and women are seen as those of content and the degree of emotional intimacy. Men talk less and do more together and men are sociable rather than intimate (Pleck 1975; Seiden and Bart 1975). Their needs for intimacy are, it appears, met within marriage (Lowenthal and Robinson 1976). What happens to them afterwards we do not know though the suggestion in the literature seems to be that the loss of intimacy through widowerhood makes men vulnerable to depression and psychosomatic illness, and accounts for increased mortality following bereavement. In general, though, the literature tells us little about the emotional needs of men in later life, or how they are met. The more recent psychological literature focusing on the life-span suggests that a convergence occurs between men and women in mid-life. Men are increasingly freed from instrumental concerns to develop the expressive sides of their personalities (Gutmann 1987). The sociological evidence offered above indicates that in terms of emotional intimacy, these psychological changes occur either insufficiently or too late for most men, though other variables such as marital status might be implicated.

The capacity for friendship, throughout the adult life-span, is determined to a large extent by the content of the marital relationship, one of the two key dyads in western cultures (Caplan and Bujra 1978; du Bois 1974; Paine 1974). The tendency to view marriage as the main source of companionship and fulfilment has developed gradually since the turn of the century. As the ideal of companionate marriage has grown the value of intimate same-sex friendships – so clear in the correspondence of middle-class Victorian women friends – has diminished (Bernard 1976; Jerrome 1984). Solidarity between women is easier after the shedding of the bonds of active kinship. In societies with polygamous traditions, in Muslim societies where the women's world is veiled in secrecy, in cultures where women's economic activities produce an active female network centred on commerce, friendship is the main source of emotional intimacy between adults (V. Saifullah-Kahn 1976; Jerrome 1979; Caplan and Bujra 1978). The tendency for preoccupations of marriage and family to undermine the quality of extra-familial friendship is underlined in the social lives of older women in Britain. Some recently detached from the obligations of marriage and active parenthood find themselves devastated by the loss of key relationships and unable to develop substitutes (Jerrome 1983). Others are able for the first time to enjoy active friendships (Jerrome 1981). In old age, the lifestyles of never-married women and formerly married women with attenuated family ties converge, centring upon the activities of friendship.

For men, too, the theoretical link between the form and content of the marital relationship and the quality of same-sex friendships holds. On the evidence of the men's fellowship, reviewed in the last chapter, it would seem that some formerly-married men derive from their extra-familial relationships the range of benefits attributed to female friendship and previously enjoyed within the marriage. The content of sociable relationships in the men's fellowship confirms the suggestion in the literature of the importance of activity as a focus of men's friendships. It also provides an insight into the consequences of bereavement for a small section of the elderly male population. Their lives are in contrast to those for whom widowerhood signals the end of emotional intimacy.

Friendship emerges in this study as one of the major benefits of organisation membership for the unattached man or woman. But the link between friendship and club membership is more subtle than one would expect on the basis of official claims and popular preconceptions. In the culture of the club the remark, 'That's what it's all about' is – as we saw in Chapter Three – used regularly to affirm the shared value of friendship and sociability. Club-going provides opportunities for social interaction with peers. In theory it introduces people to potential friends. In practice people tend to join with a friend and someone who joins alone has some difficulty in becoming integrated. An ideology of friendship and caring is expressed in formal gestures, in concern over illness, in the celebration of personal achievements and in the welcome extended in meetings. But friendship as a personal relationship involving intimacy, mutuality and shared leisure activities is generally restricted to relationships founded outside the clubs and cutting across them. Club-going emerges as an activity of friendship, the club providing a wider network into which pairs of friends may integrate.

The activities of friendship

Pairs and groups of friends can be identified at a glance by seating arrange-ments. Close friends sit in such a way that the maximum amount of talk is possible. This means occupying a small table for four or six, a trestle table for eight or ten or a row of chairs, depending on the layout of the room. Conversation appears to be the main activity of friendship, apart from club-going itself. Although some friends visit each other's homes for a cup of tea quite regularly (especially if they are neighbours) and others gather for cards, they tend to see each other mainly at the club. The question, 'Do you see your friend outside this club?' typically brings the response, 'Oh yes, we also go to X club together and Y'. Club-going, especially the sampling of new clubs, is a pastime made all the more enjoyable by being shared. Once in the club, regular seats are taken up and groups of friends waste no time before catching up on each other's news, commenting on people as they arrive, and enjoying a sense of camaraderie as the collective identity en-joyed in this particular setting is taken on. Known as 'our gang' or 'your gang' by outsiders, a friendship group is identifiable by the noise it makes, sometimes at a time when silence is the norm. One such group consists of eight women, and the brother of one of them, who is tolerated as long as he does not intrude. Indeed he says very little, speaking only rarely to tell one of the women to shut up when the barely concealed whispering makes it difficult to concentrate on the game of bingo. The seating pattern on two sides of a trestle table never changes (see Figure 5.1):

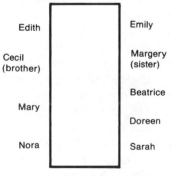

Figure 5.1

Nora and Mary are best friends, as are Edith and Emily. So are Doreen and Sarah, though in their case the closeness is a product of their restricted environment rather than mutual attraction. Both disabled, they lean on each other as neighbours while disapproving of each other's personal style and outlook. Sarah visits Doreen daily and picks her up on the way to the club, which is for both of them the only outing in the week. Nora and Mary accompany each other on club holidays which invariably means sharing a room. They also have tea together several times a week as they live in the same street. In addition to their meeting at the club, Edith and Emily play cards together once a week with Edith's cousin, Mr R, who now sits at the top table as the club secretary. He and Emily are romantically attached and for years have gone on club holidays and outings together.

As a group the six women stand out for the intensity of their interaction. Gifts are exchanged: in return for Doreen's bread-pudding, Edith gives some coconut ice which Doreen consumes with relish, for it is strictly against doctor's orders, to the accompaniment of cries of envy from the rest; Christmas cards are exchanged, and it is red roses all round when Doreen is due to move away from the area, for the others to remember her by when she leaves. A win at bingo is a triumph for the whole table, and a winning raffle ticket a shared success. The jokes and banter which have won the group a dubious reputation as the noisiest table occasionally degenerate into wild horse-play, resulting on one occasion in a packet of tea spilt on the table after a fierce struggle hampered by breathless laughter. Such behaviour is recognised by participants as belonging to childhood, in remarks offered defensively or in explanation: 'We behave like kids when we get together'. This brings to mind Hochschild's comment about elderly people being protected within the peer group from society's censure of those who violate age expectations. The link between the playfulness of early life and the camaraderie of older people has been noted in the studies of peer group behaviour in a variety of cultures (Spencer 1987; du Bois 1974). Gatherings of peers reinvoke the natural play of childhood. The sense of community is rooted in the play and the spontaneous enjoyment of childhood which are carried over to the private domains of the older peer group and protected in a ritualised setting. Within the elderly per group we can observe what Lambeck (1988) calls 'a playful kind of collective regression' involving gluttony, sexual joking and reminiscence.

In groups of friends in the club, conversation is punctuated by humour. The jokes are often about age and sex, the gain of one and the loss of the other being unpalatable facts which older people, being in the same situation, can appreciate. In this company the ribaldry is acceptable for 'we are all widows and need to let our hair down'. It is the sense of shared circumstances which helps to forge a collective identity: 'We are a filthy lot!' (in reference to sexual jokes); 'He's favouring our enemies' when the bingo caller picks the wrong number. Sexual joking, freedom from constraint and

Good Company

lively personal encounters have been noted as features of older women's discourse (Gutmann 1987). Even in Islamic cultures the bawdy older woman is observed cackling obscenely with her cronies.

Topics of conversation between friends reflect the typical concerns of club members. They talk about how many people have turned up and unexplained absences which are clues to people's state of health; and the weather and its effects on participation. These routine topics constitute ritualistic opening gambits paving the way for more personal topics. The happenings of the past week, the welfare of mutual friends, details of health and domestic organisation, difficulties with builders, the size of heating bills, threats to personal safety and changes in appearance are noted and commented on. These intimate concerns occupy the attention before the meeting, over tea and sometimes through the card-playing too, often to the irritation of the organisers who have different objectives. In fact, it is clear from the lack of attention to play that, for such groups as these, the game is not of central importance. It merely provides a pretext for talk. Although enjoyable the game is secondary to the social exchanges it facilitates. This is a cause of irritation to any serious player who happens by mistake to join a table of friends. Arthur, for instance, was moving from table to table in search of romantic attachment. With one group of friends he finally seized the cards from the dealer in exasperation and dealt them himself. His irritated remark on the side, 'Don't Flo patter when she gets started!' summed up his view of the talk as idle chatter, essentially meaningless.

The significance of talk

Arthur's discomfiture underlines the point that the women, unlike him, have come to talk. The importance of talk explains the apparent inconsistency of Lilly's reluctance to attend the local day centre where 'they don't do anything but play bingo!' when she would not miss the weekly session of bingo at St Anthony's Club for anything. The talk meets important social and psychological needs. Through questions and answers about recent and expected movements (had Mabel had her hair done: it was looking unusually nice! Was Rene planning to come on the outing or would the prospect of the coach journey deter her?) a life is exposed to scrutiny. Its difficulties and achievements are acknowledged. The past as well as the present swims into view and the whole is put into perspective. This process is particularly effective between old friends, though new friends can perform a similar function, as the following example shows. Daisy and Jean, Jessie and Eva talked of hair-styles during the war and subsequent changes in appearance, for good or bad. This was followed the next week by an exchange of early photographs over tea accompanied by reminiscences about young womanhood. Against this background, the weekly nip of whiskey in the tea was justifiable ('we take care of ourselves *now*!' – and why not?). The outcome of conversation is often mutual reassurance that the present has its compensations and that a bit of self-indulgence in widowhood, after a lifetime of service demanded by ideologies of family and marriage, is not a bad thing. Treating oneself is condoned not as selfish but as life-preserving. In a couple-oriented society, where the unattached must work hard to achieve validation, friends perform a valuable service in legitimating behaviour. Equally, they set limits on behaviour which does not conform to prevailing standards. Nora tells how her neighbour, recently widowed, expects constant attention on her own terms. Her friends agree that Nora is justified in refusing to supply it. Doreen, crippled with arthritis, insists on reserving an extra chair for her bag and umbrella. Openly in her absence and more subtly in her presence her friends grumble about her fussiness, seeing her insistence as rigid and complaining. Whereas a nip of whiskey in one's tea is condoned, especially when it is shared with neighbours and hence a sociable activity, getting her friends to organise an extra seat when Doreen could just as easily hang her stick on the radiator behind her violates the norms of both friendship and illness behaviour. The former – norms of friendship – emphasise consideration and mutuality; the latter – norms of illness behaviour – struggle and resistance. On another occasion Doreen is talked out of a wish to end her own life, viewed as a weak and misguided intention when she has so much to be thankful for.

Conversation among women friends at the club is intimate and 'small frame'. It shares the special quality of women's talk noted by Johnson and Aries (1983) in offering a mosaic of non-critical listening and talking which meets the needs for self-expression and reassurance of worth. It establishes guidelines for behaviour at times when other sources of prescription are vague or negative. It is essentially private and backstage (D. Jones 1980), although in the case of these elderly working-class widows the arena – the club – is public and formally organised.

To counteract the impersonal and anonymous framework of the formal organisation the women colonise the space around them, making it their own. They employ a variety of mechanisms to do so. Noisy talk and hunched shoulders and other non-verbal signs of exclusivity signal their resistance to the leaders and defiance of externally imposed rules such as that of silence. The emphasis on talk supports the values of intimacy and dependency, values which women in particular hold dear (Stephens 1976). This gender difference has implications for informal communication between men and women in the club. Men and women communicate differently, both in the content and style of their speech (Spender 1980; Lakoff 1975). These differences and the essentially private nature of communications in the club disqualify any men present from joining in. In the same way, gender-specific interests and styles of communication work to prevent women from joining men's groups.

The personal content of conversation, ironically, creates difficulties for women who come to a club in order to make friends. The universal

Good Company

complaint seems to be that it is hard to get to know people or that clubs are 'cliquy'. An analysis of conversation between friends provides a clue to the difficulties in friendship formation. Friends talk constantly about people and events of mutual interest. Strangers sit in silence, unable to join in. It is felt inappropriate to ask personal questions, but there is no other basis for conversation between strangers in that they are mutually ignorant and have no knowledge of each other's friends or interests. In the experience of two friends reviewing the situation, 'You couldn't really join a group of friends because you wouldn't know what they were talking about and they wouldn't know what to say to you'. In this community people either pick up personal information through mutual acquaintances or wait months – sometimes years – for personal revelations which answer an unspoken question. In one case, it concerned the manner of a husband's death which had been a source of speculation for some time. (This appears to be a feature of other clubs, too. Mogey (1956) speaks of two old ladies who had always sat together. Neither of them knew where the other lived but were very interested to find out through him.)

If the rule of avoiding direct questions applies between friends it is even stronger in the case of complete strangers. One outcome is for friends to carry on their conversation as if the strangers were not there. Another is for silence to fall. This is particularly noticeable when two clubs come together for reasons of economy to do something which on account of their size they could not afford to do alone. At the Good Companions Christmas dinner, held jointly with another small Federation club, the atmosphere was quieter and less buoyant than usual. There was no jollity. Eating was the main activity, accompanied by desultory conversation. Despite the close proximity of women from the other club and the prospect of a shared afternoon of eating and entertainment there were no attempts to become acquainted. Several explanations for this pattern are possible. One is controversial, implying that social skills are class-specific. Lopata and Maines (1981), for instance, suggest that a reluctance to enter into potentially intimate relationships with strangers is a feature of working-class subcultures. Evidence from North America indicates that working-class subcultures often lack the pre-conditions necessary for the conversion of acquaintances into friends.

> Fear, lack of trust, lack of self-confidence, the presence of negative self-images and lack of familiarity with norms outlining steps in friendship formation combine with the inability to protect privacy and the wish to hide past or present events so as to hinder the development and maintenance of achieved voluntary relations aside from relatives and lifelong associates. (Lopata and Maines 1981).

It has been noted elsewhere that there are special difficulties in the integration of working-class immigrants in middle-class communities. The suggestion, again, is that their linguistic limitations and ignorance of social routines inhibit membership of established organisations and informal groupings (Bott 1957; Willmott and Young 1960). If true, this pattern of social intercourse might, at the psychological level, be a product of a lack of experience, poor social skills and low rewards, operating in a vicious circle. Many people in the wider society have difficulty in pacing the exchanges that provide the foundation for friendship, converting an acquaintanceship into something more intimate (Duck 1983). Maintaining 'polite companionship' without an invasion of privacy requires knowledge of cultural assumptions about friendship and familiarity with ceremonies of exchange which regulate the intensity of the relationship of participants. Embarking on social relationships with strangers in the club, whose friendship beliefs one cannot take for granted in the absence of mechanisms for controlling the mutual exploration, is socially hazardous (Jerrome 1983). People might in any case differ in the extent to which they regard friendly relations as possible or desirable. In general, mutual trust and empathy – in short openness – are not thought possible or desired with more than a very few individuals in highly specific settings. This is a feature of informal social life which distinguishes North-West European and North American cultures from those of the Mediterranean, where greater emphasis on sociability in principle and in practice is a product of social, climatic and psychological factors (Boissevain 1974).

At the Christmas party, the social mix of intimates and strangers had come about for practical rather than normative reasons. It was not thought necessary for strangers to be integrated into existing networks. This is not the case at the normal club meeting where value is attached to sociability, among the organisers at least. Committee members see their role as introducing the unattached newcomer to established members. But for the reasons I have just outlined, the object of friendship is difficult to achieve. The difficulty in conducting a conversation with a stranger is compounded by a more fundamental problem arising from the gap between official and unofficial friendship strategies.

An ideology of friendship

In the professed ideology of the club, friendship has no boundaries. An ideology of friendship is expressed in public gestures of concern, warmth and acceptance. In the official view, the club exists to introduce people to potential friends and to consolidate the bonds of friendship. The aim of the organisers is 'a friendly club' and the often stated belief that 'we are all friends together' is reflected in seating arrangements and in rituals of solidarity.

The crucial nature of seating arrangements is recognised by the organisers and reflected in the amount of thought and energy given to the issue. Since movement is limited during the meeting, interaction is restricted to those within reach: with whom eye contact can be satisfactorily made and who are in earshot. People tend not to know or even to recognise those on different tables or in different rows. In one club, three different arrangements were tried before the organiser – Mrs L – was satisfied that she had achieved the maximum amount of social interaction. She had started with trestle tables in a long line with up to fifteen people on each side. When this arrangement seemed unsatisfactory the trestle tables were separated to make three units. The final arrangement consisted of eight small tables seating four people each, scattered at random throughout the hall. Other clubs retain the first or second pattern. Some have no tables at all as they take up space and limit the potential size of the club. The largest clubs have chairs in rows, either in straight lines or with some set at an angle to maximise eye contact and improve the view of the platform. In the Good Companions Club the rows had been replaced by a circle of thirty chairs when a gradual drop in numbers through ageing and death was sharply accelerated by a conflict among the leaders. In the case of Mrs L's club the rearrangement of chairs was a deliberate attempt to promote general friendliness and resist the process of exclusive friendship formation, or 'clicks' as identifiable networks are known by organisers. In the Good Companions Club the radical decision to replace the formal arrangement of rows by a circle was part of a campaign to boost membership by fostering an informal, intimate atmosphere.

Not only is the seating plan designed to promote friendly intercourse; there are also rules regulating access to seats. Officially, anyone can sit anywhere. In the leader's view seats cannot be reserved for friends. In cases of infringement, horror stories are produced to maintain open access. The case is recalled of the newcomer Mrs X who stood around waiting for a seat (all the empty ones were being kept for friends) then went home, never to reappear. Such practices, if they become widely known, can ruin a club's reputation. Somewhat surprisingly, the seating issue emerges in the more instrumental clubs too. Despite its overtly political aims and instrumental orientation, the National Federation of Retirement Pensioners' Associations recognises the expressive needs of older people. At an area council meeting I attended, the Federation was said to stand for friendship. The local meeting exists to satisfy members' needs to 'sit and talk, a release from the silence of living alone'. As in non-Federation clubs, the tendency for members to reserve seats is seen as a major problem.

The aim of 'a friendly club' is expressed in different ways. Frequent statements from the platform underline the importance of friendship as a goal and the anxiety of the committee that they should succeed in this. Loneliness and the desire for friends are seen as the main reasons for attendance, the main justification for the club's existence and for the efforts of the executive committee. Frequent reminders of this are offered. On successive weeks, leaders at Stamford Road Club called for assurances from the members that they were succeeding: 'You come back because you meet all your friends here, you know them all!'. This statement met with noisy affirmation. The following week, congratulating people for turning out, the chairman said 'Of course you meet with your friends don't you?' to which the ritual response was a rousing, 'Oh yes!'. The equation of success and friendliness emerged clearly in the way I was introduced on one occasion. My comment, 'I've come to see how people enjoy themselves on a Sunday afternoon' was translated by the organiser: 'This lady has come to see what a friendly club we are'. After the meeting she enquired anxiously whether they had passed the test.

The opening prayer at St Brelade's Club regularly includes a plea to 'bless all clubs trying to promote friendship'. References to the benefits of friendship and the trust it inspires are made in prayer, song and readings from 'the little book'. *The Book of Friendship* by Francis Gay has been discussed already. The moralistic tone of the text makes it ideal for devotional purposes and in one club a passage is selected every week together with a thanksgiving prayer to close the meetings. A typical example read to the Sunday Club is the story of Mrs M, who didn't want to open her front door ('none of us do!'). But she did, and the two young people who were standing there said quickly, 'We want you to be our granny'. She responded and they became her greatest friends. She started to bake cakes and pastries again and her days of loneliness were over. Despite initial looks of resignation a round of applause greeted this satisfactory ending, which affirmed the value of friendship and the need to grasp opportunities when they arise. The content of the message in this particular case was somewhat diluted in the ensuing discussion which arose spontaneously about the folly of elderly people opening their doors to anyone, particularly youths, at any time of the day or night. The ending of the story, while it made sense in terms of the principle of reciprocity, was far removed from the reality of friendship in the experience of club members.

Two views of friendship

Despite the good intentions of the organisers and the ideology of friendship which pervades meetings, clubs are not, it seems, a place in which to make friends. The problem lies in the multiple meanings attached to friendship in the culture of the club. When used in a collective ritual context it is close to the Christian notion of fellowship, meaning solidarity, mutual forbearance, social acceptance and a shared identity in relation to outsiders. But when used between individuals it refers to a dyadic relationship based on mutual attraction. The bond between pairs or groups of friends establishes boundaries which include some people and exclude others. In the official view you come to the club to make friends. But in practice, 'You need a friend to join with or it's hard to get to know people'. Friendship in the sense of intimacy, mutuality and sharing of time, leisure and confidences is restricted to relationships founded outside the clubs and cutting across them. The tension between these two contrasting understandings of the term produces dilemmas for the organisers and conflict over seating

arrangements. It also accounts for the difficulty newcomers have in pene-
trating existing friendship networks, although they have the organisers'
support in their efforts to do so. Seating arrangements designed to promote
general friendliness tend to inhibit the growth of dyadic relationships. The
principle that anyone can sit anywhere conflicts with members' wish to sit
with their friends. Reserving seats – which means arriving up to half an hour
early – meets with official disapproval; but the alternative is a drop in
numbers. The choice of a seat becomes a symbol of resistance to unpopular
leaders. The politically astute member manipulates the seating rule to keep
friends at hand and unwelcome people at bay. In the following case a
member ignores the rule on one occasion and upholds it on another to
promote her social interests.

Jean arrived early and took up her seat at the long trestle table. Her
friends Gladys who had been absent for some time reappeared and took up
her customary position opposite. She disappeared for a moment to buy
raffle tickets. In her absence two relative newcomers, who the previous week
had taken over Gladys's seat and the neighbouring one, appeared and
expressed annoyance at the sight of Glady's bag. Jean didn't like them
much so she sat up and said sharply, 'It's Gladys's seat, she used to have it
before you arrived and can have it back'. The two women recognised the
force of the argument and withdrew. Gladys didn't come again and the two
women managed to establish themselves at Jean's table. A few weeks later,
they arrived a bit later than usual to find that their seats had been reserved
with a bag and a stick. The owners had gone off to the cloakroom. Indig-
nantly they protested, 'They're our seats.' Seeing her opportunity to be rid
of them once again Jean drew herself up firmly and reminded them that,
'Seats don't belong to people!' Again they withdrew. Inconsistent applica-
tion of the seating rule can thus be seen as a way of controlling movement
into and out of friendship groups.

People who successfully retain their seats are more likely to establish
intimate relationships. Familiarity makes the chat more satisfying. It is
possible without preliminaries to resume conversations broken off the
previous week, in a climate of trust and predictability. Resistance to strangers, especially men, is made easier by some seating arrangements than
others. At the Sunday Club Bessie, May, Jean, Edna and Laura come to talk
rather than to play cards. They go through the motions without concentrating. The missed turns and haphazard dealing pass without comment. There
is even a bit of half-hearted cheating which does not create the tension that
would be generated on the more 'serious' tables. To discourage anyone else
from joining, for there is just room to squeeze one more chair in and the
organiser is circling with a strange man in tow, they do their best to convey
a sense of completeness as a group. The noisy talk and laughter, the
heads drawn together around the table, and their obvious familiarity with
each other, successfully distance them from adjacent tables. The message

conveyed by the hunched shoulders is that they care less about cards than about each other. Failing to catch anyone's eye, the organiser passes on.

The tension between personal needs for intimacy and the organisational aims of a friendly club surfaces in different ways. It is the basis of arguments about seating. The executive committee of the Good Companions Club have struggled for years to build up the membership. They are baffled by the failure of their friendly atmosphere and lively programme to gain new members. The problem lies in the seating arrangement itself. The circle of chairs is at once too intimate and too public. Unless it is whispered to a next door neighbour, everyone is party to a conversation. Inadvertently establishing eye contact with someone on the opposite side requires acknowledgement, but the rules governing this kind of communication are uncertain. Unable to slip in at the back, the newcomer also feels exposed.

Ironically, the organisers' insistence on free access to seats in the name of friendship ultimately defeats the goal of integrating the newcomer, as the following case shows. Miss C doesn't feel she really belongs to the Sunday Club. She had originally been invited by a friend but got there before her. She was turned away from two tables where the empty seats had already been reserved and finally went home. On the way she met her friend who later told the organiser what had happened. The organiser was angry with the members of the two offending tables and ordered Miss C to move from table to table in future. Miss C, a shy and unassertive woman, obeys but has no real friends in the club: she drifts in and out permanently on the margin of things. Women like Miss C are in the minority, even in this club set up by a charitable organisation specifically for lonely people (defined by the organisers as those living alone). A preponderance of people with her needs would, in fact, make the club unviable. Participation in a social club populated by people as lonely as each other is an unrewarding experience which contributes to the low success rate of such organisations (Jerrome 1983). In a sense, women like Miss C are ineligible for friendship, even in a friendship club (set up to help isolated people make friends). The very fact of membership in a club for lonely people makes them unattractive to each other for it reveals their own need for friends and lack of success in making such relationships by conventional means. Club members know too much about each other for comfort; they are too much alike to help each other. Membership of a friendship club is itself a demoralising experience, an admission of social failure. In interaction with others, the lonely woman's low self-esteem is reinforced by seeing herself reflected in those around her: unattached, ageing and lonely in a society which values youthfulness and family life, where value is attached to sociability, and where social life is couple-oriented. Lacking in confidence and unpractised in the skill of self-presentation the lonely woman finds the unstructured setting of the social club for unattached people, where there are few prescriptions for behaviour and where first contacts are hindered by the knowledge that she is being assessed as a potential friend, especially daunting. The Sunday Club is officially for the socially isolated older person but is in fact dominated by women who are socially active and well-connected. Miss C provides an exception. But her experience confirms the point that if the club were just for really lonely people like her and attracted no others it would be a failure.

Boundaries of friendship

People rarely join clubs on their own. They join with friends or relatives – an aunt, mother or sister, cousin or spouse – or follow them to the club when circumstances change. Just as it is normal to join with a friend so continued membership in his or her absence is seen as difficult. Efforts are made by the committee to hang on to someone after a friend's death or hospitalisation or re-housing, the assumption being that sentiments cannot be easily transferred from this unique personal relationship to another. But the woman or man who stays on is the exception who proves the rule. A partner's absence is felt, especially on club outings, as the following extract suggests. It comes from a letter I receive after the end of my field-work. 'I am still going to the club but shall not be going on the outings as you need a friend to go round with and as you know Maud and I always went together and I feel the old saying is true, as while you have someone to sit with you need a friend to go round with when you get to the destination. Another two years and my "other" friend will be retiring and will be able to come.' On the telephone she added, 'It's a pity about the outings. But you don't want to be a third person. When people have been together for years you feel in the way'.

A friendly club, in short, is a club where people are welcoming, prepared to talk and allow you to join in their conversations, and make space for you to sit down. But members do not automatically become friends. Fellow club members are friendly acquaintances though they may in some cases become friends over time. But the norm is not to intrude on another friendship unless invited. Shared membership does not establish a right to friendship. My friend's friend is not my friend, even if we have sat either side of her for years. I cannot assume they will want me to accompany them to club X even though we three are very friendly at club Y. Friendships *are* made, especially when the object of membership is to find a companion for a specific leisure activity or mutual interest, such as theatre-going. Friendship for its own sake is harder to achieve, for 'it would take weeks to tell a new friend about my family. Old friends are acquainted with family events as they happen'. Some women establish new friendships successfully, but in general the experience of this group is in contrast to that of middle-class women among whom the establishment of new intimate same-sex friendships is not uncommon (Jerrome 1981; Armstrong 1988; Matthews 1986).

As we saw at the beginning of the chapter, groups of friends are discernible by the intensity of their interaction. On outings they go their separate ways, each group barely acknowledging the other's existence. If they pass in the street their separateness is underlined by humorous gestures such as noses thrust in the air. If they are less kindly disposed to one another the outing is enlivened by gossip and speculation: poor old Len has got in with a bad lot at the back of the coach. How will they pass their time in Tunbridge Wells? Members of one group gaze avidly into a shop window hoping not to be recognised while 'the bad lot' pass by on the opposite pavement.

The distinction between friendly acquaintance and friend creates further subdivisions within the friendship group. The sense of solidarity generated by the shared circumstances of old age and widowhood does not obscure the divisions between close friends and casual friends who convene in groups for the purpose of recreation. The infringement of a rule of privacy within the dyad brings accusations of eavesdropping. Sociability in this context is problematic, as Sarah found out when she joined in a conversation between Mary and Nora sitting opposite. She ruefully acknowledged her mistake by signing her Christmas cards MYOB (Mind Your Own Business). The incident rested on a misunderstanding about the scope of relationships around the table. The lack of consensus was further underlined by joking references to the initials by other members of the table on subsequent occasions. The humorous response also implied that Sarah's mistake was tolerable. She could be forgiven for mistaking her casual friendship for the close one she desired. The status of the relationships in the group was ambiguous. Its permanence as a group made it more than a set of 'cronies' but in the setting of the club the dyadic emphasis faded into a type of small group interaction in which intimate disclosures were less appropriate (du Bois 1974).

The notion of intruding inhibits acquaintances who would like to become friends. Strangers are at an even greater disadvantage. They must be careful where they sit but they are unlikely to be invited to take a seat. The onus is on them to become integrated but social mechanisms enabling them to join in conversations are inadequate. Sitting alone for whatever reason is problematic in this atmosphere. The question, 'are you on your own?' is more than an opening gambit from one unattached person to another. It is a request for significant information about accessibility. If two regulars find themselves without company on a particular occasion, the anomaly will be removed by a speedy closing of the gap as one is invited to join the other. If a woman is one of a threesome on a coach trip and the other two are sitting together, the response to the question, 'are you on you own?' may be a brusque, '*No I'm not*', as if the question were an insult.

Friendship is problematic in the context of club life. The exclusiveness of friendship groups ('clickyness') is a recurrent theme, an organisational problem, and a criterion for the evaluation of clubs. The tension between personal needs and organisational aims is highlighted by the seating issue.

As I have said, the problem lies in the multiple definitions of friendship. There is a contrast between the collective use of the term in an impersonal ritual context to mean general friendliness and social acceptance, and the more intense personal relationships developed by individual members. For them friendship is an exclusive category, while for the club organisers it is inclusive. An analysis of sociability in clubs suggests that club organisers, desiring general friendliness rather than the establishment of emotionally rewarding dyads and groups or cliques, foster the first at the expense of the second. The two sides of friendship are problematic also from the members' point of view. The exercise of inclusion and exclusion means that within a group of friends people are left out of dyadic communications. The exclusiveness of friendship sets up boundaries within groups as well as between them and the rules governing interaction across these boundaries are not always clear.

Club-going is one of the main activities of friendship for these women. Within that context conversation is both a pastime and a means of communication. Both express women's emotional needs and values. The need for intimacy and the fact of dependency are acknowledged and celebrated. Through friendship both the social and psychological needs of the ageing woman are met. As I have suggested earlier, support in difficult circumstances, the consolidation of new identities, socialisation to new roles, reassurance of personal worth and the integration of past and present are achieved through conversation with friends. To be alone in these circumstances is problematic. But the social mechanisms which exist to integrate unattached newcomers are inadequate. The strong sense that you need to join with a friend to get to know people might reflect the difficulties strangers have in entering into conversation between friends, or it might be a rationalisation for shyness. A cultural interpretation focuses upon norms of friendship and points to the conclusion that the club environment is not conducive to friendship formation, despite the intentions of the organisers.

SIX

In sickness and in health

'It's all very well getting old, people say aren't you marvellous! But your body doesn't work the same as before. I can't jump out of bed as I used to. If I did I would feel dizzy and might fall down, then I couldn't get up again. My fingertips have lost their sensitivity and I can't sew. Today I feel unwell, exhausted. But I dare not go to bed for the day in case I shan't get up again. You quickly lose the use of your limbs. That's what's the trouble with a lot of these old people you see using zimmers: they have been in bed.'

'Mrs S was unique, a wonderful woman. She was ill but you wouldn't know it.'

These quotations reflect a particular view of health and illness in old age. They also indicate a public and a private face of sickness. Issues of health and ill-health tend to dominate the lives of organisation members. They influence the content of meetings and informal communications in club and fellowship. The presence of sickness is discernible from the first moment of gathering, when greetings are exchanged to the last, when members are admonished to keep well and sent on their way. Members of old-age organisations are relatively fit, compared with non-joiners, but their social activities conceal chronic conditions the control of which takes much energy.

This chapter examines the role of peers in both alleviating the problems caused by ill-health and promoting health and fitness. The chapter falls into several parts. It starts with the prevalence of ill-health in the club and fellowship population and its salience in their lives. It analyses the importance of friends in the confirmation of health status and in the construction of norms of illness behaviour. It goes on to consider individual concepts of illness and the strategies to which they give rise. The last part of the chapter concentrates on the role of friends in coping with illness and disability. It looks at the nature of friendship and those features by which it is distinguished from other intimate relationships. It challenges the views of those contemporary writers who argue that friendship is incompatible with the provision of health care.

The perception of sickness

If health statistics are to be believed, the majority of old people suffer from a range of debilitating conditions apart from the life changes which are a product of normal senescence. Indeed it has been said that multiple disability is so common as to be almost the rule (Williams 1979, p. 38). Disorders range from arthritis which afflicts one-fifth of late middle-aged people and presumably considerably more of the elderly; minor disorders of the feet, experienced by 80 per cent of those over 65; and swollen ankles, to chronic bronchitis and angina (Gray and Wilcock 1981). These conditions are in part related to living conditions and personal health histories: they are more prevalent in working-class than in middle-class old people (Victor 1987; Ford 1985). The high incidence of long-standing illness or disability, even that which is felt to limit mobility or the capacity to engage in the full range of activities, is not reflected in subjective ratings of health. Feeling well and enjoying good health does not depend on the absence of physical illness in old people. Some severely disabled people are known to regard their health as good. Health is defined as the absence of acute sickness like having a temperature or feeling exhausted or weak, rather than as difficulties of immobility, pain or breathing – relatively common experiences in old age (Copeland et al. 1986).

The spirit of optimism and determination not to let physical illness get one down, observed in health studies of elderly people in the community, inspires elderly participants in club and fellowship. But the presence of sickness and concern for its consequences are acknowledged. Public pronouncements and private conversation dwell on health matters. An opening prayer records the concern with health: 'Oh Lord, bless and strengthen the sick of this club and those who care for them'.The business part of the meeting is largely taken up with details of sickness, starting with the 'sick news', going on to the sick news recorded in the minutes of the last meeting, and under 'business arising' an update on the state of people mentioned there. The sick news is detailed and lengthy. 'Bob R – it's very sad … Mrs Hawks is going in X ward (Groan!). Lawrence is no better. Winnie K is very, very poorly and wishes to be remembered to you. Mrs G is very poorly and Mrs I is still in hospital. Mrs V has bad legs and can't come out today …'. The chairman follows this up with news of people who have returned after a period of ill-health. They are formally welcomed back with a round of applause and even cheering. The rest are admonished to stay well: 'We want no more falls and illnesses, we want a healthy, happy club!'. The business moves on rapidly to affirmations of the importance of good health, with the birthday announcements. Good health and the achievement of a long life are celebrated in song, gifts and applause. The juxtaposition of ill-health and deaths and birthday announcements is significant. It affirms the positive outlook of members and reminds them that they are here to demonstrate their capacity to survive, to lead an active life and overcome adversity. The chairman lightens the atmosphere by introducing an element of humour: 'No more falls: take more water with it' – the improbable suggestion of intoxication earning a ripple of laughter. At the informal level, too, the despondency at the presence of sickness is tempered by humour, when concerned questions are met with frivolous replies:

'Where's Lou today?' 'She was lame and we shot her!'

'You look better now – how are you?' 'Ill in bed, worse up!'

'You're nice and brown [i.e. suntanned]'. 'That's rust ... or dirt!'

Health – one's own or other people's – is a source of interest and fit subject for comment. Concern is expressed in one corner when the social secretary's eyelids are seen to droop. Is she all right? She wakes up from what has simply been a doze. Relief is expressed, but someone points out that she hasn't looked so well lately. Similar remarks can be heard over tea. Doesn't X look ill! And Y has gone really old (frail) recently. These observations, offered with some relish, betray more interest than anxiety. When contemporaries get together at the women's fellowship annual tea-party a variety of parallel experiences are recalled, from courtship in the 1920s to current health issues. Medical histories are recounted, to provide a context for current difficulties.

Contemporaries commiserate with one another and also compare the roles they play in relation to sick family members: spouses and siblings. In some cases the object of assistance is present during the discussion. The salience of ill-health is nowhere more obvious than in the case of the physically disabled who approach their seats with great difficulty. One couple attracted attention by a noisy whispered conversation during the closing prayer, wondering how they were going to get up again. But mental infirmity, also, exists in the form of a few confused members described as 'not too good', 'not all there', 'not too well'. The mentally infirm member tends to be ignored until her confusion and forgetfulness put her and fellow members at risk. She is distinguished by her incompetence at cards or bingo, her irregularity in attendance and unreliability on club outings. Like the physically disabled member who depends on others for transport to and from meetings and for collecting raffle winnings from the top table, the confused woman needs help in functioning. If they are feeling charitable, her neighbours will check the number on her raffle ticket, write down the dates and times of forthcoming events, and shepherd her about on outings. At best they are benevolent and tolerant, adopting the terms and tone of voice suitable for a child. At worst they take no notice of her – 'She never listens anyway' – or react with impatience to her difficulties.

The other women on her table wonder why Vera, deaf, confused and forgetful, comes to the meetings at all. She does not play bingo or join in the conversation but looks on, smiling vaguely. Vera and others like her illustrate the point that for this population of elderly people issues of health and ill-health dominate daily existence. Life is lived within strictly defined limits imposed by health. Accommodating to ill-health becomes a governing principle. At one extreme this means exclusion from the club. This happened to Lou, a stroke victim whose incoherent letter to fellow members from the institution where he now lives conveyed a deep sadness at the loss

of their companionship. Others continue to attend but not as full participants. Vera is slightly better off than Lou, for she can still attend meetings –
but that is about all. A sense of powerlessness pervades her life. 'No, I'm not
going on the club holiday; I'm not allowed to' (touching her head to imply
'I'm mentally incapable'). She doesn't play bingo either, saying sadly, 'They
took it away, stopped me doing it as I can't cope'. Even the control of her
financial affairs has been taken away, for her son now seems to be managing
them, though she does not remember agreeing that he should.

Even the apparently fit and well members' activities are curtailed by
routine health checks which interfere with social participation. Reluctance
to alter medical appointments which clash with club meetings reflects both
class-specific regard for medical authorities and the priority accorded to
health maintenance. The weather is much more intrusive in the lives of the
physically vulnerable than in younger, fitter people. If gait is awkward and
mobility slow, heavy rain must be avoided and so must high winds. Dependence on walking-sticks limits both speed and access and increases vulnerability to bad weather. Health problems are compounded by unreasonable
or severe weather through its effect on morale. Hence the belief that the
weather is to blame for the fact that Mrs K who was 'doing nicely' after her
recent depression, triggered by bereavement, is now 'down again'.

Time budgeting is geared to health needs. More time is needed to
accomplish tasks involving physical exertion. Dolly S, for instance, who
suffers from severe arthritis, sets off for home in the wrong direction after a
meeting. She cannot climb the slight hill to her flat, half a mile (about one
kilometre) away, and must make a huge detour involving a downhill walk
and two bus journeys, in order to get home. Slight physical problems reduce
opportunities for leadership roles as do sensory impairments such as deaf-
ness. Hearing loss is often given as a reason for avoiding office and possibly
accounts for the emphasis on audibility generally. Members are as keen as
organisers to uphold the silence rule since if others break it hearing becomes difficult. One of the commonest disabilities is high blood pressure,
which hampers movement and reduces the capacity for stressful activity. It
lies behind the avoidance of office and resignations tendered reluctantly.
Occasionally, someone's self-image and total life space are dominated by
health considerations, as the following case shows:

> Penny is relatively young – 61 – but suffers from multiple handicaps.
> She has survived a number of life-threatening health crises since
> childhood and thinks of herself as a walking miracle. She recounts the
> details of her various illnesses frequently, drawing attention to her
> facial disfigurement, which is obvious enough. Once attractive, she is
> still carefully dressed and groomed. Walking with sticks and almost
> blind, she nevertheless struggles to attend her clubs. But she feels
> stigmatised on account of her health. Club X is a friendly club – 'The
> girls are very kind to me' – but it is different at a dance club she

attends. 'They don't seem to want me there'. She feels shunned – 'People don't like you if you're disabled' – but has a strong sense of injustice. Penny feels that she has been abandoned after a life-time of helping other people. She experiences acute housing and social problems as a result of her poor health. Doing battle with the authorities, whom she regards as unsympathetic, and struggling to accomplish the routines of daily life against heavy odds, seem to keep her going.

Penny's friends at the club are anxious that she should get home safely but are not prepared to escort her to the bus-stop, which would mean a slight detour. The women Penny refers to as friends are friendly acquaintances who are sorry for her, a relative newcomer, who is manifestly handicapped and alone. Her isolation and lack of real friends (in the sense of other women with whom she shares a variety of activities and information, with a high degree of mutuality) are attributable in part to her preoccupation with health. There is admiration and sympathy for the coper, but only if she does not proclaim her virtue too much.

Norms of sickness behaviour

In general there is a tendency to deny the extent and gravity of ill-health and to avoid behaviour which might be construed as complaining or self-indulgent. People expect to cope alone with chronic health problems such as arthritis. To be met and accompanied to the club by a friend, for instance, is to be spoilt. Health crises are minimised, partly to save a friend's feelings and partly to avoid the fuss and attention which would be generated, unwelcome in their indulgence. Stoicism is a virtue but there is another reason for minimising one's condition. Some people show a capacity to rationalise about the signs of ill-health, to screen out unwelcome possibilities. Old Mr M, for instance, has had difficulty in the last month in hearing with his right ear. The nurse syringed it 'but she's not too good at it'. This comment was repeated then there was a pause while Mr M pondered. 'Unless it's ... but I don't want to think about that ... '.

People with health problems are expected to be sensible and avoid taking risks though exceptions can be made. Only the mildest disapproval is expressed by the chairman when Vic, known to be dying of cancer of the throat, is seen helping himself to a cigarette. In his terminal condition there is only gentle discouragement from this forbidden pleasure. But Mrs H is viewed with mixed feelings when she sets off to walk to her son's house two miles (about three kilometres) away, having suffered from a gastric disorder for the past three weeks. Edna, who refuses to have a telephone despite her heart condition is a source of irritation to her friends who know she can well afford it. Equally, disapproval is expressed towards people who give in too easily to their symptoms, who moan and complain, who rely too much on other people, who should 'buck up' and face adversity. There seems, then, to be a contradiction in attitudes, for people who embrace the sick role too readily and those who deny it altogether are both the objects of criticism. The former are guilty of making things worse than they really are, of being self-indulgent and morally weak. The latter are criticised for being too independent, for coping with their disability at the expense of other people. In their case admiration is replaced by anxiety and resentment.

The talk is of responses to symptoms rather than the symptoms themselves, and value judgments are invariably attached to observations. Initially, the recurrent talk about aches and pains appears to the observer as morbid and tedious. When focused on personal experience it strikes the youthful observer as self-centred, consistent with a popular stereotype of old age as egocentric, dominated by a self-preoccupation with one's health and a search for sympathy. On closer inspection, however, a vital process of negotiation is apparent within the social network. The outcome is a set of norms of behaviour in sickness and in health. Through the comparison of symptoms and responses to them, individuals collectively derive a standard against which to measure their own performance and evaluate other people's. Endless details are offered and assessed in order to establish what is appropriate behaviour. Within a group of friends a typical conversation runs as follows. Why does X carry on being involved in the club when Y in similar circumstances does not? If Y is open to criticism for not trying, is Z who feels that there is a limit to what she can cope with and therefore does not try, also failing? Nellie has rejected attempts by her friends to help her lead a normal life after her heart operation. She is surely exaggerating its effect on her life. Why doesn't she carry on as before, when Jean's husband's brother and Bessie's sister do? She has the wrong attitude. She is not trying. Nellie claims to have lost confidence in her ability to get about, but surely it's a vicious circle. The heart pacemaker should have given Nellie the opportunity to carry on as usual, without any period of recuperation. On the other hand, Bessie's hip replacement operation was also supposed to do that, and it has not. Could the same be said of her? Jean and Edna consider this point and reassure Bessie. She is not to blame. She has had three operations and none has been entirely successful. Her present predicament is not her fault.

The friends move on to consider the case of Ruby, recently returned from hospital and as helpless as Nellie. Is she behaving appropriately? In her case, dependency is created by her daughter's tendency to do everything for her. In Jean's family the roles are reversed. Jean, who is actually older than Ruby, does everything for her daughter. (Perhaps she should stop!) Behaviour judged to be self-indulgent or likely to spoil someone else by giving in to unreasonable demands for assistance is critically examined.

In the course of these conversations there emerges a double equation: good health plus correct attitudes equal fitness, which equals performance. Participants agree on the desirability of an active life, and the ingredients for it: they are reasonable health and a positive attitude which acknowledges the importance of effort and endurance. Together, individual old people establish norms of behaviour in a situation where guidelines are lacking, or social expectations are negative. Any topic relevant for the creation of norms is popular in conversation. Discussion of a housing difficulty, a health problem or strained family relationships, involve judgements of the rightness or wrongness of a view or course of action. The unreasonableness of someone's position, based on a faulty assessment of the situation, is meat for discussion. Unproblematic behaviour such as someone else's self-imposed and contented isolation is not.

The following case illustrates the role of friends in the process of establishing norms of behaviour. It concerns Edna, a never-married woman in her 70s who ignores signals from her social network that she is acting inappropriately. Edna's friends are anxious because she is at risk of a breakdown in health; sad because she is unhappy and they cannot help her; and cross because she is causing them worry and ignoring their advice. Her behaviour is in one sense a breach of the norm of friendship which stresses consideration for others, even in illness, and an acknowledgement of a friend's natural concern. But her behaviour in another sense preserves the friendship. Edna fears becoming dependent on her friends and undermining a relationship which is based on reciprocity.

Edna had been ill on Monday, arriving late at the club. She found it hard to keep awake or concentrate on the game, and she was seen getting on the wrong bus afterwards. (Her friends never did establish how she got home.) Jack felt obliged to visit her to see how she was, but got sent away. Everyone knew that Edna didn't welcome visitors, but Jean – her closest friend – said 'tell her I sent you', not caring if Edna became angry with her so long as she was alright. Edna stayed at home on Wednesday but went to the Thursday Club, where another set of friends was duly alarmed by her behaviour. But she seemed better than she had been on the Monday, according to Jean, who had been present on both occasions. By Sunday she was ill again. Her three friends at the Sunday Club were alarmed. She smiled vacantly, couldn't speak clearly and was very emotional. Her walk was unsteady. Every time Edna was out of earshot there was an anxious pooling of information. Olive had seen Edna cross the road safely on Thursday, according to Bessie. But it was noted that she refused to use the pedestrian crossing, despite the heavy traffic and her impaired gait. Bessie has had similar symptoms and knows what Edna is going through. 'You are anxious, depressed and reluctant to stay at home in case anything should happen to you there', she told the others. Edna was arriving for meetings very early. Was she losing her sense of time or making sure she left her flat while she was able?

The problem which most exercised the friends was how to keep a check on Edna's condition. Her only relatives – two cousins – did not visit very often and although Jean had their telephone number it might be out of date. Edna refused to have a telephone and her neighbours were uncooperative. A fellow club member who had lived nearby used to ring Jean when she thought Edna was not very well, but she had moved away. Bessie who also lived nearby wanted to help Edna, too, but is unsteady on her feet herself. Jean, the fittest of the group and also the closest to Edna, takes responsibility for the next move. The formulation of the plan of action occupies most of the meeting on Sunday. If Edna does not turn up at the Monday Club Jean will not worry too much, as there is a steep climb to the building. If she misses the Wednesday Club, which is supplied by a good bus service, Jean will brave Edna's anger and go to her flat, hoping to be allowed in. 'All right, leave it until Wednesday evening'. Jean, Bessie, Olive, Jack and Laura are all concerned about Edna. Jean is the main source of information but the lines of communication go between the others as well. Edna hates making a fuss and has assured them that she is well. They must not let her know they are talking about her. So the urgency created by her failing health is complicated by the need for discretion. Over a period of two-and-a-half weeks there is anxious reiteration of the events which have signalled her illness, endless comparison with earlier illnesses, speculation about her feelings, anticipation of her movements over the next few days, and the development of contingency plans. The friends are inclined to blame the new tablets supplied by Edna's doctor. Why did she choose this one, who lives some distance away, when her old doctor died recently? Edna is urged by her friends to change her doctor or at least return to the current doctor for a new prescription. They assure her that her condition is normal, that it is reasonable to question the prescribed treatment, that her doubts about the present drugs are justified and her efforts to rectify matters not self-indulgent. Edna finally accepts their definition of the situation. The drug treatment is changed and her distressing symptoms disappear.

Edna's case illustrates the role of elderly peers in the social construction of health and illness. Social reality is defined through conversation and non-verbal signals. Through talking with friends in the club, members of the social network convey information, monitor performance, assess behaviour and make judgements which are conveyed either subtly or bluntly. The process works most effectively for people with firm social connections. In the absence of an active social network health crises are harder to cope with. The person who is not socially integrated – by chance or by choice – lacks a framework for interpreting experience (a state of anomie). Such a view of reality as socially constructed has much in common with Vesperi's (1985) analysis of ageing in Florida. In 'the city of green benches' individual actors are guided by messages about age coming from the social milieu of friends, neighbours, relatives and service providers. Members of the social network – which in this case includes fellow club-goers and co-worshippers – are vital in contributing to the formation of attitudes about health and illness. It is largely through informal exchanges that private experiences are transformed into shared, public knowledge and attributed with meaning.

Health as a social phenomenon

The case of Edna underlines the social nature of health and illness and indicates the value of social connections. Illness has an effect on friends, creating anxiety, even resentment, when denial undermines the base of friendship as a relationship of mutual concern and trust. Reciprocally, friends influence the perception of illness. They confirm or deny the status of symptoms and establish appropriate ways of responding to them. A review of the literature of social support confirms the influence of peers and significant others in the perception of one's condition and control of its emotional consequences (Craney 1985). Variations in reactions to illness are strongly associated with the nature and quality of social relationships (Robinson 1971). Relatives have views on the legitimacy of sick role behaviour. A balance must be struck between the costs of caring for someone assuming the sick role and the threat to his health of denying the status of sufferer (Ford 1985). Health and illness are not clearly defined aspects of reality. Illness has a highly subjective nature, for it is defined in terms of inactivity (Herzlich 1973). One is ill because one is unable to fulfil social obligations. Exclusion from the world of the healthy occurs by virtue of the social roles and activities one is no longer able to undertake. The existence of other roles and social contacts are therefore crucial for knowledge of one's condition (except in extreme cases, say a high temperature or crippling pain).

In this view, illness is created or recognised by society. One cannot be ill by oneself and know that one is ill. The person who is alone cannot be sure of the status of her feelings, for she has no chance to test them out in prescribed or chosen activities and relationships. It is possible, Williams suggests (1979), that symptoms go unreported because some elderly people – those in isolation – simply do not know that they are ill. The unattached elderly person excluded from the social world of the club or fellowship or friendship network lacks a reference group and thus the opportunity to attach a socially acceptable meaning to symptoms. For organisation members interpretation is made easier by the consensus about the salience of physical and mental symptoms, evident in conversation and formal activities. Whether or not people 'go sick' at any age is thus a question of their social situation (Alonzo 1979). In old age this might be viewed more broadly as one of lifestyle (Ford 1985; Taylor and Ford 1981), the lifestyle of voluntary association participants having very different implications for health than that of, say, the house-bound carer.

Symptoms are interpreted in terms of their effect on activity and by comparison with the performance of peers. This interpretation of attitudes to health and illness in the club and fellowship population finds support in the literature of medical sociology which suggests that older people tend to adopt a functional rather than symptomatic definition of health (Craney

1985). In common with other old people the majority of members would rate their health as good. Their subjective health is considerably higher than objective measures – the presence of symptoms – would warrant (Copeland et al. 1986; Victor 1987). The discrepancy lies less in changing expectations of what constitutes good health as people age (Victor 1987) or apathy, fear and ignorance (Williams 1979) than in a view of health as the ability to be independent and fulfil role expectations. Responses to health changes are set by demands for normal functioning. If I am able to get to the meeting and participate in the normal way, I am well. The incessant reference to ill-health reflects the uncertainties surrounding the issue. Good health is not a source of problems and there is no talk about it. The interest in other people's physical and mental condition arises from several needs. In part it reflects a desire to enjoy good health oneself. The relish with which details are discussed might rest on fear of one's own loss of freedom and a valued lifestyle, as Stephens observed in the social world of the occupants of retirement hotels in New York (Stephens 1976). There is comfort to be derived from the knowledge that others are worse off. Hockey draws similar conclusions in the residential establishment where fitter residents become increasingly fearful that their own disorders might represent the onset of decline and death (Hockey 1985). An additional reason for such comparisons, however, is the need to establish guidelines for behaviour in a realm of experience where cultural prescriptions are vague.

The standard against which health behaviour is measured is a moral one. There are good and bad ways of behaving, right and wrong attitudes. At one end of the scale is the uncomplaining attitude which enjoys approval. At the other is the self-indulgent stance which is seen as morally weak. Illness and incapacity is thus a moral category, a condition for which the sufferer is partly to blame. Whereas disease is an affliction which happens to you and is bad luck, illness is something which should be resisted, a condition of mind as much as of body (Blaxter and Paterson 1982). This attitude accounts for the impatience with which some sick people are viewed. They are people who give in too easily, who don't help themselves, who are their own worst enemies. It is nowhere clearer than in the lack of sympathy extended to disabled George, confused Cecil, and frail Olive whom no-one will accompany on holiday because of her habit of having 'bad turns'. 'She's a drag ... when you are on holiday you want to get up in the morning and rush out ... She holds you up ...'. The lame are urged to think twice before inflicting themselves on the able-bodied. Inviting bookings for a forthcoming outing the leader of St Brelade's Club said firmly. 'People who can't walk shouldn't come. The rest want to enjoy themselves and won't if others are dragging on them. If the lame *must* come they should get someone to help them who doesn't mind'.

This unsympathetic attitude extends to the confused as well. Vera, referred to earlier, is the object of scorn and amusement. When the social secretary comes to collect her money for the outing and remind her of the date the others look on. 'Take her purse!', they chortle, when she fails to hear or understand what is required. There is no embarrassment or sympathy for her plight, though the other women on her table find her general situation of helplessness and vulnerability shocking and are critical of her son for not looking after her properly. Vera has a sense of humour which makes the rest of her table laugh, but otherwise they ignore or mock her. They have no sense of responsibility for her and make no attempt to dissuade her for her own safety, from going on the outing although she is known to wander. There is, rather, a sense that what happens is 'her own funeral'. If anything, righteous indignation greets Vera and others who would take personal risks at the expense of other people's pleasure and peace of mind.

The unsympathetic attitude in the clubs (absent in the church community, where consideration for others is itself a virtue) may be accounted for in different ways. Possibly fellow club members cannot afford to be magnanimous from a position of relative weakness. They themselves have struggled through ill-health and earned the comforts of normal living. Disability is seen as moral weakness and bystanders are absolved from responsibility for the sufferers. Distancing themselves from the handicapped and blaming them for their misfortune not only exonerates the righteous but protects them from the knowledge that they too might suffer and that this could happen to anybody. The noisy dissociation of the fit from the confused and feeble has been observed in residential settings too (Hockey 1985, 1989; Gubrium 1975; Hornum 1987).

Concepts of health and illness

The healthy (in subjective terms) believe that they owe their condition in part to the care they take of themselves, their sensible routines and positive attitudes. In some cases precautions are taken as soon as suspicious signs appear. In others the symptoms of illness are not acknowledged until they impinge on normal living or until friends and relatives insist on remedial action. The readiness to acknowledge the need for action depends partly on the view of sickness held by the sufferer. This analysis of illness strategies owes much to the work of Herzlich (1973) developed in respect of elderly people in Britain by Williams (1980). In her study of health and illness in an age-mixed population of Parisians, Herzlich identifies three conceptions of illness which produce a variety of strategies. When illness is seen as destructive, annihilating existing roles and identities, it is denied and the patient refuses to accept the sick role. Illness can also be seen as a liberator, freeing the patient from existing social obligations. In this case it is welcomed. A third concept stresses illness as an occupation. Social participation is retained but the role changes to that of invalid. The strategy here is to struggle to overcome the illness, pleasing caretakers by working hard to get better.

The commonest initial response to symptoms of illness in the club and fellowship population is denial. A minority continue to deny that anything is wrong, for example Edna whose case was described earlier and the old woman quoted at the start of this chapter. The price of acceptance· is annihilation: of a lifestyle, of friend relationships, of identity as an independent individual. This position is marked by a refusal to make any concessions to ill-health or to seek any treatment which would amount to an acknowledgement of the condition. The majority move from initial resistance to a position of acceptance, in most cases grudgingly. Illness is a setback which is acknowledged reluctantly, and resisted as far as possible. Most members are determined to keep going, and struggle against the pressure to give up or at least modify their lifestyle. Some succeed in retaining their position. Others adapt, incorporating elements of the invalid role into their lifestyle. Their lives become restricted by ill-health. Though judged morally less worthy than the former position, surrender is legitimate after a struggle: it is preferable to total collapse. The strategy of adaptation is legitimised by the commands of superior beings – health professionals or occasionally adult children. The strategy of both the strugglers and the adapters is not to be ill. Another response involving adaptation produces the opposite strategy. Illness can be seen as liberating, and surrender is based on the desire to assert what Herzlich calls non-conforming aspects of identity. The following case illustrates this well.

Nell and Edna had got on the same bus to attend the Sunday Club meeting as usual, but Nell had got off early and returned home saying that she did not feel well. Edna travelled on alone and alerted Nell's friends to the fact of her illness. Nell did not appear at the Thursday Club either, and there was no word from her. By this time, Jean and the others were getting worried. Jean, getting no reply to her repeated telephone calls, paid a visit and learned from a neighbour that Nell had collapsed in the street on the previous Sunday and had been rushed to hospital with a suspected heart condition that no-one had known about. The friends blamed themselves for not doing something earlier. Edna in particular came in for criticism as she had not escorted Nell home on that fateful Sunday afternoon. Details of Nell's whereabouts in hospital were obtained and announced at her three clubs so that people could visit. Surprisingly, Nell did not seem very receptive to their attentions. She wanted no visits and as time went on it was not clear what was happening. Word went round that she was no longer in hospital, but whether she was at home or away convalescing was not clear. At the Thursday Club meeting the subject of Nell dominated the conversation. Had Mary, the club registrar, visited her? She had, but Nell had been non-committal. Had the women in the row in front been to see her? Unsuccessfully: they had taken flowers and chocolates but Nell had refused to answer the doorbell. What about the woman in the row behind whose obsession with cats had earned her the title of 'the cat lady', had she rung? No, the cat lady had forgotten but would do so immediately after the meeting (that was what she had said last week!). Perhaps they should approach Nell's landlord. But last time Bessie and the landlord had by chance met at Nell's bedside there had been an unpleasant confrontation. Nell had said, 'You must *never* ask my landlord for *anything*'. 'She thinks he's God apparently,' grumbled Bessie.

To provoke a response Jean wrote asking Nell to leave some magazines she had borrowed on the doorstep, so that Edna could collect them. The magazines did not appear. The friends were in a dilemma. They did not know whether Nell was there or not, alive or dead. Finally, Jean made contact on the telephone. Nell announced that she was a very sick woman who after a serious operation could not leave her bed and should not be disturbed. This news was relayed to friends at the club who pondered the significance of Nell's refusal to get well after what had been, in fact, a relatively simple operation. Jean wrote again, expressing concern and urging Nell to return when she was able. Nell replied that 'it takes a long time to recover from a serious illness' and that she was unable to go out. Nothing more was heard and Nell's friends decided to leave her alone to recover in her own way. Shortly afterwards it transpired that Nell was up and about. She had been seen at a new club and was going about with Rose who belonged to a different part of the Thursday Club network. She had sent word that Rose was welcome to come and visit her but that she was glad to be rid of 'those people at the club who were not friends at all but simply people she knew'. In subsequent months it seemed that Nell had severed her old connections and made a new life for herself.

Nell's refusal to get up and her anger at being disturbed suggest a different conception of illness from the one which dominated the thinking of club members. For her, illness was a chance to withdraw from her existing commitments, recoup her energies and change direction. Total surrender to her illness was a tactic in her bid for a new life.

Although sharply defined here for analytical purposes (see Figure 6.1),

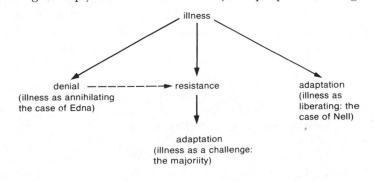

Figure 6.1 Concepts of illness

in reality the concepts of illness lack clarity and are surrounded with ambivalence. There is movement between concepts and a shift of strategies as individuals recognise the constraints of reality or bow to pressure. A position of denial is frequently modified to become one of adaptation and struggle. Grudging acknowledgement of symptoms leads to their incorporation into a new concept of self.

These shifts may occur with the passage of time. A range of factors influences the conception of illness favoured. Factors include nearness to death (in chronological terms); ideas about the naturalness of physical decline with age; and the possibility of recovery. All these incorporate the notion of time left to live, and what can be done with it. A further factor is the views of other people – friends and relatives – about what is reasonable and morally acceptable behaviour in certain conditions.

The influence of these factors becomes increasingly obvious with the advancement of years. At a certain age it seems reasonable to heed the advice of doctors, relatives and fellow members to cut down on activities. Office holders think twice before seeking re-election or opt for less strenuous commitments. Failing energy and a reduction in time left to live make the prospect of long-term commitments less feasible. 'At 80 you don't want to take on anything new' is a comment frequently heard but never explained, resting as it does on shared assumptions. The sense of time left to live emerged clearly in a conversation with Mrs E, 85, who is about to have her third heart pacemaker and will this year break the twenty-year-old pattern of annual holidays with her friend, Miss D. She had hoped that the current pacemaker installed four years ago, would 'see her out'. So did her doctor. She hopes that this new one will last the rest of her life for she does not want to live to her 90s. At the same time she engages in life-preserving strategies, sitting in her front garden where the sun will do her good rather than going to a meeting of her women's fellowship. She also avoids going out in the rain, since she walks slowly and a soaking would be both uncomfortable and undermining in health terms. Mrs E. and others like her keep to the health habits of a lifetime, being careful, taking sensible precautions to avoid ill-health, making the best of diminishing physical resources. Through talk with others they learn whether they are doing more or less well than their contemporaries. Their accomplishment of small routines is a source of pride and to some extent health is a competitive affair. The talk of symptoms and responses to them helps to boost individual scores in the competition to defeat ill-health. Membership of a social network of peers is vital in this process of comparison and self-evaluation.

Frailty and friendship

So far we have examined the association between health and peer group support in cognitive terms; we have analysed the influence of friends and fellow club members on the perception of ill-health. Friends assist in the interpretation of symptoms and help to define correct responses to them. Through interaction with friends the club and fellowship member learns what ill-health means and how to be ill. I have suggested that old-age associations provide a setting for socialisation to frailty. The emphasis on resistance and struggle is expressed in club rituals and reaffirmed in private conversation. Ill-health is to some extent seen as inevitable but can be resisted, like old age itself.

Friendship influences health not only at the cognitive level but in practical terms as well. Fellow members offer practical and moral support to the sick in the form of visits, letters, gifts and encouragement to regain health and stay well. Friends have a practical role in coping with illness and disability, a role which is ignored or even denied in other accounts of friendship and primary group relationships in old age.

In the contemporary British writing on friendship and ageing a division of labour is seen to exist between kin, neighbours and friends. One set of intimates – kin – is concerned with the alleviation of problems caused by ill-health, principally by providing practical support Another set – friends – is important in the maintenance of morale and the cultivation of a lifestyle conducive to good health. According to this view friendship is distinctive in a number of ways. A comparison of friends with neighbours shows that there are differences in the basis of the relationship, its core characteristics, the content of interactions, the causes of breakdown and the implications for social policy (Wenger 1987).

As we saw in the previous chapter, friends are normally chosen on the basis of shared interest. Friendship is voluntary and highly personal, the content of the exchanges a matter for individual negotiation. It is an expression of individuality. The relationship is characterised by intimacy, dependability, mutual support and reciprocity. Friend relationships are typically one-to-one and long-term. Not all are long-standing, however, just as there are variations in the extent of physical distance. Friendship is primarily expressive in orientation. The activities shared by friends include the provision of emotional support, reciprocal visiting, mutually enjoyable social activities and help with transport. There is a marked degree of mutuality and empathy. Friendship is not primarily instrumental. The criteria in choice of friends are comparability and liking rather than usefulness. To say that friends are not chosen for instrumental reasons is not to say that friends never help each other, or act instrumentally. In the typical relationship friends do help and make use of one another. This situation is acceptable and indeed expected, provided the relationship is not sustained solely for instrumental reasons. 'Instrumentality should not be the basis of the relationship but an expression of it: friends behave instrumentally because they are friends rather than being friends because they are useful' (Allan 1986).

Within the friendship literature it is suggested that friendship does not endure when the circumstances of one of the friends is altered in any major fashion. Shifts in social status, geographical location and domestic circumstances create changes in the friendship network as early relationships become less rewarding and new ones more appropriate. Friend relationships in old age are brought to an end by death or a change in the personal circumstances of one partner which makes him or her less attractive as a friend. Most damaging to friendship in later life is mental infirmity or another disability which creates a one-sided need for additional help and destroys the ability to reciprocate (Wenger 1987). However willingly friends provide help for each other initially, most friendships will die away if the need for caring continues indefinitely (Allan 1986). This is one of the major differences between friends and family members. The latter can in principle be relied upon to provide long-term care as an obligation of kinship, the help given not contingent on the returns. Such an imbalance is unacceptable in most friendships. Those friends who do provide extensive help and support are described in different terms: they are special, quasi-kin, a 'true friend' and 'like a sister to me'. Such relationships belong to a different category from ordinary friend relationships. The difference in quality is not, apparently, simply one of degree. The less committed friend cannot be easily transformed into a 'real' or 'true' friend despite the fact that the latter is closer to the popular image of friendship (Matthews 1983).

In short, it would seem from the literature that the dependence of one partner through ill-health is a problem which threatens the continued existence of the relationship. Friendship, typically based on reciprocal exchange and the provision of mutual enjoyment, is of little help in the solution of problems caused by sickness and has limited chances of survival in circumstances of long-term ill-health.

But not all friendships are impaired by the onset of frailty. The friendship literature gives too limited a view of the effects of ill-health in old age. A range of possibilities for its accommodation is evident, possibilities which are ignored in the literature. The ideal type fails to take account of the special nature of long-term relationships and involves a misunderstanding of the ageing process. The suggestion in the literature is that as the balance of reciprocity becomes difficult to maintain, either the dependent partner or the depended-upon, or both, will withdraw; that all but the strongest friendships are likely to become much less active and eventually be of little consequence; and that in any case, elderly people – those most in need of care and support – are likely to have relatively few friends to turn to since their situation is universal (Allan 1986). Allan's 'reasonable expectation' that old people need care and that they are likely to have only friends who themselves need care is confounded by empirical evidence from studies of relationships in old age (Armstrong 1988; Jerrome 1981, 1986; Wenger 1984, 1987; Wentowski 1981; Matthews 1986). The speculation about the universality of ill-health in old age (for factual evidence is missing from Allan's analysis) betrays an unfounded assumption about the nature and direction of change in old age and its permanence. The fact is that periods of ill-health come and go, just as friendships wax and wane; that the balance of reciprocity is disturbed but that relationships survive; that friendship networks are often active and extensive until extreme old age, reduced finally by death rather than escalating demands for support which friends feel unable to meet. Other questionable assumptions are that the provision of pleasure is the main expressive goal of friendship and outweighs others such as emotional support, affection and caring ('friendship is not normally about need, but about sociability and enjoyment' [Allan 1986, p. 7]) and that mutual pleasure is incompatible with growing incapacity in one partner. Both of these assumptions are challenged by the evidence of behaviour in old-age organisations.

Intimate relationships, especially long-term ones, have a resilience which reflects the particular pattern of rewards and contributions evolved by the partners over time. Reciprocity in friendship need not be immediate and is often delayed, even to the point where it resembles kinship in its non-contingent character. To understand the pattern of reciprocity in long-term relationships a longitudinal approach is required (Kart and Longino 1987; Wentowski 1981; Armstrong 1988; Matthews 1986). Normative expectations for the exchange of support in friendship vary considerably and rest on the previous history of the relationship. In long-established friendships the obligation to reciprocate might be waived altogether in favour of beneficence. Disproportionate investment or gain is not necessarily seen as unfair. Altruism, the need for status consistency, rationality and competition are alternatives to reciprocity as the basis for deciding whether exchanges are fair or not (Dowd 1984).

As friends become very old, the need to reciprocate loses its force. The recipient of support does not inevitably feel disturbed by the experience of dependency (although Edna's case, quoted earlier, might appear to contradict this). Studies of the relationship between social support and morale suggests that being at the receiving end does not either raise or lower life satisfaction (Kart and Longino 1987). Even for those doing the giving, who might feel less happy about unreciprocated help in an exchange relationship, there are certain conditions under which expectations for reciprocity or exchange are suspended. Impending death is such a condition. As we shall see in the following chapter, when the very old are near death and cannot reciprocate, friendship is bestowed as a gift. Its acceptance by the dying partner is highly gratifying to the remaining one. The rules of friendship, indeed, require that the frail person accepts help and advice when it is offered, even when this involves an imbalance. Friendship requires the demonstration of concern through the giving of advice and support, *particularly* in times of need when the possibilities for reciprocation are limited.

The rejection of such support in the name of equality amounts to a breach of the norm and creates frustration and resentment. This was evident in Edna's case, where her friends demanded the right to care, despite her resistance.

The norms of friendship as practised by the old people I studied thus permitted, even required, a state of imbalance. This model departs from the ideal type found in the literature and perhaps in popular thinking. The requirement is on both parties to accept benefits as a sign of friendship. Friendship in later life is thus problematic. In contrast to the conventional meaning attached to care and dependence, elderly friends measure a caring attitude by the ability to receive care without feeling the need to reciprocate immediately. They recognise dependence on someone else as a sign of dependability. Such variations in meaning are familiar from cross-cultural studies (for example, Leninger 1988; Van der Veen 1988). We should consider the possibility that in the West, the importance of equitable exchange might exist less for the social actor than the social scientist, whose view of human behaviour reflects his culture and who seeks constantly through his analysis to confirm his beliefs. The cultural obsession with equity blinds us to the possibility of satisfactory inequitable relationships and the link between being able to receive and being a good friend.

What is required in the analysis of friendships – old and new – is the elaboration of the concept of mutuality to include behaviours which do not conform to the limited notion of reciprocity in the literature. In effect, we need to modify the ideal type to take account of the non-reciprocal elements in friendship.

SEVEN

Encounters with death

Introduction

Members of old-age organisations are frequently confronted by death.
Death is a regular occurrence. It impinges on activities and consciousness in
a number of ways. Empty seats are a reminder, for they are created largely by
the deaths of former occupants. There is a high turnover in old-age organisations but the main progression is through death, hence the sadness
associated with change. Activities which are taken over from other people
have similar associations, though they are not always viewed negatively.
When asked how she had acquired the job of distributing cups of tea, a
relatively young member replied nonchalantly that 'there used to be a
regular team but they died'. Grateful recipients of her services commented
only that it was a change not to have the tea spilt in the saucer.

Succession to vacancies created by death – carrying dead women's trays,
if not walking in dead men's shoes – is taken for granted in this setting. The
successor is often the spouse, if there is one, or closest same-sex equivalent,
an arrangement which causes the least social disruption. For the person
concerned, there is both pleasure and pain involved in it. Performing a task
previously undertaken by a deceased spouse or friend is a reminder of his or
her presence and of the significance of former social roles. It does not
mitigate the sense of loss as Mrs J discovered when she took over her former
husband's delivery of the church newsletter. Her presence on the doorstep
served as a reminder of his death, and a year later, 'people only tell me how
much they miss him'.

By the time a person reaches old age death has been encountered several
times in the family from childhood onwards. But the deaths of elderly
contemporaries have a significance not shared by the deaths of elderly
relatives. In the family death is always present as older members make way
for younger people. But friends have been chosen, are objects of identification and emotionally more significant (O'Laughlin 1983). The removal of
old friends cuts deeply into the foundations of life, for friends are a link with
the past, have shared recollections and common attitudes towards the
present. When friends die, 'It makes you wonder ...' and, 'All my friends are
dying, soon there will be only the dot in the middle – me'. The last remark
was made with great sadness by an 86-year-old woman who had 'lost' four
friends in the past year.

The language of death in old-age organisations is interesting. Death is
sometimes alluded to directly, especially in public announcements from the

platform. Often it is referred to less directly in metaphors which imply a gulf or dividing line between states, as 'passing over' or, if moribund, 'waiting to be called'. More direct references to the end of earthly existence are implied in the description of the dead as simply 'gone', the very old as 'near the end'. But in general the word itself is not often used. The elaborate language of death is consistent with the evasive attitudes in society at large. The reluctance to acknowledge death in western society has been well documented (for example, Elias 1985; Ariès 1981; Butler 1978; Harris 1975; Gorer 1965; Glaser and Strauss 1968). There is substantial agreement in the literature about attitudes to death and dying in western society, and about their origin.

The literature of death and dying

The distinguishing feature of western beliefs is a separation between life and death. According to the western concept of the life-cycle, death is outside the self. To be a self one must be alive, in control, and aware of what is happening. The emphasis on individuality and control makes death an outrage (Butler 1978). In contrast, the oriental view of the self is broader. The self, the life-span and death are placed within the span of human experience. Life and death are familiar and equally acceptable parts of the self. The separation of life and death in western cultures has its origins in related historical processes: secularisation – the decline of organised religion – the growth of individuation, and the medicalisation of death. No longer 'promoted to glory', in the words of the Salvation Army, death is the end. Earlier, religion offered solace in promising another world in which the self would spring to life again. The process of secularisation has created a void. This prospect is frequently met by avoiding and denying thought of decline and death and forming self-protective prejudices against old people (Butler 1978). The restriction of death to later stages of life is itself a new phenomenon. Death typically comes at the end of a long life; it is predictable not capricious (Marshall 1986). It also tends to be the culmination of a period before death now known as 'dying', a contrast to earlier times when the process was more rapid. The meaning of death must now incorporate the notion of completion. This demographic change, coupled with the decline of explanatory systems rooted in traditional religious and philosophical thought, has meant the loss of a shared set of beliefs about the meaning of death.

Elias (1985) talks of the silence which spreads gradually around the dying. The living fear and avoid the dying because they represent the finiteness of human existence. The process of dying is concealed. The living are embarrassed in the presence of the dying, inhibited by the narrow range of words available for use in these circumstances. The shift towards informality over the last four decades has produced suspicion and embarrassment at the use of ritual phrases. The task of finding the right word and gesture falls back on the individual. The expressing of feelings is inhibited also by the demand for self-control in highly emotional situations (in Anglo-Saxon cultures at least). The lack of spontaneity in expression, and reluctance to touch the dying, makes it harder to give proof of affection and tenderness. Dying is thus a time of great loneliness. The dying person is excluded from the world of the living and is left with a sense of profound insignificance.

The difficulties of verbal communication extend to the dying person too. The presence of death is inadmissible on both sides. The expression of pain is inhibited by the requirements of self-control on one side, by the values of modesty, discretion and privacy on the other. The dying person colludes with the living to deny death, to the point where acknowledgement becomes impossible, as Tolstoy demonstrates vividly through his fictional character Ivan Illyich, used by Ariès (1981) to illustrate the invisible nature of death in twentieth-century Europe and America. The ritual 'death bed dances with the truth', described by writers such as Glaser and Strauss (1968) arise from a desire to protect both the living and dying from the knowledge of the latter's true condition. In his study of the behaviour of terminally ill patients and their relatives, Hinton (1974) describes the isolation of the dying man whose true condition is never mentioned in his presence but whose relatives 'weep tears of bereavement from prognosis-laden eyes', and whose doctors and nurses terminate treatment prematurely. At the organisational level, too, death is denied in the lack of concern to provide the resources needed to care for the dying.

In recent years, the taboo on death has been lifted slightly, mainly to accommodate the needs of the bereaved. Public attention has been focused, in response to pressure from social scientists and the social work professions, on the pathological effects of the failure to mourn properly. Since the 1960s the discussion of death has been reopened but only to accept it as a technical fact, an ordinary thing, insignificant and spoken of with feigned indifference. The real image of death is repressed; death is still invisible. In North America funeral homes are much in evidence, and are big business. But their object is to beautify death. Embalming and the use of cosmetics are less to honour the dead than to help the living overcome their resistance to death. In Britain, where these processes are less evident, the invisibility of death reaches its peak (Ariès 1981). Most recently the tragic element in death has been submerged in the meanings constructed by 'the happy death movement' (Marshall 1986) whose adherents think of the good death as a personal growth experience.

Viewed in terms of social roles, the place of death has diminished. People live longer and die in hospital. Their deaths are solitary events lacking in ceremonial or witnesses, for there is no need to emphasise changes in status either of the deceased or of the survivors whose rights and responsibilities are largely unaltered. Here, death is not the final role change as in those cultures where the deceased (those worthy, at least) become ancestors who continue to influence the affairs of the living. In societies where there is no after-life, death amounts to an expiry of roles.

The meaning of death is expressed in ceremonial. A funeral takes place because there is a body to dispose of and because there are feelings of loss to be expressed. But it also reflects the significance of death and the life that has gone before it. If death is seen as transition to another existence it requires the solemn celebration appropriate for an irreversible leave-taking (Harris 1975). If it involves transition to another status within society, such as ancestor status, or to a transcendent society as in the Christian view, it is a significant event and must be celebrated as such. For most people in Britain neither of these conditions obtain: death is a tragedy. But far from being treated as a tragedy death is ignored, regarded as natural and inevitable and marked by the simplest of ceremonies. The implication is that the life thus terminated has been pointless, has had such little intrinsic value that its termination has become meaningless (Blauner 1966). The futility of death points to the futility of life. The scant attention paid to death symbolises that the significant loss – of social personality, of autonomy and of agency – has already occurred. The problem facing the dying and those around them in a secular society is of making death meaningful in terms of life as it has been lived.

The point of physical death is itself problematic. Today, the point of death is *not* the point of death: medical technology makes it possible to lengthen the moment at which it occurs. Doctors distinguish between brain death, biological death and cell death. The old signs – the cessation of heartbeat and respiration – are no longer sufficient. The measurement of cerebral activity has replaced simpler measures and become the criterion by which in certain well known cases the certification of death has been withheld. The development of medical and surgical techniques, involving complex equipment and specialised professional skills, bringing advances in resuscitation and the relief of pain, has meant that the majority of people are sent to hospital when death seems imminent.

The transfer of death to hospitals has caused a redefinition of death. It has also limited the expression of grief if, indeed, the survivors are present to witness the event. It imposes a particular style of dying on the patient which reflects the professional preoccupation with health and life, with the control of pain and suffering, with doing everything that can possibly be done to ameliorate the condition. The traditional notion of a good death is inappropriate in this setting. A good death – in bed, having taken leave of kin and made both sacramental and material preparation, facing death knowingly and with a recollected mind – is reversed by the typical death which takes place in hospital. The occurrence of sudden death is now more acceptable. Dying without pain, 'slipping away' without ever regaining consciousness is increasingly seen as being 'the best way to go' (Ariès 1981).

To die in one's sleep, in ignorance of the event – the kind of death wished only on one's enemies in the Middle Ages and Renaissance period (Beckmann and Olesen 1988) – is a good death today. An explicit and noisy death, with both the dying and their relatives expressing the fear and pain of departure, is disturbing and threatening. Discouraged for medical and administrative reasons, it is regarded also as indiscreet and an invasion of other people's privacy.

The growth of the hospice movement reflects awareness that the acceptable style of death in hospital might violate the needs of the terminally ill and their intimates for a 'good death', a death with dignity and on their own terms (Taylor 1983). Hospices are often founded on religious principles too, which confer a meaning on death and life running counter to prevailing views. Above all, hospices attempt to reduce the isolation of death. In an individualistic society, the belief – and the practice – is that people die alone as they live alone. A death is dealt with not as part of *all* death but as a unique event. In the hospice there is continuity between life and death; preparation for death is about crossing the boundary (Hockey 1991). As in former centuries, in the hospice the entourage (to use Ariès' term) accompanies the dying person to the point of death.

Outside the hospice, the unwillingness or inability of the living to discuss issues of mortality with those near death is well known. Their reluctance extends to discussing death with the fit and active old person, too. It is rationalised in terms of old people's anxiety about death (O'Laughlin 1983). In fact, death anxiety in this population tends to be relatively low, though some kinds of loss can increase it. Studies suggest that it is the process of dying that people fear rather than death itself (Diggory and Rothman 1961; Collett and Lester 1969). In old age the belief in an after-life increases. The very old, especially, claim to see their dead again and to talk with them.

It is significant, but not surprising, that the literature of death and dying tends to ignore the subjective experience of the moribund and even of the fit old person. The perspective is that of younger people. Accounts of 'social attitudes' and 'cultural perspectives' in the literature refer to the middle aged, those at the commanding heights and responsible for the creation of knowledge, rather than the old whose position is socially marginal and whose definitions of reality are of little account.

In the remainder of the chapter we shall consider attitudes to death and dying in the club and fellowship population. The main problem in a society where death and life are somehow unconnected is to integrate the two. Being nearer to death, the old engage in this task more assiduously than other age groups. The search for meaning is conducted in different ways. We can see it in the way news of a death is received, in individual assessments of the event, in recollections of the previous shared existence and speculation about the current state of the departed. The search for meaning is seen in the arrangements made for disposal of the body, in the rules governing the expression of anguish and in collective responses to the plight of the bereaved.

A member dies

When a death occurs within the club or fellowship it is formally announced at the start of the meeting. A collective response is made in the observance of a short period of silence (one or two minutes) and in singing. Normally the twenty-third Psalm is chosen but sometimes a favourite hymn of the deceased is chosen instead. Occasionally singing is omitted altogether as a mark of respect. This is an important gesture symbolising the place of the member in the body of the club for 'without singing there's no club', Another ritual gesture is the sending of flowers to the bereaved, expressing sympathy. This is described as a 'tribute for the one left behind', signifying the club's appreciation of the partner's loss, and the importance of the relationship terminated by death. Members prefer to give flowers. The alternative – a donation to charity at the request of the bereaved – is felt to be too impersonal.

At this stage there is much talk of death, especially if it has occurred suddenly or involves an important member. The sense of shock is powerful in these circumstances, even if there had been chronic ill-health before-hand. Over tea, those who have heard the news already, because they were close to the former member, tell and retell how the information was received: how the regular weekly telephone call was answered this time by the son instead of his mother, Mrs P. Mrs L reflects that Mrs P had given her a tea-cosy and frequently invited her to sample Mr P's famous cooking, an invitation which could now never be taken up. Through such talk the members invest themselves in closing off the life of the deceased (Gubrium 1975). Sharing the news allows them to become involved, to compensate for the feeling of impotence aroused by death (Gubrium 1975; Keith-Ross 1977: Myerhoff 1978).

In repetition of events leading up to the public announcement, the bereft friend goes over her feelings of shock and dismay. At the same time, through recollections of their shared existence, the death is placed in the context of an ongoing relationship. The departed is remembered as some-one who engaged in shared activities, who gave pleasure and who accepted the friendship of the survivors. Earlier activities acquire a new meaning in the light of the subsequent death: 'Little did we know that that was the last time we would be drinking her health'. The dead person's fine points and strength of spirit are rehearsed and significance is conferred on his or her final words. Thus the chairman recalls from the platform the gratitude with which Mrs P thanked him as she left her final meeting. She said, 'I've had such a lovely afternoon'. He remembers the pleasure of old Frank after being taken for a drive just before his final illness: 'That made my day!'.

With tears in his eyes the chairman recounts the happy moments spent with Bob R, a personal friend and fellow-member of the executive committee. He starts with Bob's interests and fine points: 'Bob R has passed away peacefully. Bob was a man of peace. He was quiet and patient, a musician and conductor of choirs. He enjoyed things that were beautiful. Bob and I used to go on holiday together. We used to sit and watch the waves. We watched the waves on one occasion and Bob was quiet. Bob is quiet now. He was a good member of the club'. After a minute's silence Bill went on, 'Please watch the papers for details, as to date we have had no arrangements notified'. This was a reference to the cremation ceremony.

News of the death, whether given publicly or privately, is always accompanied by the date and method of disposal of the body. The assumption is that friends in the club will want to attend the funeral and that members of the committee *should* do so. In fact, not many people go, even in the case of a well known and respected member, unless the ceremony is easily accessible by public transport and does not conflict with a club meeting. The failure of the secretary to attend a funeral is a source of embarrassment for her and of indignation for the next of kin and closest friends.

The manner of disposal, mainly by cremation, is a matter of interest, even to those who have no intention of going. Possessing important information and passing it on heightens one's sense of involvement and status as a person who knows things. The ritual element terminates earthly existence, and establishes connections between those who participate in it. The majority of the members, themselves widows, are curious about the handling of an event they have themselves organised in the past. The practical arrangements are discussed in the same breath as the emotional consequences of the event, albeit in hushed tones. The following case illustrates several of these points.

The death of John R, former club treasurer, had been expected for some time. Nora his wife had missed the previous meeting, called to John's bedside. He died a few days later, and by the following Friday Nora was back in her usual position – as club secretary – in the circle of chairs. The chairman, Kate, announced John's death. It had been expected, but ... They observed a minute's silence standing. A member of the committee wept silently but Nora herself displayed no emotion. The singing of the 'Lord's My Shepherd' was slightly delayed when the pianist, 86 and fairly deaf, did not hear the request to begin.

Immediately after the singing the mood changed with the birthday announcements. It was the fourth time Mrs K had been sung 'Happy Birthday' that week, she announced with pride and pleasure. Then came apologies for absence, caused by illness, another bereavement, and two visits. Next, as part of the business, details of John's funeral were announced. He was to be cremated at the local crematorium and a service would be held beforehand at his own church. His favourite hymn would be sung. His ashes would be placed in the family grave. Nora talked about the arrangements in a matter-of-fact voice tinged with sadness. Her house was full of greeting cards, she said with a wry smile – birthday, 'get well' and sympathy cards! Members of the National Committee of the Federation had written. John's name would go in the National Federation Memorial Book in the Blackburn headquarters, as a good and loyal member.

The members wanted to know what kind of a death it had been. 'Were you with him?' asked Ann. 'Yes,' Nora replied quietly. 'He had a terrible end. At around 6 o'clock he was in great pain. I asked for a pain-killer. He was given it. He knew me and clung to me. I couldn't understand what he was trying to say. He gasped until 9.15 then breathed his last'. Nora's sister had been there too. At that point the nursing sister had made a cup of tea. She was nice; black. Ann pursued the matter with a statement: 'He was out of pain'. This acted as trigger for Nora's next remark: 'It was a relief after seeing him in pain. He had a good eleven years while he was with me'. Another member, picking up the last remark commented, 'You have nice memories'. Then, after a brief pause, she spoke again, in a different tone of voice: 'Who's doing the funeral? Newman's?' 'No, the Co-op'. 'Thank you for telling us [all this, how it happened].'

John's death is thus experienced collectively. Through the opening rituals this personal tragedy assumes significance for all the participants. In this interpretation, ritual does more than simply provide something to do at a time when nothing can be done (Keith-Ross 1977), just as talk is seen here as more than simply a way of passing the time (Gubrium 1975). Ritual gestures and verbal exchanges, I suggest, influence the meaning of the event for the participants. John's end is described in the context of his life with Nora, their joint work for the National Federation, the years of a happy second marriage which had come towards the end of his life. For her part in making his last years happy, Nora could feel relief and satisfaction. The retelling of the events leading up to his death changes its meaning from a process of painful extinction to a timely end of a worthy life.

The juxtaposition of news about the funeral, about absentees, and about birthdays which happens in all meetings is significant. The discussion of the practical details and emotional implications of John's death helped to provide a sense of continuity between life and death. This had been even more apparent the previous week, when members had gathered in anticipation of celebrating Nora's birthday, Kate's engagement (to her third husband) and the anniversary of VE day. Feelings were mixed: pleasure at Kate's forthcoming marriage, excitement about the VE-day party, and sadness at John's illness. As Nora was absent, having been called to John's bedside, they missed out the birthday song. But the party would go ahead, for 'we go on ...'. This remark acquired deeper significance as members joined in the old songs, reminders of the distinctiveness of their generation. The intense pleasure associated with wartime camaraderie, and recollections of the war experience renewed now in singing and dancing, compensated for the shadow cast by John's impending death.

A good death versus a happy release

Different kinds of death can be identified in the club members' assessment of the event. It is clear that some kinds of death are judged better than others. John R's was a good death, marred by pain but passed in his wife's arms after a fruitful life. Bob's death was also good, as he deserved. The notion of a good death includes several elements. The dying person is philosophical, composed and fulfilled. The last hours or days contain 'lovely times' – good experiences which affirm the value of friendship. It is the loving gestures on the part of friends – a journey to the park, a trip in the car – welcomed by the dying person which are remembered with relief later on, and which are assumed to have eased the journey to death. A sudden, unexpected death is also acceptable if it comes at the end of an exemplary life and the appropriate rituals are conducted in the club. Mrs S, for instance, was known throughout the club network as a great woman. She had been active in the work of the Federation throughout her adult life and had built the club up to become one of the most successful in the town. Her sudden death, following a massive haemorrhage at home, was discovered by a neighbour. Although she had been suffering from a variety of serious handicaps, her death was greeted with shock and defined as a tragedy. Members wept during the brief silence called in the meeting to commemorate her death and during the singing of the twenty-third Psalm. Her funeral was better attended than usual.

Mr B also died suddenly but the news of his death was not acknowledged in the same way. Through a misunderstanding the club secretary failed to pass the message on when Miss V, a friend of the widow, gave it to her. By the time other members heard it it was too late to attend the funeral. At their next appearance Mrs B and her friend Miss V, showed how offended they were by the lack of support. Because the current procedure had not been followed they felt cheated of a proper death. Anger and bitterness seemed to crowd out grief. The bitterness and disappointment of Mrs B and her friend are reminiscent of scenes in Les Floralies when residents are deprived of the right to acknowledge death in the usual way, with ritual (Keith-Ross 1977).

Deaths like Mr B's are 'bad deaths'. So are lingering deaths following a stroke. These are seen as unjust, if a happy release in the end. A limited existence, bed-bound, semi-conscious or confused, is a tragedy after an active and purposeful life. The contrast between the two states is referred to with sadness before death and afterwards, though as with the other cases described, the meaning of death is understood largely in terms of the active productive years and the dead person's contributions to club life. Sometimes a meaning for the discrepancy is found in the actions of the deceased or their kin. A bad death may be the person's own fault. 'She did too much' is a criticism of the stroke victim rather than an appreciation of her enormous efforts on behalf of the club. A sudden and inappropriate end is occasionally blamed upon close relatives, as in the case of Sally, the elderly pianist, whose death certificate said hypothermia. She had felt unwell at the club and waited for a taxi on the draughty doorstep in a lightweight coat. This was held to be a dereliction of duty on the part of her younger sister, Edie, who 'should never have allowed it'. Another 'bad death' is marked by faulty procedure. As in the case of Mr B above, important actors in the drama forget their lines, miss their cues, fail to give other people the signals they need in order to become involved. In the following case, Edna's death was not an affirmation but a denial of friendship, for which she herself was largely to blame.

Edna rang her best friend, Jean, to say that she was in hospital. She had collapsed in her flat and her neighbours had rung the doctor. The circumstances surrounding the illness were puzzling, for Edna who had been known to be suffering from one condition was diagnosed as having an altogether different one. This was a disturbing element in the case – though not the first, as Edna had all along denied the gravity of her condition and made it difficult for her friends to help her.

Jean visited Edna several times in hospital. They discussed her future. Edna's closest relatives, some cousins living sixty miles (about ninety-six kilometres) away, wanted her to go back with them to convalesce, but Edna was refusing to do so. This was worrying. Jean felt that Edna was too independent. You couldn't afford to be so independent at her age (77), it was a worry to other people. Jean was generally unhappy about the situation, for other elements were not right either. She was not being properly informed. Edna and her cousins had been ringing Jean's daughter Tessa rather than Jean herself. On the last occasion she had been babysitting for her daughter and had taken the call herself. (Admittedly Jean was rarely at home and Tessa had for years treated Edna – her mother's closest friend and a spinster – as an adoptive aunt.)

Jean does not really understand what is happening. She says several times, 'It's neither here nor there'. She can only wait for a telephone call or a letter. Edna's behaviour is open to criticism, not least because of her lack of thought for other people's feelings. She has allowed her cousins to return home without her, then decided to convalesce with them after all, and they have had to drive down again and collect her. After all, they are getting on themselves and '*they're* a bit funny, too'. The telephone call finally comes to say that Edna is dead. The message is abrupt and without detail. Jean feels helpless. She doesn't know how or why her friend died or when the funeral will be, or what the cousins' telephone number is. She knows only that it will be a Co-op funeral. She will have to ring the Co-op funeral service for news. The other friends and leaders of Edna's four clubs are relying on Jean to produce this information for the usual announce-ments to be made. The announcements – a ritual of social recognition and concern for the bereaved – are duly made. The funeral is expected to be an unhappy and uncomfortable affair and Jean will be glad when it is over. No-one goes to the funeral apart from Jean and her daughter, and Edna's three cousins. After the funeral the cousins invite Jean and her daughter back to Edna's flat. Jean demurs but they insist, as Edna's best friend.

Weeks later Jean and her friends are still trying to find a meaning for Edna's death. In the search for an answer to the questions troubling them they cast round in their memories of Edna's behaviour and attitudes and the roles taken by other friends and acquaintances before her death. It is recalled that N – who has since left the club – had been in the habit of dragging on Edna's arm on the way to the bus-stop. The implication is that she had contributed to Edna's untimely and uncomfortable end.

This case illustrates well the need for correct procedure and a manner of dying which affirms important principles. Jean is unhappy with the situation imposed on her by Edna's independence and the uncommunicativeness of her cousins. In failing to keep Jean informed, to allow her to help and to heed her advice, Edna has violated the code of friendship which has been the basis for their companionship over the last forty years. In the circum-stances Jean does not know what meaning to attach to the event or what rituals to perform. The task of informing everyone in their circle of Edna's death is accomplished with difficulty because of the suddenness and ab-sence of 'proper' preparation The disjunction between the years of close companionship preceding the death and Edna's isolation from her friend in her final hours cannot be resolved.

A bad death, a death which is marred by unsatisfactory elements, is best forgotten. A good death, which confers meaning on life, is remembered. Like the telling and retelling of Jacob's death in the Jewish senior citizens' centre in California (Myerhoff 1978), a good death in the club brings continuing references to the departed member.

Life after death

A club secretary told me, 'Sick people are sent one pound and flowers if they die'. The implication of this curious expression describing club prac-tices is a continuity of ontological status before and after death. Death marks the end of direct involvement in the club, but indirect involvement continues, sometimes for months. In the religious organisations there are explicit references to continuity of existence, to 'eternal life' and continued membership of the collectivity, the 'communion of saints'. Elsewhere the nature of existence after death is not clearly articulated. That 'Bob was quiet when watching the waves and is quiet now' implies continuity in one sense though the reference conjures up the stillness of a corpse.

There are other examples implying the notion of an existence after the earthly one. 'Isn't it strange, we are talking about her and she can't hear us' was heard in one intimate group. In another, Gladys, recently devastated by the loss of her sister, startled her friends by seizing upon a joking reference to death. Someone had said 'I feel half dead today!' giving Gladys the chance to raise a question which had been on her mind for some time: 'Yes, I've often wondered, where do people *go?* Where do they all *go?* All those thousands watching football; where do *they* go?' Unable to respond to such issues of mortality, Gladys's associates stared thoughtfully at their tea. The Great Stadium in the Sky was not a usual topic for discussion and after a moment's silence the conversation moved on to more familiar ground.

Speculation about the departed is normally related to specific individuals who are missed. In the case of particular well known or well liked members the references go on for weeks, even years. Soon after the event bereaved sons and daughters write with gratitude for 'the flowers, friendship and happiness at the club'. Favourite songs are sung in their memory, monologues are given 'as X would have done it' to entertain the club. They are remembered in prayer, 'dear old friends, may they rest in peace'. Money is donated by members who miss their services in – for instance – organising outings. Club activities trigger off recollections of the departed member's distinctive style of participation. 'Old X would have enjoyed that', and 'Old Y used to sit here; he would have loved it'. This process is reinforced by the annual cycle of events which reminds members of the gap in their ranks. Who will take part in the church quiz in the absence of Mrs X who had represented them last year? The deaths of members recorded in the minutes of the annual general meeting are brought to consciousness again as the minutes are read the following year. Prayers are said for them and a brief silence is observed yet again.

These references bring to mind Ariès' (1981) notion of the cult of memory, which has replaced the cult of the tomb in western society over the last few decades. The ceremonial visit to the cemetery is no longer the main means of incorporation of the dead into the world of the living. They live on in memory, their existence expressed in religious ceremonies – the memorial service – in informal remarks, and in dramatic or musical performance. Ariès suggests that the increasingly personal and private nature of death, for both the dying and survivors, has affected the way in which the memory of the dead is cultivated. Mourning has become restricted to intimates of the deceased, and memory is cultivated within the home rather than at the tomb. In extreme cases, the possessions of the dead person are kept exactly as they were in his lifetime, a practice described by Gorer (1965) as mummification. The transfer of death and mourning to the private sphere is a product of the increasing proportion of cremations rather than burials. But whereas Ariès maintains that memory can be cultivated only in the home or at the tomb, and increasingly the former, the evidence of encounters with death in club and fellowship culture suggests another possibility. In the circle of friends and acquaintances the boundary between life and death is encountered publicly. A personal tragedy has significance for them all. Collective acknowledgement of death provides a supportive framework both for the dying and the survivors.

Peer group support: the behaviour of survivors

The vast literature on the consequences of bereavement offers a united view of the difficulty encountered by survivors in the dominant culture in Britain. The silence which spreads around the dying engulfs their relatives too. The ugliness of death, a sense which has developed over the last century, includes the tears of the bereaved as much as the physical ravages of disease and death. Viewed historically, the emphasis on containment of feelings and their expression only in private is relatively new. It is also ironic. The current reduction in the range of emotional investments means that the loss of a close relative or friend has a devastating effect on emotional life. The absence of ritual and social recognition increases vulnerability in the bereaved, and leads to maladjustment, even death. A tendency to deny the loss, rather than to work through the associated feelings of grief, produces serious suffering in a significant proportion of cases. Studies of bereavement have underlined the importance of being allowed to grieve. Those who are deprived of the opportunity are more likely to remain distressed and incapacitated (Hinton 1974; Gorer 1965; Cartwright et al. 1973; Bowling 1988) – a condition in western cultures which is socially unacceptable. Gorer's early analysis, of historical, cross-cultural, class and regional variations in the style of death demonstrated clearly that the behaviour of the bereaved is culturally prescribed. In this culture, the phases of grief and mourning which elsewhere are ritually initiated and terminated are a matter for personal discretion. Rules exist for the expression of anguish but they demand a high degree of self-control and are perceptible mainly in the breach.

Members of the club or fellowship respond to a bereavement both individually and collectively. They acknowledge the death and consequent feelings of bereavement; they provide practical and moral support for the bereaved; they provide guidelines for behaviour in these circumstances; and they help the newly bereaved to acquire the identity of widow, widower, orphan, bereft sister or friend.

The announcement of details of the funeral is a ritual which expresses concern for the survivor, recognises the legitimacy of her feeling, and announces a period of mourning when she will be partly incapacitated, and from which she will emerge into full membership of this society of the widowed. The strong identification with the bereaved arises from shared experiences. The personal knowledge of suffering is expressed in flowers, in offers of help and in the concern to keep the mourner in the organisation. There is an expectation that the member will drop out in the absence of the partner or friend with whom participation in the club or fellowship had been shared. But 'we hang on to them'. This is both a factual and a normative statement. It describes the efforts made to encourage continued participation and reflects a belief in the devastating effect of this kind of loss, and in the role of the club in meeting social needs.

Practical support is offered to widows who need help with the paperwork of death, and with clearing up possessions. Moral support is even more important, for in this population the pain of loss is a familiar feeling. In the Good Companions Club, the chairman expresses this on the members' behalf: 'X is dying but fortunately there is no pain. The pain will be with M now. We have all experienced these things, haven't we? We will have to make sure she gets a lot of comfort'. When M returns as a widow sympathy is expressed in the ritual singing of the twenty-third Psalm, and in informal enquiries into her emotional state. The last moments of the dead person's life are discussed and the practical details of his disposal are established. In giving a final account of their life together the widow is in some sense absolved. As we saw in the earlier example of John's death, with the help of friends and fellow club members death is put into perspective and acknowledged as a part of life.

Within the peer group, a set of rules exists for the expression of grief. As we have seen already, much of the talk that goes on informally involves the establishment of acceptable standards of behaviour. Tears are expected and encouraged, especially if emotions have been over-contained in the period leading up to the death. It is recognised that grief must have an outlet. The response taken by friends depends partly on the personality of the bereaved. In one case the widow, known to be a 'poor thing' whose husband had done everything for her, was met at the door by a friend and shepherded to her seat. Another friend steered her to the lavatory during the interval. She said little after a muttered 'it's so hard', and was told that 'it will take three months' to settle down. Later she reminisced a little, 'fixing the past' (Hockey 1985), and the friends joined in with their own recollections. But within days concern was being expressed over her failure to think positively. Her closest friend was warned by another to avoid doing too much for her. A year later the widow's friends are getting impatient. Their suggestions have been spurned: she has no interests or resources, and is a hopeless case who won't help herself. There is disapproval of the widow who makes no effort to come to terms with her loss, who is over-reliant on neighbours or friends. The ideal response to loss is to return as soon as possible – within weeks rather than months – to a normal life, developing new activities and interests where the departure of the deceased has left a gap. It is known that life will never be the same again but that in some respects it need not be worse. The newly bereaved person is in good company. Uncomfortable emotion, if not suppressed, can be sublimated in horseplay and ribaldry at the club.

The sympathy extended to the newly bereaved is available to the dying , too. Relatively few active members are known to be dying, for death generally takes place after the period of active involvement has ceased. Death either comes at the end of an accumulation of disabilities or suddenly, without warning. The one situation in which people confront dying in the club or fellowship itself involves members known to be suffering from a terminal illness. In this situation, members witness the potentially demoralising sequence described by Hinton (1974), which begins when the ability to continue rewarding pursuits is impaired. In a terminal condition the progressive loss of function is inevitable. It is part of the process of loss and separation from the body which is experienced by the fatally ill person.

The surrender of independence, and the recognition that one's existence can change and finish, is a feature of extreme old age which is accelerated and underlined in a condition of terminal illness. Awareness of the condition alters attitudes to the self, a change which can be helped or hindered by witnesses, depending on their degree of openness to the imminence of death. The challenge of Hinton's work in the hospice was that of making death acceptable, particularly to relatives whose readiness to admit the possibility of death is often out of phase with that of the dying person. In the club and fellowship there appears to be less resistance to the idea of death. Once cancer has been diagnosed in old age, death is felt to be inevitable. The course of the illness is noted and although the word is not mentioned often, preparations for leave-taking are made calmly and quietly and without fuss. When Vic (whom we met in Chapter Six) dying of cancer of the throat and with only weeks to live, asks if he may be excused his usual job of collecting the welfare contributions, his friend Bert is asked to take it on immediately and without comment. When Vic is seen lighting up a forbidden cigarette, the chairman (who is also a personal friend) chides him gently. His observation is a comment rather than a reprimand. Heads turn briefly but no-one adds anything, for they understand why Vic should seek this forbidden pleasure in his terminal condition.

Another member of this group is also dying of cancer, though she is too weak to attend meetings. Her friends report on the progress of the disease. Winnie is said to be remarkably philosophical. She has made all the necessary arrangements, even down to choosing the hymns for her funeral. With her friends she talks openly about her death. Her husband also, not a member of the club, talks about his impending loss with them. But according to Winnie they do not discuss it between themselves. Their openness to death falls short of the ability to mention the word to each other, though each knows that the other is fully aware and working through the implications with friends.

At the funeral, Winnie's husband cries for the first time and Winnie's friends encourage him to release his feelings. The respective roles of family and friends in preparation for death are difficult to establish on the basis of this study, for it did not include interviews with kin unless they were involved with the organisation in some way. Other studies, such as Cartwright's (1973), suggest that the majority of bereaved people find that their families meet their need to talk. Friends were the main listeners in only 22 per cent of cases. But the literature on primary group relationships in old age (Dono et al. 1979; Litwak and Szelenyi 1969) and on social processes in the elderly peer group (Keith 1982, 1983) would lead one to expect that similarities in life position might make friends crucial in encounters with death.

Difficulties with death

It is suggested in the medical literature that anxiety about death is heightened more by the loss of friends than of relatives (O'Laughlin 1983). Friends have been chosen and are therefore objects of special attachment. Their death constitutes a special kind of loss, and as age mates it also brings intimations of mortality. The contrast is perhaps indicated in the comment of a club member who remarked with some surprise that she had cried less over the sudden death of her husband than at the news of the equally sudden death of the friend whom she was expecting to meet for lunch. Her distress in the second case was a product of shock, but also of the difference between an emotionally unrewarding marriage and a close and companionable relationship with a woman friend. Support for the view that the death of friends brings anxiety-provoking reminders of one's own mortality is found in the behaviour of a minority of members. There are some who consciously dissociate themselves from death by leaving a club 'because too many are dying', by refusing to visit a dying friend in hospital 'because he was once such a marvellous figure of a man and is now wasted away', by refusing to attend the funeral of a friend and fellow committee member because his widow 'doesn't want all this stuff, she wants to forget it!' This withdrawal from intimacy with the dying or newly bereaved arises, as one of the comments suggests, from a horror of the physical process of dying, a horror which we have seen to be typical of the wider society. It sometimes follows near-death experiences which leave the person emotionally vulnerable.

Apart from cases such as these, the presence of death is accepted with equanimity in the elderly peer group. Interestingly, the views of death reported here contradict those of some other groups of old people. In the Jewish day centre reported on by Hazan (1980) and in a rural community in Northern France studied by Okely (1986) death is a taboo subject, encountered with the reluctance reported in other age groups. The difference in response between these old people and those described in my study needs to be explained.

A number of studies deal with death in old age in the context of the peer group. Some, like Hazan's and Okely's, indicate the resistance identified as typical in western culture. Others, like Myerhoff's analysis of elderly Jewish immigrants in California and Hockey's material dealing with residents of an old people's home in the North of England, and Gubrium's and Hochschild's work in segregated living environments in North America, resemble this study in the more open attitudes to death and dying which they identify. The sharpest contrast is between the two studies of Jewish immigrants, by Myerhoff and Hazan.

In Hazan's interpretation, death is unmentionable because the members of his Jewish day centre in London have created a particular kind of reality for themselves (Hazan 1980). Poor, rejected by their successful, assimilated offspring, adrift and culturally dispossessed by their remoteness from childhood environments, they have cut themselves off, developed a self-protective solidarity and set of values emphasising mutual help and fraternity. They are in a state of limbo between life and death, disengaged from the dead as from the living. Death has been cognitively eliminated from the centre reality, along with the erasure of the past and the invalidation of other realities. In this state, death is irrelevant and inadmissible. Mention of it is seen to be improper and strange. The rules require that it be done out of earshot or in a special therapeutic group.

Death occurs, of course, and many of the centre members are widowed but attitudes towards grief are ambivalent. Members wish to ignore death but need to integrate the newly bereaved person, to help him or her to become 'centre-centred'. He or she is given a sympathetic hearing but encouraged to forget. Death is normal and the bereaved person should come to terms with it as quickly as possible, by contemplating the recovery of others in similar circumstances.

Despite objective similarities, the elderly Jews in Venice, California, approach death differently (Myerhoff 1978). For them death is a part of life, and a good death occurs among family and community. A death in the day centre brings people together, with embraces and intense discussions. Rituals of death – a funeral, a memorial service – establish connections between them, and are symbolic displays of unity. The rituals engage them fully, for they celebrate the cultural distinctiveness of this group of elderly emigrés, cut off from the past and abandoned by their young, who represent the future. In the funeral rites the old people behave with a certainty that is missing in much of their day-to-day activity. Myerhoff observes an intensity of life and passionate engagement with the affairs of the centre. She interprets this as being a result of their proximity to death. The emotional urgency she observes has little to do with the content of their exchanges, which is often mundane and trivial. The members compete with each other for time and attention, as if wanting to be heard before it is too late. (This brings to mind historical accounts of early modern Europe. Then the focus on transience produced a hugely enhanced intensity of life: nothing could be taken for granted – Beckmann and Olesen 1988.) Their survival of the pogroms in Russia, their difficult lives in the new country and their present impoverishment produce an intense search for meaning. In their search they turn towards ritual and symbolic life. Ethnic rituals, Myerhoff points out, are especially important in generating a collective identity in old age. These elderly Jews are more afraid of oblivion than pain or death. To counter it they engage in intense narrative activity, telling and retelling the stories of their lives.

A similar emphasis on talk about the past appears in Hockey's study of Highfield House. Residents share with the old people in the other two studies a sense of discontinuity. Like the Jews in Myerhoff's study, they search for meaning and coherence through reminiscence. In talking about the events and turning points in their lives, they are 'fixing a dissolving past' before it is swept away with oblivion in the next, unfavourable stage. The present, in the institution, can be seen as a framework through which the past is now viewed, some of its aspects taking on new, pressing meanings, others fading into insignificance (Hockey 1989). The verse of an Easter card, set to music and sung at a Christmas concert reveals the way in which these old people think about themselves and their situation (Hockey 1983). Bereft of reference points, previously taken for granted, the resident confronts 'a solitary one-way journey into the indeterminacy of the future'. The sense of uncertainty and insecurity is enhanced by changes in the body, changes which occur against a background of timeless and repetitive institutional routine. The song acknowledges the nature of the journey into the future.

It appears from Hockey's account that it is the very old and frail who reminisce the most, who have a sense of urgency in their need to provide an account of their lives. Their proximity to death sets them apart from the fitter residents who take care to retain the boundary. The care staff, in particular, are unable to respond to the residents' need to talk about death, a phenomenon noted in other studies (Gubrium 1975; Keith-Ross 1977). The residents do not, themselves, appear to address the issue directly but express their solidarity through the song, which was produced by the fitter, more independent ones, and articulates the concerns and preoccupations of them all.

Compared with these research populations, people in the clubs and fellowships appear to be quite distinctive in their handling of death. Their situation is, perhaps, more typical of old age, though as we saw in Chapter One only a minority of the retired population participate in such organisations. Comparing the experience of old people in this study with others, several reasons emerge for the willingness to confront death. Unlike the Jewish immigrants, they are not overwhelmed by problems arising from immigrant status; the issue of continuity is resolved largely through satisfactory personal relations with younger generations; and a personal death does not so directly promote the decline of the group as a cultural unit. At the same time, parallels can be drawn. The sense of a decline in values and traditions dear to this generation is not so urgent but, as we shall see in a later chapter, the issue of cultural continuity and survival does influence the content of interactions in the organisation. Perhaps the main reason for club and fellowship members' ability to confront death is that, although ever-present, it is not personally imminent for most of them. It is sufficiently close in the form of sick and bereaved members to call for acknowledgement and sympathy. But death is the antithesis of vigour, activity and a positive approach to the problems associated with ageing. The average member – whose participation in club life attests to her belief in these values – is invulnerable. She does not need to deny death; participation in club life is proof of her ability to survive the hazards of ageing.

Put in the context of broader cultural understandings of the termination of the life-span, we can see in the management of death in the club or fellowship a search for meaning. This is achieved in the way a death is acknowledged, the language of death, and rules governing the expression of anguish. In the club, the elderly member confronts death in a supportive setting. The implication for the living of the rituals surrounding death, of the frequent talk about deceased members, their manner of dying, their possible whereabouts and their loss to the community, is that death is a part of life, not outside it. A life is put in context; there is continuity between past and future. Above all, death is normal: 'Death? That's life!' And so members are prepared for loss and their own eventual deaths.

Ritual plays an important part in all this. Ritual observances range from the formal announcement and silence, the singing, and expressions of thanks and appreciation, to the repetitive words of the funeral service and formal reintroduction of the bereaved person as a widow. In rituals of death, the themes of time and continuity are thrown into sharp relief. Ritual alters the participants' sense of time. It repudiates meaningless change and disorder by emphasising regularity, procedure and order. In Barbara Myerhoff's words, ritual 'uses repetition to deny the empty repetitiveness of unremarked, unattended human and social experience'. The experience of elderly Jewish immigrants contains starker contrasts to those of elderly English organisation members, but the search for the meaning of death is a universal experience in old age.

EIGHT

Beliefs about ageing

In the culture of old-age organisations there is a close association between ill-health and self-definitions of old, a phenomenon widely noted in the literature (Stephens 1976; Williams 1986). The popular expression, 'You're as old as you feel', is close to the meaning ascribed to old age by club and fellowship members. Old is a state of feeling and behaving, rather than of years or even appearance. It is the product of accumulated experiences, good and bad.

> Count your garden by the flowers,
> Never by the leaves that fall,
> Count your joys by the golden hours,
> Never when life's worries call,
> County your nights by stars not shadows,
> Count your days by smiles not tears,
> And on every birthday morning,
> Count your age by friends not years.

As the last line suggests, The Silver Threads Club birthday song is a devaluation of chronological age in favour of accumulated experience. But more than that, it is sung as a celebration of long life and an affirmation of the positive aspects of the ageing process. It implies a balance of losses and gains, expressed in metaphor, and challenges youthful definitions in which old age is a profoundly negative experience.

In the fellowship and club population, old age exists when ill-health produces a change in a middle-aged lifestyle. In the 'sick news', shifts in age status occur as individuals are deemed to have moved, through chronic ill-health, into a new category. 'X is still very ill. The trouble is he's *really* old now'. When 82-year-old Mrs. J, an active church worker, talks of visiting old people, she refers to their health status rather than their chronological age Mr S, a relatively young church worker in his early 70s, insists that he is old: 'Well, I *feel* old, anyway; I've got arthritis in my neck'. The difference in perspective between young and old is revealed in wry smiles over Mrs J's activities. In physical terms Mrs J is older than her clients as are several of the elderly women who serve lunches at the church lunch club. The relative youth of the diners – who include Mr S – is seen as an anomaly by younger people and to some extent by the workers themselves. The discrepancy is resolved by the workers who refer to the unfortunate circumstances of the diners – they are lonely, widowers, unable to cook. The diners either adopt these ascribed roles or deny the implication that they are needy, hence inferior in status. They turn the relationship into a contractual one, claiming that they have had good value or grumbling that the food is not worth the (nominal) amount charged.

Among the old themselves, old age, like ill-health, is defined in terms of functional capacity. Responses to both ill-health and old age are similar. Struggle and resistance are seen as possible and desirable. Surrender without struggle is a sign of moral weakness. Social participation is more than simply a strategy to avoid loneliness and inactivity, as organisers tend to think. It is an expression of a notion of ageing well.

Age as a rationalisation

Age enters people's calculations in a number of ways. In the church it is used as an excuse for giving up responsibility, at any age from 60 onwards. 'When you get older you want to stop, you've done your bit, you get past it ...'. 'You lose your exuberance, it's time to give up working with children ... Well it (Sunday school teaching) takes a lot of time, the preparation ...'. As this last remark indicates, age is used as a socially acceptable excuse in place of the real reasons for giving up: boredom, lack of interest, changing priorities.

The use of age to discontinue former practices occurs at the organisational level, too. In the club, people are said to be too old to parade around in Easter Bonnets, an explanation which conveniently overlooks the less flattering facts: a misunderstanding last year between the secretary and the adjudicator, the ill grace of the losers and their friends, and so on. It is said that members are too old for a fellowship holiday, not that there is no-one willing to organise it; that another group is too old for a theatre trip, rather than admitting that arguments about where to sit began to spoil their last outing.

The same sort of rationalisation goes on in the case of people who use age to avoid taking office. No-one wants to do the job, for 'we're all getting old, near the end ...'. In most cases the people concerned have never held office but now they use age to justify their position. Age is used widely to defend one's level of commitment as part of a personal strategy to conserve energy. At the same time age is used by younger people as a basis for allocating jobs to their elders. On the assumption that older people need an occupation, have plenty of spare time and are not the best judges of their own capabilities, the services of retired unattached men and women are sought determinedly by younger people – organisers of voluntary agencies, church workers – who have work to be done. Their unattached status is even more crucial in the perception of these older people as available than their retirement from paid employment. They lack the signs of intimacy which provide others in the wider society – married people particularly – with a moral justification for existence. Whereas married people achieve validation as people in relation to each other and their narrow concerns are supported by an ideology of partnership, the unattached have to work hard to achieve a moral justification for their existence and way of life (Ward 1979). Some people turn to voluntary work or intensity their 'good neighbour' activities to avoid the guilt associated with living for oneself and 'being selfish' (Jerrome 1981). Whatever their strategy, the absence of a supporting ideology for singlehood in conjunction with the value attached to product-ivity makes elderly unattached people vulnerable to appeals for help.

To outsiders it might seem that the elderly incumbents are hanging on to offices in the church. In reality it is often made impossible for them to retire. The pressure upon them to remain in office is backed up by an ethic of service to the community, the need for purposeful existence, the importance of activity, of doing rather than being, and other cultural values. These assumptions were present in the case of Mr S, already referred to, who in his mid-70s and suffering a lot of pain was anxious to cut down on his church commitments but had his protests brushed aside; Mrs R, in her 80s, who felt unable to continue with the secretaryship of her women's organisation for another term but was prevented from giving up. The pressures are there in secular organisations too: there was Bill, whose skill with the camera was exploited for the benefit of a number of clubs; and Molly, who felt equally exploited when it was assumed that she would be available to play the piano whenever required.

In general then, age is used in different ways to justify lines of action. the different and contradictory ways in which it is used reflect the cultural vagueness surrounding this dimension of experience. The absence of clearly-defined roles and statuses in old age gives a sense of both freedom and confusion. It provides scope for manipulation and the promotion of personal interests. Cultural ambiguity provides calculating, resourceful elders with a set of possibilities for innovation and exploitation of the deregulation which characterises retirement (Myerhoff 1984; Rosow 1967).

Brett and his friend are good examples. Brett is adept at exploiting the popular belief in old age as a time of inactivity and incapacity. He left his last club explaining in a note to the chairman that he was too old to continue. He did not disclose the real reasons – boredom and the achievement of his initial goal, a new 'lady friend'. Having met Mrs S, Brett spent his Monday afternoons in more enjoyable pursuits. Brett felt the need to justify his affair with Mrs S, a widow of the same age (82) and did so in age terms: 'Two lonely old people: no harm in that, is there?' The problem was that Mrs S's landlady disapproved and would not let him visit. Mrs S adopted the same line as Brett. The landlady was foolish to uphold sexual taboos. The old are sexually innocent. But her next remark, a coy 'but it was just as well, as I was in the shower!' suggested that she and Brett were indeed sexual beings who should not be put in compromising situations. The popular assumption of asexuality in old age was exploited by these two people to manipulate the landlady. (They were unsuccessful, perhaps because she herself was an elderly woman who would not collude with them.)

But the notion of individual freedom and scope for manoeuvre must not be taken too far. Social situations cannot be defined unilaterally. They have to be negotiated (albeit on one person's terms). Individual freedom is limited by other people who can either confirm or deny the subjective account (as did Mrs S's landlady). Again, the association between old age and ill-health is close. Personal constructions of old age are dependent on confirmation by others. This principle – the intersubjectivity of experience in old age – is clearly at work in the church community.

Age in the church

Officially age is not an organising principle or criterion for distinction in the church. Unofficially, popular stereotypes and theories of ageing abound. The view of old age from below is largely unflattering. Old age is a state which has little to recommend it. As a way of behaving, it is rigid, old-fashioned and conservative. It involves loss of health and fitness, of social contacts, of the ability to concentrate, to reason and even to sell jumble. The impression given in prayer is that old age is an affliction like alcoholism and drug addiction: the elderly join the 'needy and suffering in the world', who include the hungry and thirsty, the homeless, the unemployed and unemployable, alcoholics and drug users, the sick and the lonely. An equally gloomy picture is painted in another prayer, offered by a younger person who was doing his best to identify with his elderly audience by entering their world as he saw it: 'We need support and help when our limbs don't obey, and life seems a burden, when we are alone and feel deserted'. When this was followed up by a humorous remark about failing memories the more assertive members of the group bridled and reminded him to 'speak for himself!'

This younger man's painstaking identification with older people, which backfired when his sympathy was misplaced, underlines the gap in experience between the middle-aged and elderly. A complete lack of identification is revealed in the behaviour of a group of younger women who were celebrating the twenty-fifth anniversary of their organisation. When an invited guest hoped he would be invited to their fiftieth party one of the younger women did a quick calculation. She announced that by that time she would be … 'no, its incredible, impossible … 85!'. There were shrieks and groans all round at this horrifying and unbelievable fact. There was no regard for the feelings of the two members who *were* in their 80s, both smiling enigmatically during the outburst. In this particular age-mixed group, the old women, who are in a minority, tend to be either ignored or patronised. Such descriptive terms as dear old thing or sweet little thing, or active little body, are often heard from the young in reference to the old whose behaviour pleases them. 'Sweet' implies quaint, droll or cute. 'Little' in this context is a diminutive term of affection, rather than a reference to physical size. 'Thing' implies an object so cute that it defies description as a woman. As an aspect of deference behaviour, such terms indicate the relatively low status and bargaining position of the people concerned.

Other remarks betray assumptions that the old think slowly and lack persistence. Old Hilda, at 85, is held to be remarkable at the beetle drive, 'So quick for her age and she *keeps going*!' Young Anna, responsible for the coffee morning rota, finds the weekly session 'a bit of a tie', but 'the older ones like it, don't they?' Her assumption is that older women have no ties, commitments or alternative skills which might interfere with their partici-pation. She is surprised to learn that for them, too, the coffee-making is an onerous chore undertaken from a sense of duty. Older people are seen as being limited in outlook, slower, inclined to resist change but 'on the whole very good about it' (the implication here being that they do not initiate it, but only respond, negatively at first). They like their own pew and their own little circle of friends, not liking 'masses of people around'. These assump-tions ignore similar tendencies among young people, and deviations from the supposed norm.

Above all, the state of being old is seen as undesirable, 'terrible', impossi-ble for oneself. The prospect is either inconceivable or highly unattractive ('ugh!'). It is assumed that old age should be concealed and denied by those in that condition. The term 'old' is itself an insult. The delicacy of old age as a topic of conversation revealed itself several times in age-mixed groups. Two exchanges in particular are revealing, the first an acknow-ledgement of the rudeness of using the term 'old', the second suggesting that it is highly ambiguous, meaning different things to people of different ages. In the first, a man (55) was telling a small group a story from the bible which referred to an old woman. Immediately and in some confusion he turned to the oldest woman present, in her 80s, and began to apologise: 'Sorry N, I didn't mean to (offend you) … mean anything by it.' Another group was discussing plans for a forthcoming service which involved invit-ing an outside speaker. This brief and rapid exchange at a meeting of the worship committee illustrates the variety of meanings attached to age.

Bill (74):   *Briskly* 'Is [the proposed speaker] an old person?'
Sue (55):   'Oh, quite young.'
June (65):   'Careful!' [Mind who you're calling old.]
Olga (50):   'People can be old at 20 or 60.'

The earlier remarks refer to chronological age and seek to establish that of the speaker in relation to their own: age is relative. The third comment implies that 'old' is an insult. The fourth suggests that 'old' describes a kind of behaviour of which anyone is capable. This exchange also suggests that attitudes to age in the church depend to some extent on one's own position in the age system.

60-year old Pat, mainstay of the drama group, has leapt on and off the stage for forty years. She is made ruefully aware of her relative position in the age hierarchy when one of the men, a few years her junior, warns her to be careful. It is a reminder of the discrepancy between how she feels and others' view of her. Coming to terms with being treated as 'old' when one feels young is one of the existential dilemmas of ageing in this culture (S. de Beauvoir 1977).

But positions of relative youth and age are retained as the generations move through time together. Pat's friend Jane at 50, only ten years her junior, belongs to a different generation. 'The same age as me? Certainly not! She was in my Sunday school class!' A similar relationship occurs between G and D, who are close in age (67 and 59) but whose personal timetables place them in different generations. Although friends now, the fact that G used to accompany D's mother to their club when she was alive is significant in their relationship.

The view of age from above contains as many ambiguities as that from below. The youthful notion of old as decrepit is complemented by the elderly view that 'old timers' become 'old crocks', physically frail and lacking in vitality, out-of-touch and intellectually flabby. But this negative image is rejected by those older women who took offence at what they perceived as insinuating remarks from the middle-aged clergyman about frailty and dependence. Their interpretation of age-related behaviour is more positive. Thus while the tendency for one or two members of the older women's group to doze during meetings is taken by younger people as proof of a general inability to concentrate, older women themselves see it in terms of the inappropriate content of the programme. Apart from the hymns, which they enjoy singing, the religious content of the programme is less congenial. They have their own ethical positions well established and deserve something more entertaining.

Officially, distinctions based on age are not significant. Formal criteria of worth exclude age, gender and ascribed characteristics generally. An ideology of family and fellowship unite people across the generations. Distinctions are made on the basis of adherence to these shared values, and perfection in the performance of Christian duty. Hence Mr M and Mrs Y are thanked in the church newsletter in identical terms for their work following Mr M's resignation (he is moving away from the area) and Mrs Y's retirement. The differences in their ages – forty-three years – and length of service is not reflected in the language used.

Age is no barrier to participation in The Work. The activity principle is applied by the young most vigorously in the case of older people whose involvement is functional. If, in response to pressure to carry on, they stay in office despite personal misgivings, they are held in high regard. They are treated with deference by those at the commanding heights of church organisation (in their 50s and 60s). They become folk heroes and heroines, even legends in their time. Such is old George, a role model for at least three other men in his men's group. George is the oldest member of the congregation, a veteran of the First World War and witness of all the changes – social, structural, doctrinal – which the church has gone through in the last eighty years. He has held every official position in the church, some several times over. He is active in the men's fellowship, gives talks to the women's fellowship and writes for the church magazine. He has recently survived the loss of his wife who occupied a similar position in relation to the women of the church and is now remembered in prayer. He is much admired by the younger men (in their 70s), who want to age like him.

Patterns of deference show that old people like George and Mrs J, (mentioned at the beginning of the chapter) are repositories of cultural values (Maxwell 1986). They are spoken of with admiration and respect, honoured as embodiments of the values of the church community. They are, in themselves, a cultural resource. The respect they command is in contrast to the lack of deference towards those elders who behave differently, who try to avoid responsibility on grounds of age. The loss of personal resources has produced a shift in deference behaviour (Dowd 1980, 1983). Conversation is important in conveying esteem and superiority. Identified by social scientists, the process has been vividly illuminated by novelists such as Tillie Olsen (1980) and George Simenon (1972). Third parties are drawn into exchanges by means of facial gestures, the winks and eyebrow movement which Goffman includes in his list of deference rituals. Communication techniques such as interruption, shouting down, avoiding eye contact and initiating new topics establish control over the conversation and express shifts in the balance of power. Being involved in age-mixed conversation can be a costly business. This happened repeatedly in the case of Mr S, who protested that he was not the best person to undertake a variety of tasks ascribed to him but was not taken seriously. The exchange over the church quiz was typical. Mr S protested that he would not perform well and should not be asked again to represent the group. The response was unequivocal: 'Don't give us that!' and aside to me, 'He tried to get out of it last year, too'. Turning to Mr S the speaker added, 'We know you can do it, you know more than us', and the conversation was closed.

This exchange shows the youthful intolerance of those old people in the church who do not conform to the expectation of active and willing service. It also suggests that age can be invoked by a younger person, but not an older one, to promote collective interests. The cultural vagueness which allows for manoeuvre in private life thus influences the organisation too. In the absence of clear rules for transition into and out of positions of responsibility pressure is applied to the elders to produce conformity to a model which is functional for the organisation. The result is a pattern which does not always accord with individual capacity, as in the case of Mr S, who continued unwillingly in his various roles but died suddenly at the relatively young age of 75, and Mrs R, who felt unable to continue with the secretary-ship of her women's organisation for another term but was prevented by the younger membership from giving up. The election of officials at the women's fellowship AGM is worth considering in some detail for it illustrates well the problem of age placement.

The leadership issue

The annual general meeting was preceded by chat, in small groups. The main topic of conversation was the forthcoming meeting, which would raise difficult issues. In particular, there was the perennial problem of finding a successor to the secretary who was known to be unhappy with her role. Already people were offering reasons for their own inability to take it on. 'No one has the *time* to be secretary,' Bettie told her friends, who felt the same way.

Many people had been approached over the last couple of years, both inside and outside the meeting. Within the dwindling membership those who felt comfortable in office had reasons why they could not accept this one. The most popular reason was a combination of age, health and other commitments. The very old had already done the job before and were handicapped by failing sight or high blood pressure. Others were unable to spare the time from domestic responsibilities – the need to clear the house after a husband's death; the demands made by a mentally ill son. Two younger women couched their reluctance in terms of their recent retire-ment from paid employment and their wish to be relieved of 'that kind of thing' – administrative responsibilities – for a while. Mrs R herself had taken on the job several years ago as a temporary measure to help the incumbent, a sick woman who had died shortly afterwards. She had stayed in post to keep the fellowship going, for it would come to an end without a secretary. Every year the threat to close it was made by the minister and Mrs R had always felt obliged to continue as secretary.

This year she had had difficulty carrying out the role, with health prob-lems and a sense of increasing memory loss. When the item for the election of secretary arrived, Mrs R wearily gave her resignation. She said that she had wanted to give up for the last three years, and felt she was too old for the job. 'I *do* forget things – I *have* forgotten things, it's a worry'. (This was in reference to a recent mistake involving a double booking, an embarrass-ment Mrs R felt would not have happened in her younger days.) There were immediate disclaimers from four of the younger women in their early 70s. 'We *all* forget things. Go on! You *can* do it.' An older woman, herself protected from the risk of being asked to take on the job by her residence in a different town, remarked privately to her neighbour that it was clear Mrs R wanted to give up.

The problem facing the secretary emerged as one of arranging speakers. As Mrs R recounted her difficulties numerous suggestions were made to help her. After some discussion the chairman suggested that Mrs R could perhaps cope if she had an assistant. Under pressure but determined to resist, Mrs R said in some distress that the job was getting too much for her. She did indeed look unwell, flushed and agitated. Bettie responded on behalf of her friends, a group of younger women who had been most vociferous in their opposition to Mrs R's departure: 'We're all in the same boat there, all getting older. I wish I was twenty years younger. We can't do much now, your men won't let you.' Someone else in the group referred to an absent member: 'She isn't here today but she's younger than most. She's very good, very efficient.' Without any real knowledge of her efficiency, they proposed Mrs C as assistant secretary, in her absence. The acting president spoke up: 'Isn't there *anyone* who'd like to help?' Bettie responded with emotion: 'We'd like to but *can't*. We're *just not capable*'. Here the discussion was abandoned and Mrs R was assumed to be willing to serve for another year. After the meeting, Bettie and her friends were still trying to justify themselves over their refusal to take on the secretary's role, although they were fifteen years younger than Mrs R and much fitter:

'What do you do with *your* time?'

'I've got children and grandchildren.'

'Of course, you must ... [honour family commitments]. It's your life, if you want to ... [spend it that way].'

'I don't go out in the evenings, I'm not fit, can't be relied on ...'.

These comments contained an implicit reference to the contrasting position of Mrs R, a widow with presumably more time at her disposal. The next day Mrs R was feeling slightly better and confessed to getting 'all hot and bothered' at the meeting the day before. The trouble was, they were all getting old, and no-one wanted to take on jobs. Her assessment was confirmed by another member, a youthful and active woman in her late 70s: 'We're all getting old, we don't want responsibility.'

The conduct of the women's fellowship election serves as a useful illustration of the ways in which age is used to promote personal interests. Bettie and her friends had never held office but now used advancing age to justify their position. Age was not, however, a factor which should stand in Mrs R's way. Her pleas were disregarded in the interests of the organisation.

Ageing is often given as an excuse for inactivity but, paradoxically, activity is assumed to be good for people who are ageing. This view is held by both old and young, the latter particularly when the old person plays an indispensable role in the church, and when he or she is functionally competent. Old people who perform their tasks incompetently are thought to be 'past it'; the beneficial effects of activity are disregarded in their case. The person who hangs on to office in these circumstances is subject to criticism but there is not much that younger people can do about it, given the emphasis on personal service and active involvement in church life and the official view that age does not matter. The pressure on the functionally competent old person to stay in office is withdrawn from the incompetent.

Age brinkmanship

But ironically the ambiguity surrounding old age can be exploited by the determined old person whose personal requirements conflict with those of the organisation. One case illustrates this particularly well. One of the few old women heavily involved in committee work is 85-year-old Mrs N, a widow born into Methodism and brought up in the church. Church business now occupies her five days a week. She attends meetings of the women's fellowship and church services. She comes also to supervise the cleaning, arrange the flowers, inspect the building (in her capacity as a property steward) and arrange room bookings as keeper of the church diary. She also takes her turn at running the lunch club one week in four. She sits on a variety of committees. During the peak of the cycle in the spring she is occupied by meetings several evenings a week. She has not always been so busy but is reluctant to slacken the pace of her activities. Boredom, loneliness and pain (from an illness suffered since childhood) are minimised by the ceaseless round of church business. There is virtue also in the accomplishment of daily routines and the completion of an impressive range of tasks. It is with pride that Mrs M exclaims, 'I am too busy to look out of my sitting-room window!'

Several years ago she gave up the secretaryship of the women's fellowship as she 'was getting on', and took on the treasurer's job instead. She left the choir too, for 'when people are past it they should give up!' but she shows no inclination to reduce her commitments in other areas, where her performance causes concern to younger church workers. Giving up singing protects her from the knowledge that she is hanging on too long elsewhere. Mrs N continues to do the things she enjoys. The value attached to activity and service in a context of life-long cooperation makes it difficult for others to intervene. By applying the activity principle selectively she is able to beat younger people at their own game. Her attempt to delay upgrading – old-age brinkmanship (Plath 1982) – works. Mrs N is on the threshold of extreme old age. She is between the stages of active involvement and inactivity before transition to the communion of saints. She is kept at the brink by resisting physical frailty and hanging on to her responsibilities in the church: positive signs of her relative youth and capacity. Mrs N's old-age brinkmanship reflects her view of herself as an active and independent person pursuing a continuous course through time. Other members of her network, under biographical imperatives of their own, have a vested interest in the outcome of the negotiation. The dispute over Mrs N's placement is intimately connected to their own needs and relative positions. The problems of definition (am I old, or simply late middle-aged?) and those of placement (at what point have I crossed from one grade to the next?) are settled collectively within the circle of intimates, the others in our convoy (Abrams 1980; Plath 1982) whose lives run parallel to our own. Together these people decide which actions are culturally authorised and establish the life course pathways or 'long term guidelines that self and convoy mutually apply to their actions as they plot their collective course down the biographical current' (Plath 1982).

Each transition from one point of the life-span to the next is built upon a number of thresholds, some standardised, some open to negotiation. The close association between definitions of 'old age' and 'ill-health' indicates the importance of health issues in ageing. Physical disability is a major threshold in the transition to old age. It is also one capable of manipulation. As we saw in Chapter Six, health and illness are not clearly defined aspects of reality (Herzlich 1973). Up to a point, Mrs N. can deny her physical symptoms and remain in the age grade she prefers. It worked the opposite way for Mr S who was unable to convince others of the extent of his frailty. Mrs R, similarly wished to be upgraded on grounds of ill-health but her sense of duty and the need to be useful were exploited to keep her in a position which was functional to the organisation.

The strong element of negotiation implied in this view of ageing in the church departs from the rigid notion of age roles evident in some of the gerontological literature. It is in contrast to Neugarten's cognitive timetable with its prods and breaks which propel an individual through a series of age roles (Neugarten and Hagstad 1976). The difference is one of theoretical emphasis. Attention has shifted from the regulation of progress through age grades to the self-awareness of ageing (Spencer 1987).

Models of ageing

Concepts of old age in church and club, like those of ill-health, need to be understood in their cultural context. A complex of values such as autonomy and achievement, and popular notions such as the importance of activity and social involvement, combine to influence the models of ageing which provide the basis for personal strategies and evaluation of other people's performance. The relationship between these sets of influences can be presented diagramatically (see Figure 8.1). According to the model of old age dominant among club members and church-goers, to be really old is to be functionally impaired. Old age should be resisted, though surrender is legitimate after a struggle (and if the interests of the organisation would be better served).

In the Church, people are ranked in terms of their approximation to the ideal. The 'wonderful' man or woman is an achiever who performs well in the face of adversity. His or her qualities of intelligence, judgement and stoicism inspire admiration and respect. George – role model for the younger men – and Mrs R, secretary of the women's fellowship, are wonder-

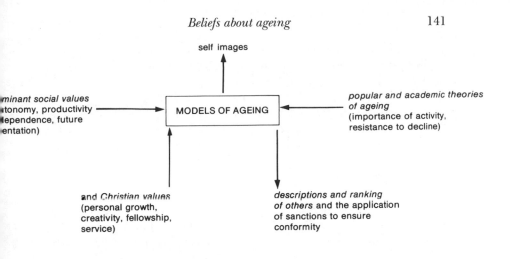

Figure 8.1 Models of ageing

ful people. So is Mrs N, though the admiration is grudging in her case. In a different category is the 'great' person. The 'great' man or woman is all these things and a model of Christian or community service too. Both the wonderful and the great are remembered after their time. Their deaths are regarded as losses to the whole community, as tragedies even, for their lives provided a standard for others to observe. In another category are the 'lovely', whose beautiful characters inspire feelings of warmth and affection. Though viewed positively, they are not long remembered after their time beyond the circle of kin and friends. In contrast to these three categories is the 'poor thing', a pitiful creature unable to cope with adversity.

This informal ranking system has its counterpart in behaviour. Sanctions are applied to achieve conformity to the ideal. Those old people whose lives express the dominant values of autonomy, productivity and independence, and in the church those who embody the values of creativity, fellowship and service, win approval. In upholding such values – the cultural resources of the group – they are objects of deference, honoured in their lifetimes and venerated afterwards. The positive sanctions of approval and deference are withheld from those whose lives do not conform to the dominant model of ageing. Disapproval is extended to old men and women who deny their ageing at the expense of the group or 'give in to it' prematurely.

The models of ageing held out to elderly people in the church, while similar to those of the club in terms of their central values, are set in the context of a church career with clearly defined stages (see Chapter Four). Movement from one stage to the next is justified not simply in terms of the individual's needs and capacities but with reference to the instrumental and expressive orientation of the group. Notions of service and struggle occur as part of the Vision (of God's Kingdom on earth) which unites believers of all ages. As we saw in Chapter Four, membership of a close-knit age-mixed organisation provides a distinctive experience of ageing, social change and replacement. The reciprocal expectations of people at different points in the church career create an effective system of socialisation and social control. Conformity to age roles is underpinned by the network and legitimated by Christian values. The very old person in the church, for whom this is likely to be the only social arena, enjoys the security of a highly integrated and purposeful existence.

Old age as a moral category

Old age is a moral category. Responses to it are a matter of virtue and moral strength, or weakness. To be happy and make the best of things in spite of pain or hardship is a moral and social obligation attached to the status of old or handicapped person. Those who fail are blameworthy, and tend to blame themselves. In widowhood, for instance, the majority in the club and fellowship population are well-adjusted; they conform to the model, and are reasonably content because they did 'the right thing'. 'I did what a lot of people do: joined the fellowship, went on holiday with a friend, did voluntary work …'. There are a few, though, for whom this strategy has not worked. The few intensely lonely and unhappy widows in the club population see their plight as being somehow their own fault, although it might be defined as situational rather than personal in origin. Their talk is punctuated with 'I should have …' and 'if only …', as old housing decisions and missed opportunities are blamed for their current malaise and become a focus for their unhappiness.

The resistance model of ageing provides an explanation for failure and unhappiness in the principle of just deserts: 'you get out of life what you put into it'. It also offers a standard against which to evaluate one's own performance. Some old people do this much more openly than others.

'I am always happy, I set an example to others …'.

'I fill my time doing good works.'

'I do so much for the church.'

'I am too busy to look out of my sitting-room window.'

'I am a walking miracle.'

These remarks suggest a need to justify existence. They are strange when set alongside cultural prescriptions for modesty as in the popular injunction, 'Don't blow your own trumpet!' There are several reasons why people might claim virtue in a way which defies the cultural requirement of modesty. A possible psychological explanation is insecurity and the need for reassurance. In sociological terms the explanation might be sought in the nature of the retirement experience: the need for new identities to replace the occupational one, the attempt to find some meaning in the process of personal change in the light of earlier achievements and the uncertainties of the future. Such remarks could be understood as a claim to distinction in relation to peers. What they seem to display is uncertainty arising from the changing basis of self-evaluation in retirement and widowhood.

Most people do not proclaim their virtue quite so openly. Strong identities and methods of coping perfected over a lifetime help them to accept their decline in status (Streib 1976). But old people in both categories – those who proclaim their virtue and those who do not – respond to the decline in status by making a career out of ageing. Old people acquire a sense of achievement from the accomplishment of small routines. Each day is a challenge and its conquest is essentially a competitive affair (Stephens 1976; Gubrium 1975). Over the years the routines may become private rituals, partly to compensate for the absence of public ceremonial marking the progression through old age (Myerhoff 1984). The significance attached to having one's own seat (or a particular place for one's bag or stick) at meetings might be understood in this light.

The changing basis of evaluation and the absence of those cultural markers which provide milestones earlier in life help to account for a certain amount of ambivalence towards the ageing process. Ambivalence is reflected in the meetings, where references to age are often contradictory. Injunctions to remain active and involved are set alongside poems on the virtue of surrender and acceptance and homilies on the importance of coming to terms with the negative changes associated with age. The message about ageing is inconsistent: resist it; accept it. The inconsistency here is close to the paradox reported earlier, in the assumption that old people need to be active, set against the use of age as an excuse for inactivity. The paradox is resolved when the meaning of old age is considered more closely. Age means decline but decline can be delayed by activity. Old people use age as a basis for reorganising their lives, which thereby acquire new meaning.

The success ethos of western society, with its emphasis on achievement and independence, is thus adapted to the conditions of old age. But there is a class difference in the mode of adaptation. For middle-class elderly the values of achievement and independence are sustained through the pursuit of a middle-aged lifestyle. The effects of illness and status loss are minimised and ageing is denied (Hellebrandt 1980; Clark 1969). Alternatively it is tolerated as an opportunity for personal development (Williams 1986). In this context age might even become the basis for an age-specific organisation whose aim is to counter status loss, as in the Gray Panther movement or the University of the Third Age. For middle-class elderly people the onset of old age is liberating in its release from the obligations associated with middle age, and by resisting the encroachments of physical age they achieve moral control over the ageing process.

Working-class elderly people vary in their response to old age. According to Williams (1986) it is regarded as a set-back: surrender is more typical than the resistance which characterises middle-class responses. But in the club population the values of achievement and independence are paramount. Their response is close to that of Williams's middle-class subjects, and indeed as we saw in Chapter Two they appear to be untypical of working-class elderly people as a whole in several respects. People in old people's clubs and fellowships are resisters. Social participation is part of a strategy for survival. All are determined to keep going, either by denying increasing frailty or by acknowledging it and coming to terms with it.

Personal ecology

Regardless of social background, health and fitness appear to be crucial for the sense of ageing. In the club population, as we saw in the last chapter, attitudes are ambivalent. Illness creates a dilemma resolved by a compromise between the ideal of resistance and the less valued response of surrender. Diminishing resources are protected by a change of strategy: a cutting down, a giving up in one area balanced by an intensification of interest in another, less strenuous kind of activity. The concept of personal ecology is a useful one, implying a strategy to conserve energy (Christiansen 1981). The strategy varies from person to person. It might mean giving something up (or trying to), it might mean hanging on to an activity in spite of pressure to give it up, or refusing to take it on in the first place. Whether an activity is avoided, taken on or given up, the strategy to conserve energy reflects characteristic ways of responding to change. Decisions are a product of a lifetime of interaction between the self and the environment.

The concept of personal ecology draws our attention to the individual life-span. A strategy for the conservation of dwindling personal resources is drawn up in relation to one's own life history rather than through comparison with the activities of older or younger groups. Viewed in this way, the decision made by Bettie and her friends at the women's fellowship AGM to avoid office on the grounds of age is comprehensible. Much younger than the incumbent, they nevertheless found the prospect of a role which had been unavailable or rejected earlier, unattractive at this stage. Their argument, incomprehensible to the presiding minister and to the older people, made sense in terms of their existing commitments (they were still wives and mothers before anything else) and their expectations that these would continue. The age of the secretary wanting to relinquish her post was insignificant except as a possible basis for manipulating her into staying.

The concept of personal ecology draws attention to the importance of a biographical approach to ageing. The biographical framework has been effective in a number of studies which seek to promote an understanding of older people's responses to social isolation, to dependence and to physical frailty (Munnichs et al. 1985; Evers 1983; Wenger 1983; Nydegger 1980). Current responses are shaped by previous experience and expectations. But they are also influenced by peer group standards. Within the peer group the formal organisation and the informal network of friends and acquaintances play a vital role in the social construction of age and in the definition of appropriate responses to age-related changes. Individual strategies and the normative consensus which exists within the peer group cannot however be divorced from the values of the wider society. A cultural emphasis on activity and individual achievement shapes the experience of ageing in a way which heightens the significance of voluntary association membership itself.

Membership of club or fellowship is part of a notion of ageing well. But individual strategies are pursued at the expense of fellow participants, as the leadership issue revealed. Similarly the need to demonstrate fitness through social activity creates a certain amount of tension. Ironically, the cultural emphasis on social participation is the basis for competition within old-age organisations, between the fit and the frail, the leaders and the rest. As we have seen, 'old age' is a moral category, and by various means old people seek to control the ageing process. Participation in club life is proof of such control and hence a source of virtue. Members and leaders are distinguished from non-members by their choice of this form of social activity, but participation in club life assumes special significance for the leadership.

NINE

Age group solidarity

By and large, old-age organisations are egalitarian. Social distinctions are made but the basis for differentiation is social age and attitudes to ageing: the extent to which someone is active or passive. In terms of objective criteria such as social class, differences can be identified, but these do not provide a basis for members' own social categories.

By conventional criteria, a number of members and proportionately more leaders are middle class. A combination of income, home ownership, the former occupations of spouses and themselves, private education, styles of speech and dress, degree of social sophistication (shown in attitudes to such things as alcohol and gambling at cards), and range of leisure activities outside the club, distinguish them. But in the culture of the club, differences of social class do not appear to create obstacles to informal social intercourse. The principle of homophilia – like being attracted to like – is upheld in the choice of intimate friends but within looser friendship networks there are distinct status incongruities.

Social background does not appear to count for much in the pattern of informal relationships, and neither is it a basis for formal organisation. Given the fact that voluntary associations are normally homogeneous in terms of both ascribed and achieved characteristics (Fry 1980; Tomlinson 1979), the inclusion of a minority of middle-class people is problematic. An obvious explanation lies in age, which might provide a basis for identification and affiliation more powerful than alternatives such as social class. Physical age and fitness are known to unite older people across class barriers in segregated housing developments (Hornum 1987). The inferior status of the 'poor dears' in Hochschild's study of Merritt Court reflected health rather than socio-economic variables. The discussion of ageing in the last chapter suggests that the same might be true in old-age organisations.

It is occasionally suggested that the common experiences of old age generates sympathies which overcome rivalries based on other characteristics (a possibility discussed in Ward 1979). But age is a complex variable. If, indeed, age is a basis for recruitment at pensioners's clubs, we might expect it to continue as a basis for differentiation within the age group (Legesse 1979). To what extent is age a source of shared identity or, alternatively, a basis for internal differentiation?

The average organisation contains a wide age range, in chronological terms. Members range from their early 60s to their mid-90s. Member's own age categories for 60–90-year-olds ('very old', 'oldies', 'old crocks', 'old dears', 'young ladies', 'young people') suggests an awareness of age distinctions within their group. But there is a shared sense of being 'old people'. There is a strong sense of common interests as pensioners, people with post-employment status, in discussion of welfare benefits and physical security. Above all they occupy the same position in relation to 'youth', those people who were too young for active service in the Second World War, who missed the discipline of military service, who have been spoiled by the welfare state, who are self-indulgent and incapable of good clean fun. The war experience does not seem in itself to have been important in group identity but it symbolises the difference between the current retired and younger generations. The solidarity of the old and their moral superiority over the young is expressed collectively through the club chairman and entertainers, and in private conversation. As a representative of this errant generation I occasionally found myself acting as a catalyst for the expression of collective consciousness.

An analysis of references to age in meetings (in private conversation, in public pronouncements from the platform, in readings from *The Friendship Book*, in jokes and sketches) suggests that youth is in general viewed negatively. The very young are seen to lack understanding, do not often act from good intentions and are potential if not actual hooligans. They are a source of fear and perplexity to their elders. The only reading from *The Friendship Book* during the field-work period which did not get an automatic round of applause was referred to in Chapter Five. Here, it is reproduced in full:

> Old Mrs. McAndrew opened her front door to be confronted by two teenagers, a boy and a girl. Now alas, all too often teenagers have a bad name in our society because of the thoughtless behaviour of a few, so Mrs. McAndrew's first reaction was to shut the door firmly in their faces and lock it – but something in their shy smiles stopped her long enough for the girl to say: 'Please will you be our Granny?'
>
> 'You see', added the boy, 'we've started an Adopt a Granny/ Grandad scheme at school, and as we know you live alone, Jennie and I chose you'.
>
> How glad Mrs. McAndrew was that she hadn't closed that door – those two teenagers became her greatest friends, and every week, in holiday time as well as during term, they called on her, ready and willing to help in any way they could.
>
> Constant days of loneliness were over and once again she enjoyed baking cakes and pastries – there was now an incentive to do so! What a grand scheme this is, one of mutual benefit, I'm sure. (*The Friendship Book*, Wednesday, 6 February 1985.)

The story was offered as evidence of the benefits of overcoming prejudice, of being responsible for one's condition, and of the mutual advantages of intergenerational involvement. But it backfired. It had touched on crucial issues of great personal significance, to do with dependency, vulnerability and the need for company. The spontaneous and out-of-order discussion which followed focused upon the dangers of opening one's door at any time of day but especially at night. The woman in the story was a fool to have done so – though she was lucky that the consequences were not bad.

In club and fellowship alike, issues of national importance such as violence at international football matches become the focus of a generalised anxiety and at such times the theme of violence is prominent. On one occasion the threat assumed personal proportions as media accounts of terrorist attacks raised the prospect of their own town being the next target. 'Don't get mixed up in any crowds when you get out of here', warned the chairman as members got themselves ready for departure. The meeting had been conducted with an air of gloom and despondency particularly apparent during the devotions. The chairman was incoherent in his distress:'To think that the Lord's prayer that our mothers taught us to say ... we've never forgotten it. Think of the last four lines! [Deliver us from evil] We've heard of nothing but evil these last few days. It's only by sticking together that we can – [protect ourselves]'.

The significance of this statement lies in its linking together of modern-day violence perpetrated by 'them' with the serene and protected childhoods of club members, and the belief that they must support each other in the battle to withstand the forces of evil. They are in a state of moral, if not physical, siege, and age is the crucial variable in the alignment of moral forces.

The most favourable comments about youth are that 'they are not *all* bad', the implication being that most of them are. Young people like the would-be grandchildren of the story and a group of children who held a dance to raise money for a club member's terminally ill grandson ('marvellous for kids of today, wasn't it?') are the exceptions who prove the rule. By implication older people have a monopoly over altruism and other virtues. There is the tendency to view the young stereotypically, even when personal acquaintances are involved, and to generalise from a single experience. Hilda, for instance, makes constant references to her only son, Richard, of whom she is justly proud. She quotes his experiences and opinions, using him as an example of modern youth. But she doesn't entirely approve of his behaviour. For instance, he left his employers after they had invested a large sum of money in his training 'but I don't approve of young people today, anyway'. Hilda's assumption is that the behaviour of one member of the generation is shared by the rest and that they are the only group to indulge in it. In general, pronouncements on age reflect the twin assumptions that moral behaviour is generation-specific and that the whole generation is affected. In public and in private, the talk surrounding age reaffirms the collective consciousness of the group as old people with a distinctive outlook and set of interests.

Despite a certain amount of social class differentiation within the clubs, members are conscious of a distinct cultural identity. They have experienced a loss of ground. This sense of being strangers in their own culture was powerfully conveyed by an address given to a women's fellowship meeting (made up mostly of 80-year-olds) by an 86-year-old man on being a Christian in his 80s in the 1980s, trying to understand the bitterness and bigotry of modern times. He confessed himself baffled by a series of contradictions – between record profits and rising prices, between affluence and protest. Mentions of youthful drug culture and the philosophy of individualism touched a chord in his listeners' hearts and the discussion ranged widely, from the Women's Peace Camp at Greenham Common (symbolising the desertion by women of their families) to child abuse and the disappearance of family traditions at Christmas time. There was incomprehension of strike action and other actions 'inspired by greed'. In group discussions in club and fellowship, events like the Juventus incident (when a riot of British football fans in Belgium ended in heavy loss of life) and revelries in London's Trafalgar Square on New Year's Eve are taken to symbolise youthful decadence. One is struck by the strength of emotional response – distress bordering on tears – to national events which reflect badly on Britain. This is an aspect of the patriotism which distinguishes this generation from others (Abrams, Gerard and Timms 1985; Featherstone, 1987).

Cohorts and generations

The term 'generation' has been used several times to refer to the elderly population of old-age organisations, particularly in relation to younger people. In the popular usage, a generation is a group of people of similar chronological age and outlook. In the gerontological literature a more specific term – cohort – is used to describe a group of individuals born in a particular time interval. A generation consists of people who may make up only part of a cohort but are a unit by virtue of their historical consciousness and sense of common interests (Mannheim 1952). The orientations of a particular birth cohort are a product of their unique socialisation experiences (Bengtson and Cutler 1976). Born at a particular conjunction of events (Mannheim's unique intersection) their attitudes are shaped by historical events which they have experienced in a distinctive way. It is this rather than chronological age as such which accounts for observed age differences in, for instance, political attitudes.

Envy, disapproval and bitterness are displayed towards post-war generations by those born early this century. These sentiments, while not a product of age as such, are to be found in all cohorts as they increasingly inhabit a world they have not made – a feature of the ageing process in modern times. (I am indebted to Dr John Macnicol, of London University, for his helpful comments on the historical analysis contained in this chapter.) They form a social generation in the phenomenal sense of feeling strange (Nydegger and Mitteness 1983) and through the collective consciousness which arises from critical early experience. But by the same process, the older members of the clubs and fellowships are distinguished from the younger members. Adopting the Mannheimian concept of generation and considering the range of historical experience of members we might find that the population of old-age organisations contains several subgroups. We need to deconstruct the term 'elderly' to produce at least two generations coexisting in the club population: the very old, born at the turn of the century and entering retirement in the 1960s, and the young old, born around the time of the First World War and entering retirement in the late 1970s. Given the age range of members, it is clear that similar personal events – marriage, parenthood – must have taken place over a lengthy time span. The period from the birth of the oldest to the point at which the youngest were leaving their childhoods behind and entering adulthood, for instance, is about thirty years (see Figure 9.1).

The following historical details are drawn not from interview material but from the literature, which provides some insight into the early experience of organisation members. The old, born around 1900, grew up with the virtues of frugality and self-restraint, particularly in the working class (Abrams 1978, 1980; Abrams, Gerard and Timms 1985). As young adults and parents in the 1930s they experienced hardship by today's standards. They had limited diets and little money for commercial entertainment. Leisure – such as there was – took different forms. The notion of the modern holiday was alien to all but a privileged few. Before 1939 more than half the population typically never spent even one night a year away from home. Social life in the 1920s and 1930s was characterised by formality in dress, in speech and manners and in countless other ways (Branson and Heinemann 1971).

After the war, as middle-aged people, the older cohort enjoyed the benefits of child allowance and, indirectly, their parents' pensions through no longer having to support them. There was free health care and better housing. By the 1950s they were in competition for national resources with a younger generation of parents (now the young old) who enjoyed the increased education spending. Abrams (1985) refers to the gulf which had developed by the 1950s between the older generation of parents, who now enjoyed the benefits of the welfare state after a lifetime of struggle, and those who had become parents after the war.

The younger cohort, born around 1915, experienced the Second World War as young adults. They built their family lives with the help of the welfare state and gave birth to the anti-establishment generation of the 1960s.

In the church community the difference in outlook is expressed with clarity in the contrast in style and activities of two age-graded women's organisations – the women's fellowship and Feminine Focus. The buoyancy

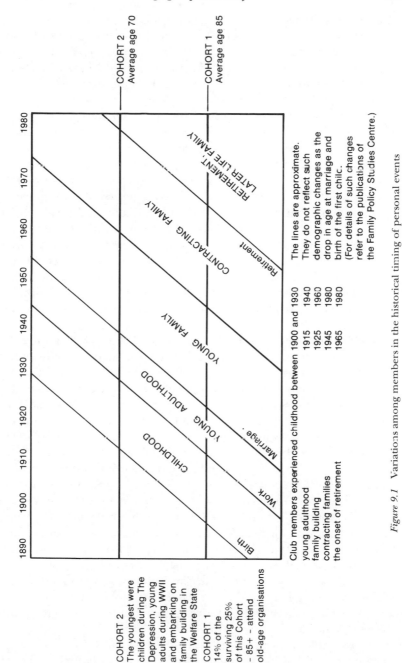

Figure 9.1 Variations among members in the historical timing of personal events

and self-confidence of the younger group, the 'daughters', and the insecurity and ambivalence of the older – the 'mothers' – are a product of cultural-historical factors surrounding their respective growths to maturity. The younger women were in their formative years during the post-war social reforms. Their high expectations reflect the optimism and exuberance of that time. The older women, in their 70s and 80s, were the parent generation in the post-war resurgence. They experienced parenthood in the aftermath of the war, when the general emphasis on home and family, peace and child-centred creativity which is typical of such times (Wilson 1980) was in full spate. Having struggled materially, they have different attitudes to authority, to gender and the respective rights of men and women, and to deviant behaviour. The younger women are more tolerant of cultural variation and more assertive individually and as a group. The two groups occupy themselves differently at their meetings: there are sharp contrasts in content and style. The older women have a more formal arrangement. They are staid and passive. The younger women are informal, noisy and participative. Their moral relativism (within limits) contrasts with the judgmental approach of the older women and is a product of the cultural movements of the 1960s. So is their assertiveness and lack of respect for male authority.

Their sensitivity to different issues showed itself clearly in their different responses to an identical talk on early Christianity, delivered by the minister. The younger women listened politely but, searching for evidence of the talk's relevance to their own lives, then demanded to know about the experience of women in the early church. They received the minister's comment about the invisibility of women in historical evidence unwillingly, but reluctantly accepted the truth of his statement. A week or so later the minister repeated the talk at the women's fellowship. He included the point about women, adding that it had aroused much interest in the meeting of feminine focus. The leader seemed somewhat nonplussed by this information but speaking up for the group she assured him that they shared the interest in women in history. She thanked him for his talk, which had filled a gap in their knowledge. She referred to the limited education of her generation in comparison with that of children today, confirming the generally poor collective self-image of the group. Her comments about education produced immediate disclaimers from the more assertive, who reversed her judgment of the relative merits of earlier and contemporary education. Once again, it became an opportunity for invidious comparisons between themselves and modern youth.

This example introduces the point that in values, too, there is a difference between older and younger cohorts. It is a difference which emerges also from the study of changing values by Abrams (1985). Abrams compares the outlook of three cohorts in relation to a set of traditional values. He finds that in the domains of family, religion, patriotism and sex, marked differences occur between the oldest (now in their 80s) and the youngest (now in their 30s and 40s). They are differences which override social class. The older people derive strength and comfort from religion. They are critical of prostitutes, homosexuality and abortion. They regard the family and marriage as important. They are proud to be British, have confidence in Parliament, and feel that law and order matter. Productivity is important to them and they have a concern for honesty and property rights. The younger people, now in their 30s and early 40s, tend to question authority and appear to condone cheating and lying in self-interest, denigrate respect for parents and disavow pride in being British. They attach less importance than their elders to public order. They refuse to accept the idea of a clear-cut distinction between good and evil and they have little contact with organised religion.

An intermediate group, the middle-aged and young retired – lie between these two positions. They are less inclined to support traditional values and by implication less anxious to defend them. But they are still critical and rejecting of the younger generation (those who were in their teens or young adults in the 1960s). In being critical of the younger and accepting of the older, parent generation (now in their 80s and 90s) they demonstrate the asymmetrical nature of social generations (Nydegger and Mitteness 1983). The young old and old old enjoy a sense of common interest in relation to younger generations. But they object to different aspects of youthful conduct. That different generations fight different adversaries is a point nicely illustrated by Posy Simmonds (in a cartoon which first appeared in the *Guardian* newspaper and is reproduced here with her permission).

The different experiences of the two main cohorts identified in the current retired population – the old old and the young old – have produced variations in diet and dress and in attitudes to age which are well known. Expectations have changed. The very old have a sense of alienation and lack of confidence which inhibits membership of formal organisations. Indeed, only 14 per cent of the surviving 25 per cent of the cohort now in their 80s attend old-age organisations though factors such as ill-health no doubt contribute to this pattern. In contrast, today's young old 'don't want to sit at home and wait to die like the older generation'. Such an attitude reflects the widening leisure opportunities and increased affluence which have altered the character of adult life in recent decades.

Within the setting of the old-age organisation the young old identify with their elders to the extent that they are both retired and both alienated from the generation who were young adults in the 1960s. Although popular songs from the 1920s do not have the same significance for the recently retired as for the older people, and they are less resistant to the social phenomena which older people view with disapproval and incomprehension, the young old, like the old old, find considerable gratification in club activities. They benefit, for instance, from the ritualisation of generational

Figure 9.1 'U Turn', © Posy Simmonds 1986 (*The Guardian*, 6 October 1986)

conflict. Given the absence of effective symbolic expression of such conflict in family life – a major setting in western cultures for direct intergenerational encounters – and its general absence from public life in modern class societies (Legesse 1979), this benefit is substantial.

Despite differences of social class and of chronological age, members of old-age organisations are united in relation to outsiders – younger people, and to some extent to older people who possess different attitudes to ageing. Their solidarity rests on the belief in struggle and the conviction that their survival owes much to their own efforts. Life was hard in their youth and continues to be so in a hostile world which ignores their values and finds no use for the experience.

The attachment to the view that life was hard is interesting. Not everyone in this population had a hard time in their youth. Given the relationship between socio-economic status and mortality it is unlikely that many of the very old members fall into the category of the most oppressed. Many middle- and lower-class people in the south of England did not suffer unemployment and did relatively well in the depression years of the 1930s (Stevenson 1984). It is an interesting feature of recent history, though, that everyone alive in the inter-war years claims to have had a bad time. The image of the period as one of depression is so engraved on the popular imagination that no-one dares recall otherwise – a problem for oral historians. (I am grateful to Dr Pat Thane, of London University, for her helpful comments on the uses of historical material in the interpretation of current attitudes.) The envy and bitterness displayed towards younger generations are perhaps better understood in psychological than in historical terms, as a product of resentment over personal experiences left behind rather than real changes in material circumstances.

An anthropological interpretation focuses on the symbolic significance of the belief that life was hard. Regardless of actual experience, recollections of widespread suffering in the past continue to colour the attitudes of old people who lived through those years towards those born since, who 'have had it easy'. That early lives were hard is a myth – in the sense of an account of history not necessarily based on fact, but crucial for old people's views of themselves.It is a myth which unites members in the knowledge of their own resilience and belief in their moral superiority over subsequent generations. The claim to distinction covers most areas of private and public morality, from 'we know how to behave in public' to 'we know how to eat sensibly, dress warmly and look after our bodies'. One is struck by the frequency with which judgements are made and by the moralistic stance of group members, particularly in relation to the young. The sense of superiority in relation to youth pervades meetings, expressed in private conversation, in formal communications from the platform and in songs, jokes and sketches. Every opportunity is made to castigate youth and draw invidious distinctions between the generations. Occasionally, as in the women's fellowship discussion quoted earlier, the general shift in values from traditional to anti-traditional prompts a questioning of customary beliefs and the rueful acceptance of youthful values. It is acknowledged that youth 'are not all bad', and are capable of worthy conduct, even moral innovation. More common, though, is the sense of moral siege which underpins the culture of old-age organisations.

Age and social status

The moralistic stance of older people can be understood in a number of ways. A popular suggestion might be that moralising is a product of age itself, an intrinsic tendency in the ageing process. A psychoanalytic explanation emphasises the tendency for the superego to dominate as ego considerations wane in importance with age (Clark 1969). In another psychological account the moralistic tendencies of older women develop as they enter the phase of active mastery. A different kind of explanation focuses on cohort differences. The moralistic tendencies of old people might be rooted in experiences of early life characterised by higher rates of religious affiliation and a greater degree of moral consensus. It might, of course, be the case that age is immaterial, and that the population of old-age associations represents a section of the peer group whose characteristics are repeated in equivalent sections of younger cohorts; that in fact,the factors of class and education rather than age lie behind these sentiments. However, my observations of church groups suggests that middle-class elderly people adopt the same position as their working-class counterparts in the clubs. These possibilities bring to mind the early debates about political attitudes and the relative effects on them of age, cohort and historical period (Bengtson and Cutler 1976; Dowd 1980).

A fourth interpretation of the moralistic stance of the older generation places moral sentiments in the context of age relations. By elaborating a set of moral principles and giving them ritual expression in gatherings of members of the moral community, the group preserves itself as a distinct cultural entity. Their morality is an important dimension of difference and so are the ties of sociability – personal and impersonal – which link them together. The ideology of friendship, fellowship and peer group solidarity in the club has parallels in the principles of mutual help through which members of the Jewish day centre in East London define themselves in relation to outsiders (Hazan 1980, 1981). There are also parallels with the use made of ritual secrecy by freemasons (Cohen 1971), of religious beliefs by groups of expatriate Hausa (Cohen 1969), the use of religion as a survival strategy in an old people's home in Israel (Hazan 1984) and of ideologies of kinship and marriage in a Nigerian community in London (Jerrome 1973, 1974, 1979). Political groupings typically express their interests through a set of symbols. The theoretical link between symbolic systems (ritual, religion, morality, kinship) and power relations has been elaborated by Cohen

(1969b). In this theoretical model the cultural difference elaborated by elderly people in old-age organisations, expressed mainly as a difference in values ritually displayed at meetings of the peer group, can be understood as a political strategy.

In the competition for social status, values are a cultural resource. In asserting their moral superiority over youth, the elders claim to possess the correct values and thus a share of the cultural resources which confer status. An analysis of values and their control along these lines owes much to Bourdieu's (1984) concept of cultural capital, a concept which has been taken up in relation to ageing in Britain by Hepworth and Featherstone (1986).

The preoccupation with morality can thus be understood in terms of elderly people's diminishing spheres of influence and lack of conventional status attributes. A cross-cultural analysis suggests that elders in this society are claiming a role which in some other cultures is institutionalised (Clark 1969; Rose 1965). In societies where age is the main organising principle and all institutions are age-graded, the role of guardians of the moral order is assigned to the elders. Indeed in some instances the role of moral arbiter is forced upon them. By contrast, the older generations in western industrial societies take upon themselves the task of defending traditional values. The stridency with which they express their views tells us something about the degree of social recognition they are afforded.

The claim to superiority may be understood as an attempt to maintain equity in relationships with the young. A balance of contributions and benefits makes social transaction satisfying and motivates the parties to continue. An imbalance confers power on the partner who contributes the most with a corresponding reduction in status and bargaining power in the other (Blau 1964). The notion that all relationships are based on exchange can illuminate interactions across age lines (Dowd 1975, 1983; Gouldner 1960, 1966; Wentowski 1981). The old in this society more than in some non-western cultures tend to experience a decline in status as their withdrawal from key areas of social life and increasing frailty make reciprocity harder to demonstrate. It reduces them to the unenviable status of dependents (Clark 1969). Viewed from the perspective of exchange theory, the energetic defence of traditional values by old people in this study can be seen as a unilateral attempt to equalise resources in order to avoid dependency.

The importance of continuity

We have so far understood the moralistic stance of older people in terms of their relative status and influence. A different approach ignores discontinuities in status and the power differential between old and young but focuses on the personal need to maintain a sense of continuity, especially in the area of values. Of the many far-reaching changes experienced by older people during their lifetimes one of the most profound has been in values. Some of the dimensions of difference were referred to earlier. A broad distinction has been made between traditional and anti-traditional values (Abrams 1985) which corresponds to the current value standpoints of the old and the young in the wider society. The shift in values has moved in the direction of self-centredness, or narcissism (Lasch 1978). The newer emphasis on personal growth and fulfilment is attributed by observers to a sense of emptiness and lack of faith, and a retreat from public life and acts. A more profound and far-reaching change is in the attitude to life itself, brought about by the new possibilities for destruction on a massive scale.

In the apparent moral weakness and self-destructive tendencies of the young, expressed in heightened suicide rates, through various forms of self-abuse, and in violence, the old witness a genuine age difference which in their view justifies a sense of moral superiority (Fiske and Chiriboga 1985).Young people lack a special quality of life, a power available only to those 'seasoned by the struggles of decades'. Such power comes from the extensive cultivation of images and forms having to do with loving and caring. It is rooted in a lifetime of commitment to parenthood and generativity as well as to work and mastery (Lifton, quoted in Fiske and Chiriboga 1985). Older generations have, as a result of the stabilising and integrating forces experienced in their youth, a sense of human continuity lacking in their offspring.

But the sustaining power enjoyed by the old is vulnerable. The gap in values threatens their stability and security. The widening generation gap threatens to deprive older people of a sense of generativity (Fiske and Chiriboga 1985; Coleman and McCulloch 1985). The tragic breakdown of the self in old age becomes more prevalent in times of great change. It is well known that clinical depression has a high incidence in the retired population and that rates of demoralisation are even higher. The symptoms of demoralisation are less dramatic but they are more diffuse and more difficult to change because of their associated characteristics: loss of motivation, apathy and the neglect of potentialities.

The relationship between psychological change and social change is complex. In a rapidly changing society, adjustment to old age is in part an adjustment to changes in society's norms and values. In the last decade developmental psychologists have begun to think deeply about psychosocial change in late life. Their evidence of individual modes of adjustment illuminates the process which has been seen to occur collectively in settings where old people gather together.

The change in values and lifestyles is a problem which old people cope with in various ways. Some feel defeated by modern values and suffer a decline in morale. Others reject the present, valuing the past more highly. But they do so with self-assurance, confident that they have seen the best. They have a high moral estimation of the old and a low estimation of the young. They are not simply alienated from the present, they positively value the past. They therefore enjoy high morale in a way which does not fit in with conventional views on adjustment to old age, with their emphasis on acceptance as the route to integrity.

People are brought up to accept certain standards and it is difficult to overthrow them. To deny the validity of one's values would amount to denying the validity of one's life. Coleman and McCulloch put it this way:

> Rejection of the values by which one has lived is hard to endure, and as many elderly people disapprove strongly of modern values, successful adjustment to old age can often only be achieved by emphasising the superiority of the past (1985, p. 253).

Modern society may actually be inimical to older people, preventing them from developing their potentials (Gutmann 1987). At a personal level they need to feel that the principles they have stood by will survive them. Ageing people need a sense of permanence to make the fact of their own impermanence bearable.

Recent psychological work, then, offers an important clue to the behaviour of old people on an individual basis. Writers point out that far-reaching social change is unsettling, leading to the loss of a sense of meaning in one's life and the world one lives in. They underline the importance of a sense of continuity for acceptance of the finiteness of personal existence. Old people's views on contemporary morality are part of the process of making sense of the present. The rejection of modern values might lead to alienation and despair or renewed confidence and vigour, depending on the strength of the old person's self-concept.

Extending these findings to the behaviour of old people in meetings of the peer group, several parallels emerge. Through club and fellowship rituals the elderly participants express their belief in their moral superiority and defend the old moral order. The support they give each other sustains the individual attempt to resist the moral decadence which they see around them. The sentiments expressed in meetings are an act of collective resistance.

In their preoccupation with the issues of personal and social change psychologists and anthropologists converge. The issues of time and mortality which psychologists like Coleman have been investigating in their case-studies, social anthropologists have pursued in different settings; old people's homes, day centres, and hospices where the old articulate their beliefs under each other's influence. The overlap does not end with content. In research methods, too, there is a shared belief in the importance of qualitative modes of enquiry. The psychologists's in-depth interview and case material complements the anthropologist's participant observation and field-notes in providing valuable material for interpretation. The intensive method provides the opportunity to explore and develop ideas in the course of the investigation so that certain unanticipated features of social life can be identified and relationships teased out. The relationship between morale, morality and peer group rituals can never, of course, be established definitely. But with the accumulation of a sufficient body of research we might be able to achieve a degree of certainty based on comparisons and contrasts between individual cases.

TEN

Ageing associations

We have seen that the process of ageing involves coming to terms with changes in society. Rapid social change influences the ageing of individuals, sometimes negatively. Old people in Britain today have reason to regret the conjunction of events which marks their attainment of old age. No area of their lives is free from change. Even their own organisations are not immune. Voluntary organisations which an early generation of sociologists saw as 'intermediate associations' acting as a buffer between society and the individual, are themselves subject to forces of change.

A sense of decline, at best, and a struggle to survive at worst, pervades many old-age organisations. There is a strong sense that things are not what they were. The situation is widespread, affecting both secular and religious associations. In the clubs, members comment sadly on the contraction in activities. They remark upon the disappearance of Easter Bonnet parades; the shortage of good entertainers; the drop in the quality of produce at bring-and-buy sales; the lack of commitment of members; and above all, the decline in numbers.

The changes are not imaginary. The deaths of particular social secretaries have had an immediate and marked effect on the range of activities. So has the growing incapacity of members whose domestic arts and crafts, acquired in the 1920s and 1930s, once populated the bring-and-buy stalls. Travel agents specialising in old people's clubs and entertainers for their shows appear to have dwindled. A review of the club movement suggests a period of buoyancy in the 1960s and early 1970s, followed by a decline. A graph of the independent clubs I studied has sharp peaks and troughs (see Figure 10.1).

The fate of other clubs in the town is apparently similar. A coach operator reports a decline on his books from seventy to seven clubs. The National Federation of Retirement Pensioners' Associations reports a fall-off in attendance at its annual conference from 1,000 in 1938 to 270 in 1985. Some of the losses are due to collective withdrawals of clubs which feel that the Federation no longer reflects their political interests.

The decline in numbers in old-age organisations seems to be related to the age of the founders and their inability to match with new recruits the losses incurred through death and disability. The life-span of the organisation appears to match that of its founder members, who carry it forward with them. Rather than belonging to the age-grade, with older members passing out at one end and new members moving up from the grade below, the club becomes the property of a particular age group or cohort.

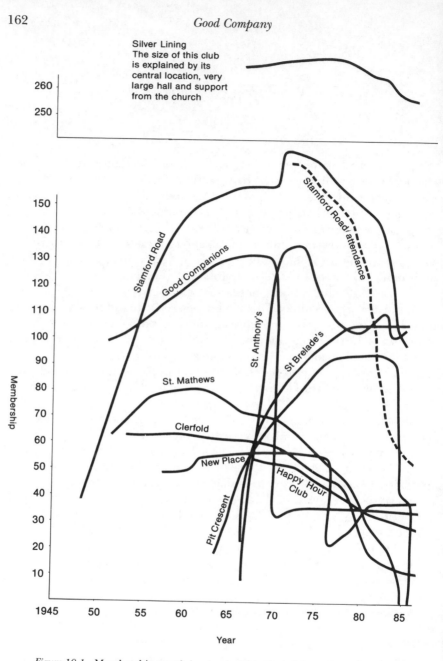

Figure 10.1 Membership trends in nine independent old peoples clubs, 1945–86

The state of decline is evident in the religious organisations too. As we saw in Chapter Four the numbers in both fellowships have steadily dropped over recent years. The membership of the men's fellowship has reached a level which threatens the viability of the organisation. The men try constantly to understand the decline. They do so in terms of other people's lack of commitment or capacity. They seek to halt the decline by advertising the benefits of membership by both impersonal means and personal influence. Valuing the experience of membership highly, they cannot really understand its lack of appeal to others. Attempts to increase the membership have failed. Discussions about modifying the programme to broaden its appeal never progress because the existing members are happy with it as it is.

The issue of recruitment

The men's preoccupation with the strength and health of the fellowship dominated the Annual General Meeting. The chat beforehand was about how many people might come. The meeting began with an opening address in which a member who was also a lay preacher reminded them all of the object of the gathering – to worship and learn the truth and pass it on. The address was followed by a hymn through which the men remembered departed members and hoped to welcome more. The secretary, variously referred to as the governor or boss, thanked the speaker for his inspiring address, and everyone for their help and support. He spoke of the uniqueness of the meeting, which was run entirely on devotional lines. But it was not attracting new members. His next remark, 'You don't need me to tell you that natural wastage takes its toll,' raised a laugh from George, the oldest member whose wife had died the previous year. The secretary described the attempts that had been made to boost the membership, and suggested another possibility. Perhaps they should be more flexible in their choice of subjects for discussion 'as the ladies are'.

The meeting proceeded with the remaining items on the agenda – the programme, finances, the annual men's service, elections. Unlike the women, the men had little use for their substantial financial surplus, derived from the weekly collection, from the tea profits and the games club balance. They decided to pay most of it to the church, retaining a small amount to cover their need for new sports equipment. The elections passed without difficulty, for the secretary was prepared to serve for a fifteenth year and the treasurer for his thirty-seventh. The pianist would carry on as usual.

The discussion returned, inevitably, to the issue of recruitment. It ranged around the content of the programme, likely areas of recruitment and the meaning of the fellowship for its members.

Charles (secretary): 'Are we on the right lines? The meeting isn't particularly attractive to outsiders but *we* all feel that we have something worthwhile.'

Fred and others:	'Yes.'
Albert:	'The strength of the meeting is its devotional nature.'
Jim and others:	'Yes.'
George:	'Do we aim to do good with our devotions, which build up the Christian fabric and produce something of lasting value to remember, or do we introduce other topics?'
Geoffrey:	'Not many people want devotional topics. But the other things – entertainment, reading matter, travel, friendship are elsewhere in abundance. We *need* some place in the church to study the gospel and know the truth.'
George:	'There aren't many men in the church who have the time to come but don't.'
Jim:	'Yes.'
Geoffrey and Charles:	'No, that's right. Reg R and Harold W won't come.'
Bill:	'If we changed the meeting they still wouldn't come.'
Geoffrey:	'Young G is interested, a bright spark.'
Charles:	'If his own organisation shifts its meeting to a different night he'll have no excuse!'
Paul:	'What about Norman P?'
Charles:	'Norman doesn't like bad weather, has catarrh, is deaf.'
Albert:	'We've been going for thirty or forty years, while others in the district have folded, so we must be on the right lines.'
Geoffrey:	'We've got several new people coming in (to the church) … the man from X church …'
Charles:	'I gave him a warm welcome.'
Geoffrey:	'He has a heart problem.'
Fred:	'We *must* keep going.'
Bill:	'It's the most important thing in *my* life.'

There the discussion ended, with the determination to continue as far as possible unchanged. The closing hymn set the meeting firmly in the context of the wider community, reminding members of its instrumental goals: we are part of a church, we have a calling to fulfil, and we seek divine guidance in this task. The Grace (a closing prayer) was said in unison, a parting ritual affirming the group's collective identity and binding the individual members together.

In the women's fellowship, too, a steady fall in numbers is matched by the sad acknowledgement that things are not what they were. In both fellow-

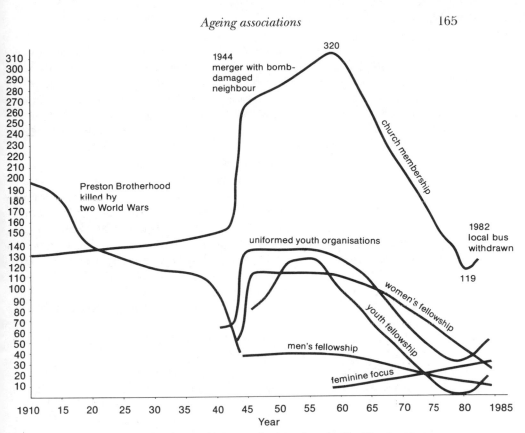

Figure 10.2 Membership trends in Stamford Road Methodist Church, 1910-86

ships the pattern of decline needs to be seen against parallel changes in the parent organisation (see Figure 10.2).

Old people in the fellowships have experienced not only the decline of their own organisation but the transformation of the parent body – the church – over their lifetimes. There is a dearth of young people in the church. Since a glorious peak around 1960 numbers in general have dropped. The reasons lie in broad cultural developments since the 1960s which have affected the whole of western Europe and North America. In Britain, *Social Trends 1985* indicated a substantial decline in church attendance, nationwide, over the fifteen-year period 1970–85. At Stamford Road in the 1950s young people packed the left-hand side of the church on Sunday nights and the youth club drew over 100 young people. Youth work was 'the chief glory of the 1950s', and several of the current middle-aged members of the church met their spouses in the church youth fellowship in the 1950s. They 'were settled' as young parents or spinsters by the time the counter-culture of the 1960s emerged, posing a challenge to the traditional moral order, and hastening the decline of community values (Gerard 1985: Musgrove 1974; Berger and Kellner 1974). But their children were affected by it. The change in intellectual direction in this period, marked by a general cynicism and burgeoning of alternative belief systems, undermined the faith of the current cohorts of 40-year-olds, then in their 20s. The decade from 20 to 30 seems to be critical in religious affiliation. The strength of established religious movements appears to be derived from their ability to replace older generations lost through death with rising generations of young people. This universal phenomenon works with particular force in church similar to the Methodist structure where continuous waves of new recruits are needed to sustain the elaborate organisational framework. The death of young people in the church is thus doubly depressing for the oldest members who, as we saw, derive some strength and purpose from their role in the perpetuation of the church as a social and cultural unit. The changes indicated in Figure 10.2 affect them at different levels, as members of a declining group and as embodiments of a set of values which no longer enjoy credence in society at large. Negative social changes are mirrored in personal decline. For the oldest members, loss and change are compounded on different fronts. Decline is a multi-dimensional social and personal phenomenon.

This might account for the air of depression which hovers over the fellowships. Both are groups facing extinction in the absence of new recruits. The awareness of decline is expressed differently in the two groups. In the men's fellowship it surfaces periodically in a desperate attempt to understand and halt the downward trend in membership. This endeavour took on an added urgency at the AGM, as the repeated pledges of loyalty and service by existing members, extending back over forty years, put their present plight in a historical context and forced into consciousness the unwelcome prospect of an ever-diminishing future. In the women's fellowship there is no talk of recruitment. The attempt to halt decline focuses on the ability of existing members to undertake leadership roles. The painfulness of decline is mitigated by reference to a glorious past. By comparison with the men, the women suffer from a collective loss of confidence which adds to the problem of recruitment among younger people and reinforces the image of passivity and marginality which they project to outsiders. Within the church there are many popular explanations for decline of the fellowships, their failure to recruit new members, and for the disappearance of parts of the programme. The explanations fall into three groups. In the first are those which attribute the decline to the ageing and dying of existing members. The remaining members are said to be too old to run things or do the things they used to enjoy, such as going on outings. This suggestion is a familiar one: other women's organisations have accounted for change in that way (Tomlinson 1979). The Townswomen's Guild saw the closure of thirty-four local branches during the 1970s due to 'the ageing of members and the failure to obtain officers and committee members' (National Union of Townswomen's Guilds Annual Report 1977, quoted in Tomlinson 1979).

The second type of explanation focuses on the image of the group and its unattractiveness to potential recruits. Members feel that they are seen as an old organisation and therefore unattractive. There is some basis for this. The younger women themselves view the prospect of joining the women's fellowship with distaste. They express themselves forcefully on the subject: 'We *wouldn't* move up!'; 'I'll *never* move up!'; 'No, I've always thought of them as "the mothers". That's not for me.'

In the third group are those explanations which emphasise the potential recruits' lack of capacity or interest. Younger men are incapable of commitment or are too busy doing other things. Younger women are seduced by other, more attractive leisure opportunities or paid employment which keeps them occupied on a Tuesday afternoon. 'Can you wonder that the fellowship isn't growing when the people who should come are at work?' There is bitterness behind this remark. The decline of the fellowship is associated with the younger women's violation of a central value – motherhood. Their avoidance of full-time home-making represents a deviation from the norms set by the older generation, whose commitment to family and children followed the post-war trends. But in fact paid employment does not account for the failure of the most likely recruits – the cohort of young retired women in their 60s – to come forward. Despite their presence in the church they prefer not to join the older women. They include two groups of potential recruits. The first are women who joined the younger women's group, Feminine focus, before they retired. They preferred to remain there when retirement freed them to attend women's fellowship meetings. In the second group are never married women who profess to be too busy with other church commitments or are simply unwilling to join 'the mothers' in devotional activity.

While their association with the older generation, or increasing incapacity may lie behind the failure of both fellowships, additional factors account for changes in the men's organisation. Friendship and the gratification of short-term emotional, spiritual and social needs appear to sustain the existing membership but possibly inhibit recruitment. As we have seen, participation in expressive associations is an activity of friendship and friends recruit each other. A homogeneous membership is necessary for ease of communication and the growth of solidarity. But the more uniform the population of the organisation, the less congenial it appears to people in other categories . To some extent the members are right to claim that it is their age which discourages new people. Shared age lies behind their intimacy and solidarity, and makes the group impermeable.

Members of the secular old people's clubs account for their own failure to attract newcomers in various ways. They talk vaguely about younger retired people having more money and a wider range of leisure facilities available to them. They talk about the attractiveness of big wins at commercial bingo and in the working men's clubs.

There are several possible causes of decline. One is the unattractiveness of club culture for rising cohorts, in the light of the unique historical experiences which have turned the present cohorts of club-goers into a generation with a shared identity and outlook.

Another explanation focuses on attitudes to ageing, within old-age organisations themselves. Club rituals express ideas about the ageing process. They can be viewed as a personal strategy for demonstrating fitness and the capacity to survive. While both members and leaders are distinguished from non-members by their choice of this form of social activity, participation in club life assumes special significance for the leadership. The assumption of leadership roles is part of a personal strategy for ageing which makes retirement from office difficult: leadership roles must be retained for as long as possible. But personal needs are met at the expense of organisational ones, seriously undermining the strength and vitality of the club. The club ages with its executive committee and ultimately expires.

Leaders and followers

Despite the rhetoric of friendship and solidarity a gulf exists between the relatively active and the relatively passive members. In their different styles of participation people in the two categories compete with each other to age well. Rival claims to superiority are made despite broad similarities in chronological age, health status and family circumstances. The most active – leaders and committee members – describe the rest as lonely, passive, demanding, sometimes suspicious and ungrateful, and often childlike. The members in turn are critical of the organisers and resentful of their privileges. They often regard club officials, their friends and people with leadership pretensions with suspicion. They are particularly critical of those who operate without any checks on their behaviour, in the form of a committee structure. This is not to deny the widespread warmth and mutual respect between many leaders and club members. But at all times a sense of 'us' and 'them' pervades meetings, matched by social and physical boundaries which separate the leaders and active members from the rest. At parties and bring-and-buy sales, for instance, the organisers put a great deal of effort into putting on a good show for the members. The latter often do not bring anything, buy anything or do anything. There are no spontaneous offers of help and none is sought. The preservation of the status quo allows the workers to regard themselves as an elite in physical, hence moral, terms. In their public achievements they find confirmation of their superiority. Their unusual energy and ability to cope with sometimes severe health problems are reaffirmed. In these circumstances it becomes increasingly difficult to give up. To surrender office would be to surrender control over the ageing process. To the extent that club work is a joint project shared by a married couple or group of friends, retirement would also have implications for one's social network. In all those clubs in the study with formally elected committees, committee members and officers were connected to each other by ties of friendship and kinship. In one case the committee of twelve included four married couples. In another, six of the eleven were close friends whose ties extended beyond the club. Shared committee work and more intense involvement on club holidays and outings (when they sat together on the journeys and passed the days in each other's company) were important social activities.

Generally, therefore, leaders remain in office until they die, and their tenure is not challenged. If people object to the style of leadership they are more likely to leave the club than to express themselves openly. Occasionally resentment *is* expressed in a formal criticism through a committee member who conveys it to the leaders. In one club, for instance, it was suspected that committee members were not paying for their tea. This abuse of authority was made the subject of an official complaint. If resentment is sufficiently widespread and senior officers are unresponsive to criticism they are voted out of office at the AGM. They may leave the club, accompanied by their supporters.

Given the expressive orientation of the clubs, and the expectation that attendance at meetings will be pleasurable, an end in itself, the majority of members do not have leadership aspirations and those that do are accommodated on the committee. Another consequence of the expressive orientation and overt emphasis on friendliness as an organisational goal is that the formal expression of conflict is minimal. There is, in any case, substantial agreement about appropriate ways of behaving in the company of peers which extends to the leadership. An array of unwritten rules relating to frequency of attendance, noise levels, contributions to collective resources and general forbearance, makes this a highly disciplined, norm-governed affair. In the clubs, informal sanctions – disapproval, ridicule and ostracism – produce conformity. Many of the rules incorporate the value of consideration for others. Members should not interfere with another's enjoyment by late arrival, noise, or bossy behaviour. Neither should leaders, and those who do are punished by ridicule. The use of unflattering nicknames ('The führer', 'the school marm', 'The Queen', 'the SS', 'The Gestapo', 'the wardress') are common and can be heard *sotto voce* when breaches are observed.

The silence rule is normally upheld as fiercely by members as by leaders. Talkative or otherwise noisy members (those, for instance, who allow their walking-sticks to fall with a clatter at inopportune moments) are sanctioned with disapproving non-verbal gestures or very occasionally by a formal complaint to the chairman. The importance of the silence rule is a measure both of members' hearing loss and the leaders' authority over the members. The way in which breaches are handled is a good indication of leaders' relationships with the club. The majority of leaders recognise that tact is required, and breaches are approached sympathetically. As one leader explained: 'You *have* to be a little bit strict, you have to have order in the club. You can't have talking while you're talking. Sometimes they get very excited about things, and talk.'

To the members another leader said: 'You *are* talkative this afternoon … silence, please … Is it because we are going to lose Henry (a committee member facing a spell in hospital) in a few days …? I don't mind you talking so long as it's not when someone is trying to address you.' Other leaders ignore minor infringements but stop and wait for silence if the noise becomes excessive. One or two achieve their object more brutally with sharp banging on the table. But this approach is not thought justified and might indeed be counter-productive.

The egalitarian nature of peer group organisations and their dislike of authority in general (Legesse 1979), extends to leaders who assert themselves without the necessary displays of respect for their members. In some instances the silence rule is deliberately flouted. Making noise is a major form of collective assertion of will, an attempt to resist control by unpopular leaders. This was particularly noticeable in two of the clubs in the study. In one, the leader persistently ignored informal seating arrangements and interrupted pleasurable activities to make formal announcements. Her rigid adherence to the timetable and hectoring style produced indignation and, occasionally, outright defiance. Members stuck firmly to their preferred seating arrangements and on one occasion persistently refused to respond to calls for silence. In another club the leader's authority was legitimated by her hard work for the club and treats acquired through her connections with the world of show business. But her style was abrasive, even rude, and her habit of calling for silence by banging on the table with a heavy wooden croquet mallet irritated her members enormously. They were regularly pushed beyond the limits of endurance and challenged her verbally, grumbling among themselves about the indignities involved in membership of this particular club. It was the otherwise congenial company, cheap theatre tickets, occasional high quality entertainment, and above all handy central location which retained their loyalty.

The leader who is domineering or rude, who is unnecessarily noisy or who operates unconstitutionally, ignores a fact of club life – that authority is bestowed by the membership. The exercise of leadership by power alone is precarious, dependent on the loyalty of a small group of personal followers while the rest respond with sarcasm (at best) or withdrawal of support and departure from the club (at worst). There is a sense in which the members themselves control the meeting, pacing the exchanges by bestowing or withholding cooperation. This phenomenon is not new. It is worth quoting again from material collected in the 1940s. The following extract from the mass observation archive reveals striking similarities with the present. It describes a familiar scene:

The meeting began. The lady secretary called the meeting to order with 'Friends, Friends, Friends ...' and she announced that there would be a draw for some cinema tickets at the end of the meeting. Chatter arose again, mainly, it seemed, because another Pensioner's Branch managed to get tickets for 'all their members'.

The secretary announced the death of a member, and asked everyone to stand. They rose, with much scraping of chairs, and chattered again. 'Shh!' she said, and everyone stood for half a minute with bowed head.

After they had sat down: 'Now', said the secretary, 'about our annual picnic'. This caused an expectant hush, and everyone strained to hear the details of the plans ... They continued to listen as a little later they were told about a tea which was soon to be given.

Then the minutes were read. During this procedure, the audience embarked on a little flurry of conversation which effectively drowned the voice of the speaker, so that this time the secretary felt compelled to say, 'Now, please, no talking. Please reserve your talking for later.' But her plea was useless. The audience went on as before ...

Soon after this, there was some reading of correspondence. Seemingly the audience again took little notice, but when an item about the system of payment of dues to the Old Age Pensioners occurred, the meeting was suddenly silent and attentive.

Next came the tea break, and the helpers busily passed round tea and scones. Someone began to play the piano, and the audience acknowledged the music by raising their voices above it ... (Beveridge and Wells 1949, pp. 47–8).

In contemporary clubs, too, noise-making is a powerful form of resistance. It conveys the feelings of the members and reminds their leaders of their accountability. Generally, this amount of protest is sufficient to preserve the status quo: the leaders stay, as do the members. Together they age and expire and the club becomes a memory to the relatively youthful remnant who move on, attaching themselves to a more vital organisation.

The timing of transitions

The crucial issue here is the transfer of authority. In traditional societies where age is the organising principle and the peer group the basic social unit, the movement into and out of office is a societal problem, managed collectively. At a certain point leadership roles are ceremonially relinquished by the ruling cohort and assumed by the next in line (see, for instance, Beattie 1964). In this society the timing of transitions is more an individual than an age-group problem, though response to the problem is sometimes made collectively. The National Federation of Retirement Pensioners' Associations has tried to halt the decline of the movement by introducing compulsory retirement from office at 80. This, it is thought, will defeat the problem of elderly married couples who not only hang on to senior posts but expel their opponents. Proposals to this effect have so far been outvoted by the over-80s on the national executive committee. It has also been suggested that elderly leaders should appoint younger deputies. But that would undermine the traditional basis of nomination and recruitment to office – a project for a group of friends and peers – and the suggestion has never been taken up.

The governing body of the Methodist church introduced a six-year rule to prevent elderly incumbents from hanging on to office. Church offices may be held for six years only, and two years must elapse before renomination. But the ruling does not extend to leadership in church societies. Hence more informal responses to the problem of age-transitions occur, such as coups and secessions by the younger element. In the club world there are occasional coups by factions who work within existing constitutional arrangements for succession.

On the evidence available, it would appear that the survival of a club or society depends upon the timely death of its leaders, timely in the sense that their departure from office occurs before the potential successors have disappeared as well. This point is born out by the contrasting fates of two clubs in the study. One of them finally collapsed after an unsuccessful appeal in the local press for 'anyone interested' to take over from the aged chairman and his wife before the club was officially wound up. The other club unexpectedly lost its chairman, a dynamic and powerful woman who 'had made the club great'. The large membership expected the club to carry on, 'as a monument to Mrs S', and a committee reshuffle produced her successor.

ELEVEN

Paths to friendship: possibilities for intervention

There are some clubs whose survival does not depend so crucially on the timing of leadership changes. In these clubs power relationships also take a different form, with a more obvious distance between the leaders and the members. These are the clubs financed and run by charitable organisations. In contrast to those clubs which are run by elected representatives of the members, these are staffed by voluntary workers under the direction of an organiser who is appointed by the charity.

Two of the clubs in the study fell into this category: a lunch club for elderly people and a Sunday afternoon club for people living alone (and by implication lonely and in need of company). They were run under the auspices of Age Concern. I was introduced to them by people encountered in the other clubs, who belonged to both. I thus came across them by chance, through the social networks of the elderly joiners in the study.

Whereas most of the associations in the study were run by old people for each other, those sponsored by the charitable organisations were staffed by volunteers who were on the whole younger than the beneficiaries although most were retired. The distinctive feature of the charitable clubs is the style of leadership. An analysis of the aims of the clubs and their leaders suggests that volunteer work, like activity in other clubs, is a strategy for ageing well. It has much in common with the way other club leaders and committee members cope with the vicissitudes of age.

Before discussing social processes in the Age Concern clubs in detail, this kind of work should be seen in an historical context. In recent decades a number of charitable organisations have devoted resources to setting up clubs, thereby extending peer group activities. They have done so in the belief that social interaction in a supportive setting, especially with age mates, brings special benefits to old people.

Goals of intervention

In 1952 the National Old People's Welfare Committee (NOPWC) published a handbook giving guidance to would-be founders of old-people's clubs and to clubs already in existence, then estimated at about 2,500. Getting old people out of the home and into the community, for friendly contact and communal pursuits, was paradoxically the best way for them to continue living at home independently. The feeling expressed in the handbook was that clubs met a general human need for social contact, for conversation and warmth.

More and more voluntary bodies have become involved in the provision of clubs for older people though the field in Britain is dominated by some very large ones such as Age Concern (the old NOPWC) and the Women's Royal Voluntary Service (WRVS). Twenty years after the publication of the NOPWC handbook the number of clubs had grown to about 7,000 (Tomlinson 1979), òne-third of them run by the WRVS. In 1977 the WRVS ran 132 all-day clubs, 1,891 afternoon and evening clubs and 93 clubs in local authority homes. The range of Age Concern provision at the national level is similar.

In Seatown, Age Concern runs three afternoon and seven luncheon clubs. Other charitable concerns which provide old people's clubs include the British Red Cross, the Rotary Club and a number of churches. Seatown Age Concern, which is exclusively concerned with the needs of this age group, is a large organisation employing five hundred voluntary workers and a number of paid staff. In addition to the clubs, it provides fitness classes, opportunities for craft work, and a range of personal services.

The aims of the charitable organisations in the provision of clubs have not changed much over the years. They seek to reduce social isolation and loneliness, seen as major scourges of old age, by introducing vulnerable old people to potential friends and providing pleasurable activities. They are inspired by a humanitarian and altruistic desire to improve the quality of older people's lives. Often the endeavour is motivated by a religious belief in the importance of helping the less fortunate. The style of intervention is supported by common-sense assumptions and the organising ability of well-meaning individuals.

Some clubs are, by all accounts, highly successful. Others are less so, even on their own terms. They all experience tensions commonly caused by conflicts of interest and perspective.

Tensions

The question of conflicting expectations held by old people and providers for old people is a central one that was identified in Darby and Joan clubs in Oxfordshire nearly forty years ago (Mogey 1956). It is still a central question. The organisers and recipients have different perceptions of leisure needs and of older people's capacity to run their affairs.

The problem over activities surfaces in the Age Concern clubs over misunderstandings about friendship. Members attend with friends and view the proceedings in terms of their capacity to promote the interests which friends share, by providing opportunities for interaction and talk. They form exclusive groupings but networks are extensive and overlapping. For club members, friendship is an intensely personal relationship which finds expression in communal activities in a public setting. Club leaders, on the the other hand, have an idealistic notion of friendship which embraces everyone in the club. It rests on a notion of friendly behaviour, summed up in the rejoiner, 'Look, sit *anywhere*. This is a friendly club'. Leaders refer unsympathetically to groupings of friends as 'cliques'. They attempt to resist the process of exclusive friendship formation by introducing newcomers to groups of friends and breaking groups up by seating arrangements designed to even-out physical spacing and social contact. In one case, trestle tables were thought to be the answer.

Years ago, the NOPWC recommended that organisers try whist drives to break up groups of friends. Committee members should also make personal approaches to each member to draw her out and integrate her into a larger group. Those members who resist the pressure to ignore friendship ties by closing their ranks are still regarded as selfish and self-interested. They are 'just being awkward', 'like children' rather than adults whom one might expect to be more public-spirited and generous. That members might naturally prefer to sit with their friends is reluctantly acknowledged, and only after the attempt to modify their preferred seating pattern has failed.

The different concepts of friendship held by members and organisers, discussed in Chapter Five, are a real source of difficulty. The organisers and volunteer helpers, inspired by Christian values of service and compassion, work with a belief in the importance of sharing the benefits of club life. No-one who is eligible and in need should be excluded. An important Christian principle is upheld in the belief that the club should be like a family, containing differences in a climate of love and tolerance. For the members, though, an open club is a contradiction in terms. A club without social boundaries or qualifications for admission loses its club-like qualities. In an instance in which this dilemma came to the fore, an elderly vagrant was finally ejected by the reluctant helper who felt that she was failing in her Christian duty but that the views of the other members must prevail. The members do not always get their own way, however. In one instance, an argument that they should have their own outing rather than combine forces with another Age Concern club was lost to the organiser whose view that 'we are all a happy family' prevailed.

Insensitivity to the friendship needs of members is reflected in the tendency to impose a timetable which interferes with preferred activities. While the interests of friends might be best served by continuing a game of cards or a satisfying conversation, there are other more appropriate items on the organiser's agenda. In a not untypical instance, an organiser interrupted a card game so that, at her instigation, a reluctant member might tell everyone of a recent experience on holiday – so that 'we can see what kindness there is about'. On this occasion the grumbles from annoyed card-players were quelled by a sharp rap on the table from the organiser, equally annoyed by the muttering at what she regarded as an entirely legitimate interruption. On another occasion players were most reluctant to finish their game during the piano interlude before tea, when they were expected to dance. On the observation of a helper that no-one was dancing, the organiser shouted loudly from the kitchen door, 'Come on, dance, get up, use those legs'. A half-hearted response by a few women who recognised the voice of authority drew a satisfied comment to the observers in the kitchen: 'There you are. That's what we're here for: to get them going!'

Members who are openly critical are regarded as ungrateful. In the same way, people who belong to several clubs at once are lacking in commitment, even disloyal. Multiple membership is not seen for what it is – a feature of a gregarious lifestyle – but as a weakness. It is a sign of acute need, the desperate search of the poor and lonely for company and treats. In fact, as we saw in Chapter Three, this is the lifestyle of the typical member. The truly isolated and lonely person for whom the club is intended is a rare occurrence.

The differences in ideas about appropriate activities arise from fundamental differences in aims. Club members do not always see eye-to-eye with organisers about the goals of the organisation. The early documents such as the NOPWC's were full of assumptions about the needs of old people which betrayed the relative youth of their authors. Old people, readers were told, do not like to sit and sip tea all the time. They do not like to sit in rows for they may not find their neighbour congenial. They are easily bored: a varied programme creates greater interest. The assumption seems to be that variety is stimulating and stimulation is a good thing. The exponents of these ideas did not, of course, benefit from current knowledge about the culture of clubs. In other ways too, the language and sentiments of the guidelines now appear to be very dated. The frequent occurrence of the word 'simple' ('a few simple games', 'a simple doll becomes a person to the old lady who has made her') strikes the modern reader as quaint if not ageist. But the club member appears to suffer from ageist attitudes even today. The experience of being treated as one of 'a bunch of nitwits' (Harrison 1975) is not unusual.

It is an attitude which colours not only the content of activities but their organisation too. The issue of leadership raises a number of problems. Although attitudes have changed since the days when the NOPWC could remind organisers that the old people themselves, at least the 65-year-olds among them, might well be able to run their own affairs, a gulf still exists between leaders and members on the issue of decision-making.

Age Concern clubs do not on the whole have elected committees. Activities are provided by voluntary helpers for the membership. One of the most striking features of the Age Concern clubs in the study is the lack of identification of the leader and her helpers with the members. Distance is preserved between the two groups by a variety of means. In terms of address a distinction is made between the leader and the rest. Miss Craddock, or at the most informal, Miss C, addresses her helpers and the beneficiaries by the first names. The seating arrangements also emphasise the social distance between people in the two categories. Miss C and her helpers do not sit down and chat, unlike the officials in other old people's clubs. The situation is not unique, however. The isolating effect of particular arrangements of tables and chairs has been noted in other clubs run by charitable bodies. 'The audience composed of small self-isolating sets of three or four people reflects the barriers to free communication between the committee and the members and is as much a defence by the group against the organisation as it is a defence by the officers against too close an identification with "their ladies"' (Mogey 1956).

The Darby and Joan Club in Oxford in the early 1950s demonstrated to the anthropologist a marked social distance between members and officers. The old people were treated in a kindly fashion, but firmly, as if they were children. Attempts to be friendly were defined as over-familiar and dealt with firmly. For example, a member who leaned forward and tickled a committee member who was pouring out the tea received a reprimand.

> There was a faint indrawn breath and then: 'You won't get a better cup of tea for doing that, you know.' The old people reacted to this with banter: 'Is it a good cup of tea then? We don't want it if it isn't good', a frame of mind which would be impossible amongst a group of equals doing things for themselves. (Mogey 1956)

The resemblance to contemporary practices is striking.

The position of the helpers is slightly ambiguous and they manage the gap by joking about it. They pretend that the work of looking after the members is hard labour, just a job, something they will be relieved to finish with at the end of the day. The banter is exchanged with one eye on the organiser and in her absence there is an air of conspiracy. But the banter itself underlines the difference in their status. The language of the formal parts of the programme is one of inclusion and exclusion: of us and you. The closing prayer is revealing: 'Thank you Lord for the fun we've had this afternoon ... [then to the members] You've enjoyed yourselves and we've enjoyed ourselves with you ... .'

What goes on in the kitchen where the members' tea is prepared is not their concern. The kitchen is the province of the helpers and entry to other people is forbidden 'for reasons of insurance'. At a lunch club in the study the very appearance of the helpers sallying forth from the kitchen clad in what appear to be aprons made of dustbin liners heightens the institutional atmosphere. The lack of identification is marked in some verbal exchanges which betray insensitivity to the feelings of particular individuals. In one instance the organiser publicly reprimanded a member who had no telephone for making the task of cancelling a meeting harder to accomplish. Identification with the organisation at the expense of individual members was revealed also in an exchange concerning an elderly couple who had recently met at a club meeting. Their wedding had been organised by the charity with full media coverage. The voluntary worker most involved was inclined to produce newspaper cuttings about the occasion and invite people to the forthcoming anniversary of 'our wedding' in the presence of the old couple and without consulting them. It seemed very much as if their lives had been taken over.

Resistance

Members resist the pressure to conform in a number of ways. The banter noted above masks the tension between helpers and recipients. A more obvious form of resistance is the failure to comply with commands. Continued noise-making and even raised voices limits the organiser's chance of being heard. When the request finally penetrates, compliance is reluctant: 'At games time the leader calls out "All change" for the card players to move from one table to the next so that different people will get to know each other but the members respond in a very half-hearted fashion' (Mogey 1956).

Occasionally there is a downright refusal. 'People come to sit with their friends and if they can't they won't come!' was the firm response at an Age Concern club to a request to change tables. On other occasions the conflict is muted by humour: 'We're glued to our chairs!' Although the more assertive members like to think that they simply ignore the pressure, it is recognised that there are limits on their freedom to manoeuvre. It is unreasonable to hang on too long to empty chairs 'for my friend' when the organiser is circulating with a new member who needs a seat. This rule explains the urgency of the initial flurry to find a table with enough seating for a group of friends. It lies behind the compulsion to arrive early. In most clubs people get there up to half an hour in advance but the situation in an Age Concern club in the study was exacerbated by a ruling that the doors should remain closed until five minutes before the meeting.

Seating is an issue in all clubs. But in clubs where the organisers are the elected representatives of the members the matter never reaches a head. Seating patterns are negotiated between rival groups of members and the accommodation of newcomers (of whom there are very few) is also a matter for negotiation.

Since tension exists in many clubs there are, clearly, features of the leadership role which sets the members apart. I have argued that this division rests on attitudes to ageing. In particular, the need to be active and in command creates rivalry between the leaders and the led, and distance between them. Another possibility is that the institutional positions of leader and member reflect differences of social class. The antagonism between the two groups might rest on differential access to material resources, power and cultural capital. A disproportionate number of the committee members were described as middle class, and the helpers in the charitable clubs are similarly privileged.

However, the point made earlier about the salience of social class in categorising old people is worth repeating. Social differences in the club and fellowship population are marginal. The similarities between members and leaders are greater than their differences, in class terms. Lifestyle, which cuts across social class in this age group, provides a more meaningful system of classification. The point is supported by an analysis of the backgrounds and motives of voluntary workers in the charitable clubs.

Volunteering as a way of life

In the Age Concern clubs the distinctiveness of the categories of helper and beneficiary masks certain similarities between them. Helpers, like the members, tend to be elderly widows. They live with various deprivations, employing much the same strategy for coping as the recipients of their services. Domestic and health problems are forgotten in the business of club life, whichever position one occupies. That one woman distributes the tea and another woman drinks it has less to do with capacity than with attitudes to giving and receiving help, with a popular association between receiving help and being old, and with a wish to care for others.

A woman who has difficulty in thinking of herself as old is deterred from using the services of an organisation so obviously associated with old age as an Age Concern club. Attendance at the club as a member would mean admitting to herself and advertising to others that she had become old. People with such a perspective attend the club not as members but as helpers. They maintain their sense of independence and integrity, and gain satisfaction from helping others and remaining socially useful as well as enjoying the benefits of club life: company, entertainment, a way of structuring time, a purpose for existence. Age Concern clubs are as valuable to the helpers as to the members themselves, and important in the same way. Through volunteering, active elderly people continue to participate in the community and contribute to the welfare of its members. The benefits of voluntary work overlap with those of paid employment. There is the additional advantage that, unlike the latter, there is no age limit to being a volunteer. Voluntary workers are often retired carers. Sometimes they have spent time in the caring professions as nurses or home helps. Generally they have cared for relatives at home. They are people who have time to fill and see in volunteering an occupation which meets their need to give, to continue caring, and to satisfy the demands of a lively social conscience: '*Someone* has to do it'.

For such people, attending an old people's club as a member might be socially unacceptable. To do so as a helper confers status and permits a sense of virtue. The motives for helping are thus similar to those of committee members in the independent clubs. Both kinds of work are an expression of a desire to age well in terms of the dominant model of ageing.

But the controls on leaders' behaviour seen operating in the independent clubs do not exist in those run by volunteers. Here, organisers who 'overstep the mark' are not responsive to pressure from the members. In order to function, Age Concern clubs require the help of volunteers who tend to have needs of their own. The helpers' needs sometimes interfere with the goals of the organisation. They take priority over those of the 'needy' people who sit waiting to be served.

The personal needs of those in positions of authority are not easily recognised and are difficult to accommodate. Given the ethos of service and self-sacrifice, it is often assumed that volunteers have an inexhaustible supply of spare time. Their goodwill tends to be taken for granted. The need for a sense of achievement and the need to care for others produces helpers who are vulnerable to exploitation. They commonly experience difficulty in refusing requests for help and risk being overloaded with commitments. The risk of over-involvement in voluntary work is thus heightened by social pressure to be useful and by a personal difficulty in setting limits to involvement. Some volunteers set clear boundaries around what they are prepared to do. If the work fits in with other leisure activities it is taken on. 'I help at the Sunday Club because it fits in nicely before church. I'm afraid I can't do more than that. I'm not all that young myself and I can't afford to get too involved!' Unless they have a legitimate reason to restrict themselves in this way, however, maintaining these boundaries can be difficult. Always in need of extra volunteers, organisers put pressure on their existing workers to take on more commitments. It is assumed that helpers with special skills – photography, piano-playing – will continue indefinitely and will also respond to increased demands.

In some kinds of voluntary work there is, not surprisingly, a high turn-over. The pressures of over-commitment, health crises, and problems at home encourage people to drop out. But withdrawal is not easy for older volunteers who lack other sources of fulfilment. While working for the charity, they have the satisfaction of doing something worthwhile, making social contacts and working in a team. The sense of being active and alive is a compelling reason to go on.

Practical implications

The importance of voluntary work as a personal experience and its place in welfare provision in Britain is well known. Concern with the quality of life of vulnerable people (older people are commonly regarded as one such group) is currently expressed in many circles. Such concern has produced a variety of projects designed to benefit older people, ranging from the efforts of voluntary bodies such as Age Concern to publicly funded welfare facilities and national research on different kinds of provision.

Academic research such as the study described in these pages has implications for social policy and practice concerning older people, though that was not its primary aim. An anthropological study of friendship, for instance, offers an understanding of the meaning of friendship and the basis on which such relationships are founded. It raises questions which are pertinent to welfare schemes aiming to create friendship opportunities.

One of the questions arising in connection with friendship is why its benefits are available to some older people and not others. There are two possible explanations. The first is that people's social networks are a product of choice. The second is that circumstances beyond an individual's control limited the possibilities for friendship. Being without friends is either a favoured option or a product of such unfortunate eventualities as relocation or bereavement.

The presence or absence of friends has been seen in these pages as a matter of lifestyle. Friendship patterns reflect the preference for passing time in the company of other people. People with extensive and active friendship networks have chosen to adopt a gregarious lifestyle which meets their particular needs. Such a view contradicts popular ideas and some professional thinking about social networks. According to these, the pattern of relationships is linked to life-span changes. The absence of intimate relationships is more a product of changing social and personal circumstance that preferred lifestyle. Loss is a feature of old age and people suffer the attenuation of ties as friends die or health, mobility and housing arrangements interfere with patterns of sociability.

The two views have different implications for social policy and practice. If the pattern of association is a matter of choice it might be inappropriate to consider intervening unless help is sought to strengthen existing ties and facilitate further interaction with chosen associates. If, on the other hand, older people suffer from unwelcome changes which could be reversed by judicious intervention then such intervention is justified. In this case it is entirely appropriate to try to draw isolated people into activities which put them in touch with others and thereby improve the quality of their lives.

Several questions arise here. First, can intervention by charitable organisations and professional groups be justified in terms of what is known about the causes and consequences of loneliness? If it can, what is the most appropriate form of intervention?

Social bonds and mental health

The literature of social gerontology supports the idea that intervention in the lives of lonely old people is a good thing. Research suggests that throughout the life course interaction with others is what sustains the individual in a variety of social roles and identities. Although self-conceptions are relatively stable by adulthood, they must be affirmed from time to time by other people. Thus, the more one interacts with others or is exposed to the responses of others the greater the opportunity for reaffirming specific role identities. Social activity in general and interpersonal – preferably intimate – activity in particular offer channels for support or reinforcement of one's self-concept. The consequences of losing such support include social breakdown and psychological malfunction (Kuypers and Bengtson 1976; Lemon et al. 1976). In terms of health and illness, as we have seen, the value of social contact lies in the capacity of associates (especially intimate ones) to provide a reference group, to foster awareness of one's health status and to establish guidelines for behaviour in the circumstances of ill-health.

There is an extensive literature on the link between social networks and health. Mental health, in particular, is seen to be related to the experience of intimacy but links have recently been made with physical health too. Intimate relationships are characterised by emotional intensity, self-disclosures and a high degree of personal involvement. Individuals need to experience intimacy in order to be emotionally secure, well-adjusted and have high morale – the components of mental health. The absence of intimate relationships has been identified as a factor in depression in old age (Murphy 1982). The very existence of an intimate tie, however infrequently activated, has a protective quality arising from the feeling of reciprocal warmth, trust and a sense of being valued. In Murphy's study of depressed old people, those who had never experienced it were the most disadvantaged. People, who had experienced intimacy in the past but no longer did so were less vulnerable; those who continued to engage in intimate exchanges were least likely to succumb to depression.

There is strong evidence that social support is perhaps the single most important factor in constructive coping. The particular kind of social support which is most effective is that which maintains and enhances a person's self-esteem. People in contact with at least one other person who cares about them and knows how to convey their concern, are less liable to succumb to stress-related illnesses (Grant 1988). The condition of being without such benefits is experienced as loneliness.

The extent of loneliness at any age is difficult to establish, partly for methodological reasons (Wenger 1983). But it is a serious problem for perhaps a quarter of people in retirement. They include a disproportionate number of the very old, the widowed and, surprisingly, people living with adult children and the still-married. The incidence of loneliness in the last two categories comes as a surprise. The assumption is that people's emotional needs will be met by family members, particularly spouses. The evidence points, however, to the importance of intimate relationships outside the family for satisfaction in life (Abrams 1974; Lehr 1987).

Contact with friends serves to reduce loneliness and increase feelings of usefulness, unlike those with kin, especially adult children. The latter do little to sustain or improve morale; it is other members of the social network, particularly friends, who perform that task (Bengtson and Kuypers 1985; Wenger 1987; Jerrome 1990). Friendship has a special role to play in retirement. Even distant friendships have a life-enhancing quality. Telephone calls might be the only contact with old friends, but 'it's lovely when you hear from them. You know that you are both still alive and getting on with your lives. People ring after a long time and you know they've been thinking about you – a nice feeling'. A telephone conversation does more than provide a few moments' pleasure and information about the activities of people the older person cares about. It offers confirmation of existence: I am thought about, therefore I am. In addition, the knowledge of a peer's activities adds continuity and a sense of perspective to one's own ageing experience. Long-established friends have a special role to play in the ageing process, however infrequent and indirect the contact.

Friendship, as we have seen, has a protective quality which brings it close to kinship in the response to ill-health and disability. Friends care for each other, as well as caring about each other, in often quite practical ways. But the affection between friends, which is responsible for this caring attitude, has a distinctive quality. Unlike kin, friends are chosen. This makes their consideration and loyalty particularly valuable, as benefits freely given and therefore a measure of esteem. The very existence of friends is therefore beneficial, promoting self-esteem and a sense of worth.

The precise relationship between loneliness, depression and ill-health is difficult to establish. Loneliness appears to be associated with ill-health, measured in terms of the amount of contact with health professionals and the use of medicines (Asiel 1987). Feelings of loneliness are consistently associated with general disability (Jones, Victor and Vetter 1985). Lonely people are more vulnerable to physical disorders and diseases. Lack of psychological resistance acts in a number of ways to increase the chance of becoming ill (Grant 1988). At the simplest level the unhappy person may neglect herself and thus have reduced physical resistance. In addition, it is suggested that when a person is anxious or psychologically distressed, the body's metabolism is significantly altered. Biochemical interactions which would normally take place only in emergencies take place continuously, resulting in damage to vital organs such as the heart. Increasingly research in psychogeriatric medicine suggests that emotional states such as severe loneliness and affective disorders such as depression affect the metabolism, producing vascular and cerebral disease (Murphy 1987). The condition of loneliness is viewed by some analysts as a potentially fatal disease which corrodes the personality to a point where remedial action is impossible. In such cases death follows from stress-related illness or suicide (Lake 1980). The literature, then, provides ample justification for attempts to reduce loneliness in old age.

Patterns of intervention

The next question for consideration is how a state of loneliness can be reversed. One of the issues raised by the study of friendship is how far this relationship *can* be created or facilitated by third-parties rather than left to emerge spontaneously between two people who find each other attractive. We are reminded here of the discussion about the nature of friendship and the extent to which it differs from other intimate ties. The suggestion is that it is unique. Its uniqueness lies in the basis on which it is formed. Friends are chosen, rather than acquired by birth like kin or by proximity like neighbours. There are similarities between these categories of primary group tie: the incidence of reciprocal help and exchange of other services brings friendship close to kinship. But generally the content is specialised. Friendship is distinguished by the exchange of confidences and the pursuit of pleasure which occurs more easily between peers, with similar attitudes and life histories.

The basis in mutual attraction supports a popular view that friends are not so much made as discovered. Potential friends quickly recognise in each other the qualities that make them eligible for friendship. Friends 'hit it off'. This is not to deny that assumption of the friendship role comes after an initial negotiation of rules or that there are elements of the skilled performance in the way friends work to overcome subsequent difficulties.

There is a view in social psychology that friendship is a skilled performance which can be taught to people who find interpersonal relationships difficult. Such a view underpins various professional interventions. An example is taken from a project developed in New Zealand. On the evidence of the Auckland day centre it is possible to help older people who are isolated and lonely to achieve a state of mutual support and trust, through skilled team work.

The Auckland programme was set up to help people who suffered the damaging consequences, both physical and psychological, of loneliness (Grant 1986; Grant 1988). Often on the brink of depression they were in urgent need of meaningful social contact. The impressive results achieved by the team of workers led by a psychiatrist rested on a carefully integrated activity schedule, one day a week.

The programme is built round a variety of different elements. On arrival the eighteen members of the group are welcomed and given a cup of tea before a one-hour work period. Work needs to come first for this cohort and the knowledge that one still has the ability to make and create is a valuable part of the recreation of a positive self-image. Next comes an exercise session, timed to relax limbs stiffened from sitting still for an hour. If members wish, there is a musical accompaniment or a walk outside.

The final hour of the morning is devoted to the group session. Members sit in a circle so that everyone can see and hear. Contributions are regulated: only one person may speak at a time. After the formal introductions (if there are new members) comes a sharing of common news about personal events – birthdays, sickness, sorrowful events and happy ones. Sickness and bereavement are especially noted. As time goes on, members become very concerned for one another and provide comfort. After a short business session the members take part in a discussion or problem-solving exercise alone or in pairs to sharpen up their social and intellectual skills.

They involve thinking, the use of memory, and speaking in the group about one's own thoughts and ideas.

In the middle of the day members share a meal. It is leisurely but formally laid out. Conversations which take place around the table can continue in the free time afterwards while the meal is cleared away. The afternoon is spent in light entertainment. The emphasis is on enjoyment and fun. The content reflects members' own interests for it is their suggestions which are the basis for the programme. As with the old people's clubs in England there have been games, music, singing, visiting speakers, concerts and discussions. The afternoon is drawn to a close with another cup of tea, then the members are driven home.

Although the centre was clearly achieving some of its goals in the early years, a formal evaluation was felt to be a good idea. This took the form of a controlled experiment. The three measures of success used in the assessment were number of social contacts, morale, and the absence of depression. Gains were achieved by the members of the day centre in all three areas. All reported increases in the number of telephone calls, friends and visits. More than half reported substantial changes in activities involving being more adventurous. In all cases people had become more outgoing and less anxious, less bored, lonely and unhappy. The incidence of depression decreased markedly. The members themselves felt that they had become more responsible.

Most felt that the group session just before lunch was the most important part of the day. The exchange of views with peers on a range of contemporary issues led to an increase in the range and quality of relationships.

Barriers to intimacy

On the evidence of the Auckland programme it is possible to create opportunities for dyadic friendship by exposing isolated people to potential friends. This is best accomplished in a therapeutic setting where loneliness is not a stigma. In the conventional club setting the lonely person is handicapped in the pursuit of friendship. Caught in a downward spiral of isolation and loneliness the lonely person is paradoxically disqualified from membership of the friendship network.

In spite of their hopes, the charitable clubs must be said to have failed to create intimacy where none existed. People do not go to their clubs in the expectation of finding intimacy. The acutely lonely and isolated people for whom the clubs were set up are conspicuously absent. For the rest, who come accompanied and for whom club-going is an activity of friendship, the maintenance of close ties in the context of the club is problematic.

At the Auckland day centre, by contrast, the professionals appear to have succeeded in creating an environment conducive to intimacy. Within the group, members have accepted newcomers and welcomed them fully as friends. Furthermore, a special capacity for friendship involving unequal contributions and rewards has emerged. After a year or two people with special problems were brought in. Some of the more long-standing members were able to offer sustained care to them. This is in marked contrast to behaviour in conventional settings where the active and well integrated old person tends to distance herself from the frail and needy (Hockey 1985, 1989; Gubrium 1975; Hornum 1987; Jerrome 1990). The sustained ability to care for each other, and the valued friendships which arise out of this arrangement, can be understood in terms of the philosophy of the group and the acknowledged basis on which each member becomes involved. The established members of the day centre have themselves received the sort of support which has transformed their lives. There is no loss of face in admitting it and extending this support to others. In addition, a strong group identity affords protection to individual members who might otherwise fear taking on potentially burdensome obligations.

Despite the apparent success of the case given above, therapeutic intervention is not without its difficulties. In her account of the Auckland day centre Grant stresses the crucial role of the key professional, the day centre supervisor. Other reports of professional intervention emphasise the delicacy of the worker's position and the special skills needed to manage this kind of intervention successfully. Sensitivity, flexibility, the ability to listen, awareness of group dynamics and high degree of skill in interpersonal relationships are essential qualifications. In addition there must be some openness to the painful issues which come to the fore concerning ageing and death, confronting not just the group members but the professional as well.

The professional worker needs to be able to act simply as a resource person, supplying specific practical help without sapping the group's autonomy. The greatest temptation appears to be to take on leadership roles (Biegel, Shore and Gordon 1984; Harrison 1975) or to overdo the parent role (Grant 1988). In addition to the nurturing behaviour which is required of the supervisor or group leader at the beginning, she must also be capable of the gradual letting go or phasing out of the helper role as the elderly people being to regain their independence. The success of the programme requires them to begin to make decisions, initiate activities and take control of the group. They need to feel competent and in charge of their own lives and to be able to embark upon the final life tasks ahead.

The analogy with the parent-child relationship is an apt one. In the professionally-run groups the ultimate goal is the achievement of independence by the participants. The parent-child relationship – at least in its nurturing form – suggests a parallel with the careful fostering of autonomy in adolescent children by their parents. The model is less suitable for the organiser and beneficiary in Age Concern clubs. There, progress to independence within the club is not on the agenda though there is the hope that an enhanced social life will lead to a general improvement in morale and well-being. Instead the issues of discipline and conformity loom large. If the parent-child analogy means anything at all in this context, the voluntary organiser reminds us of the critical parent whose own needs require that the child remains in a state of dependence.

In both the charitable and professionally-run club, control is an issue which leaders and helpers must address. Letting go or hanging on, the leaders' particular relation to authority reflects the extent of their personal investment in the job. Whereas the professional can in a sense retire with honour, the voluntary workers' needs for an occupation, an outlet for affection, an expression of their Christian principles, a sense of virtue and a justification for existence make it harder for them to accept that the beneficiaries could sometimes get on better without them. Observation of club meetings offers evidence of sets of rival interests being advanced with more or less subtlety. The battle is waged every Sunday afternoon with minor victories or defeats on either side.

But research shows that all types of intervention are needed and their popularity with the members demonstrates their effectiveness. Thinking of the charitable associations in particular, the tensions described earlier should not be exaggerated. They could be overcome quite easily if voluntary organisations chose to operate on more egalitarian principles. Given the current ideological emphasis on autonomy and selfhood in the wider society, it could be argued that a change towards self-management is desirable. The ideal of self-management through skilled intervention does not deprive the voluntary worker of a useful role, neither would it remove the *raison d'être* of the charitable organisation.

On the other hand, it could be argued that already the style of organisation in such clubs permits an adequate degree of autonomy to elderly beneficiaries. Simply by their existence the clubs allow the old person to assert her independence in choosing a place for herself and resisting the pressure towards infantilism by making gestures against authority. Clubs founded and run by bodies such as Age Concern are a valuable addition to the range of social opportunities which exist for older people. A comparison with those provided by professionals and those of old people themselves indicates that all enhance the older person's prospects of engaging in the vital process of relating to peers.

Conclusion

This chapter shows the uses that can be made of academic research. The literature on loneliness and mental health provides a justification for intervention by well-meaning individuals who react to what they see as the plight of elderly people by setting up clubs and day centres. Anthropological research can play a part in the evaluation of such schemes, if that is required. The collecting of detailed evidence 'from the inside', paying particular attention to subjective meanings and individual experience, brings a capacity to identify rival perspectives and sources of conflict.

What the present study shows is that the conventional club can and does provide opportunities for the already well-connected old person to extend the supportive network. Equally important, it provides contact with other members of the peer group. This is a benefit enjoyed by all members, even the few lonely and isolated people who lack the more intense involvement of dyadic friendships. The solidarity and shared consciousness of members of the cohort creates an environment that is comfortable, supportive and stimulating. Friendly relations in the club setting – less intense, than friendship – are of some value. There is justification for the use of public resources to assist those people and groups – old people themselves or charitable organisations who would work on their behalf – who already enjoy this kind of interaction. More important, there is a case for advancing the interests of lonely and isolated members of the elderly population by supporting those projects which try in a realistic way to renew their ties with peers.

The capacity to identify goals and relate them to outcomes suggests a practical role for anthropologists. It is one which in Britain has been defined and developed in recent years as research interests have extended beyond conventional areas of study, coming closer to home. The formation in the early 1980s of Social Anthropologists in Social and Community Work (SASCW), part of the British Association for Social Anthropologists in Policy and Practice, illustrates this process. The work of the group is a reminder 'of the fruitful link which can exist between academic research and practical concerns.

TWELVE

Conclusion

In these pages I have tried to show how elderly people in old people's clubs and Christian fellowships make sense of their social world. Their current preoccupations can be discerned from the activities shared with peers and from the strategies adopted to achieve personal goals. Through these activities the ageing process is exposed to scrutiny. It is difficult to convey the vitality and intensity of life in the setting of old people's organisations. The richness of the experience for participants and its importance in their lives is summed up in the fervent remark, 'It's a life-line!'

'That's what it's all about'

On the basis of the literature and an analysis of members of selected old-age organisations, I have suggested that joiners are distinguished from non-joiners in several respects. They are socially connected; they have high morale; and they share a model of ageing which stresses struggle and resistance. Through associating with peers in old people's clubs and Christian fellowships the typical member – a widow in her 70s – enjoys a range of benefits. Already advantaged in terms of health, income, social contacts and morale, she reaps additional benefits of a social, psychological and practical nature. Companionship, moral and practical support, recognition of her goodness and worth, and confirmation of identity, are achieved through the formal weekly meetings and informal interaction with peers. Club-going is a means of self-expression and a way of life. Through participation in club culture the member is located in a particular cultural and historical context with other members of her birth cohort. The pattern of multiple member-ship produces social networks which are both extensive and close-knit. Relationships extend across clubs and fellowships, providing knowledge of and contact with a wide range of people.

The set of shared understandings and values evident in the culture of old-age organisations binds participants together as members of a moral community which transcends differences of gender and social class. To-gether, old people establish rules for conduct within the peer group and models of old age which offer prescriptions for behaviour in all situations. Appropriate responses to age-related losses are collectively defined.

But the social construction of old age within the elderly peer group must be understood in the broader cultural context. This point is underlined in an examination of ageing within the age-mixed setting of the church. The subjective experience of ageing in both age-mixed and age-segregated settings is subject to a variety of cultural influences. Age is used in different ways to promote personal and organisational interests. A degree of cultural vagueness provides scope for manipulation and innovation. But the degree of flexibility is limited by the need for confirmation of identity by other participants.

Despite being members of a single normative system, members enjoy a degree of latitude in the construction of ageing identities. Within the peer group differences occur in personal ecology, or strategies for conserving dwindling resources. The ideal response to ageing is resistance and struggle. Joining an organisation is proof of the ability to cope with ill-health and restricted movement to lead an active, independent life. It also reduces in significance the power of death. Taking an active role in the management of an organisation brings even greater rewards. Ageing well, in terms of the resistance model which dominates beliefs about age in club and fellowship, is a virtue.

The preoccupation with health and fitness, with activity and resistance to the encroachments of age, achieves collective expression in formal meetings and individual expression in informal talk and activities. The pursuit of virtue through conformity to group standards of behaviour is understood in terms of the broader situation of this group of old people: retired, widowed, and marginal to the concerns of younger people. They are experiencing a state that has (in a work-oriented culture) been described misleadingly as rolelessness, and that has involved a shift in the basis of self-evaluation. In the literature this phase is identified as a liminal period, a time of uncertainty and role confusion, much like adolescence. At times like this the peer group assumes significance in the provision of support based on shared experience, in the definition of reality and in socialisation to new roles. Collectively, members of the peer group confront problems of identity and purpose. Answers to the questions, 'Who are we?' 'What do we stand for?' are sought in the features of resilience, solidarity and conservatism which distinguish this group from outsiders: old people with more passive lifestyles, and youth.

Through old-age organisations generational interests are expressed. In their associations old people identify with peers and dissociate themselves from younger people. In weekly ritual performances they assert their moral superiority over younger generations. Club culture appears to be associated with particular age cohorts. It expresses the interests of people born early in the century, experiencing the Depression of the 1930s and the Second World War as young adults. The link between club culture and generational interests helps to account for a curious phenomenon: the decline and disappearance of clubs. Organisations appear to age with their members. As the founding cohort goes into decline, so does the club or fellowship: continuity is difficult to achieve.

The issue of continuity involves recruitment on the one hand and leadership on the other. This issue was approached through the content of inter-actions within old-age organisations and the participants' own constructions of reality. I was struck by the powerful sense of collective identity and moral superiority underpinning the organisations. An attempt to account for the pattern of decline was, therefore, made first in terms of the attitudes and preferences of the cohorts who dominate the declining organisations. My conclusions here are tentative. They rest on an historical analysis which relies in part on the personal recollections of informants. It appears, however, that despite claims of a shared past, solidarity rests more on a unifying myth of hardship than on common objective circumstances. In view of the methodological difficulties involved, an explanation of decline in terms of cohort-historical factors must be offered with strong caveats.

A more satisfactory line of argument concentrated on social processes within the organisations themselves. In particular, it focused on models of ageing and their translation into personal strategies. On this interpretation, organisational decline is attributed to a model of ageing which stresses activity and involvement and produces a reluctance in leaders to relinquish their control to younger, fitter members. Given the range of data, such an explanation is more convincing than one which focuses on cohort historical factors. The notion of personal strategies also makes sense of internal divisions in the club and fellowship populations, which appear to be related less to cohort or generation or social class than to social age.

All in all, old-age associations serve a variety of purposes. On the evidence of this study, they can be viewed as vehicles for the expression of generational consciousness, as ritual gatherings which give form and meaning to old age, as arenas for the acquisition of virtue and self-esteem, as sources of companionship and sociability, and as contexts for the activities of friendship.

Clubs and fellowships – the individuals in them, the groups they represent, the buildings and equipment, the ideas they express – are objects of attachment. Attachment in the psychological sense of strong feelings (both positive and negative) and emotional intensity characterises members' relations with each other, with the group and with the physical environment. It is sometimes assumed by younger people that with the loss of significant relationships the potential for attachment diminished through the lifespan. But though the objects of attachment may change, people go on being attached – to people, to groups and organisations, to beliefs and values, to places and possessions, and to the self. Feelings towards the object of attachment may change from positive to negative but its importance continues, growing stronger with the passage of time. This is evident in the relationships where attraction has disappeared but where the other person is crucial to identity, providing a reason for existence and continuity between past and present. In the setting of the club and fellowship it is apparent in the strength of feeling towards seating patterns, towards the traditional beliefs and values expressed in the programme, and towards the association itself, which commands loyalty and commitment year after year.

The strength of attachment rests on the organisation's continued capacity to meet a variety of needs. It is a source of integration, providing a sense of belonging to the peer group and to a social network of intimates and acquaintances. It gives a sense of autonomy, since participation is voluntary, the result of personal choice. Whether active or passive, the style of involvement is personal, and the meetings are a vehicle for self-expression. Participation enhances self-esteem by enabling the members to acquire virtue through the public accomplishment of daily routines and conformity to group standards. Since ageing is a competitive affair, doing so successfully in the public arena of the club is a source of social status within the peer group. The sense of security which accompanies these benefits is further strengthened by membership of a moral community. Members believe in the rightness of their own position, in the importance of a set of values and in conformity to shared expectations.

The peer group offers a view of reality which incorporates issues of time and change. Personal change and decline, similar in its linear quality to irreversible negative change in society itself, is set against a background of timeless and unchanging routines and social practices within the organisation. In the presence of peers, organisation members are able to accomplish developmental tasks made difficult in age-mixed settings. Together they deal with problems of ill-health and loss, with continuity and change, and with death and dying.

There is resistance to physical decline. The need, in this culture, to be *in* the world, to be a social entity, permits an openness to the possibility of physical extinction but not to social frailty, which is the antithesis of life. The ambivalence to decline produces a need to live in the present. An orientation to the present rather than the future gives added impetus to collective rituals which emphasise the cyclical nature of time.

Old people in this setting are dealing with fundamental existential problems which are intensely personal but subject to cultural forces. At the same time they find release of a sort not perhaps available elsewhere. In the sheltered setting of the peer group they are free to enjoy cohort-specific amusements in a manner which characterises peer relations from childhood onwards: spontaneous, uninhibited and childlike.

The meaning of participation

The recurrent statement 'that's what it's all about', confers meaning on participation in old people's clubs. It is prompted by the need to find an answer to existential problems which beset people at any age but perhaps achieve greater urgency towards the end of life. I have suggested that substantial agreement exists in the club population about such things as the importance of friendship, about being active, about ways of behaving among peers, and about the value of tradition. The traditional moral order and models of successful ageing are upheld equally firmly in the fellowship population. I argued that members of old-age organisations are distinguished from non-members by virtue of their adherence to these values and their symbolic expression in distinctive forms of activity. But the notion of consensus and uniformity must not be taken too far. Members share a lifestyle, a particular way of disposing of their time. But a range of meanings is attached to shared activities. Furthermore, while organisations are strong objects of attachment for some members, for others the attachment is to club-going as a way of life, rather than to particular gatherings.

Attendance at meetings is a chosen activity involving judgement, discrimination, positive commitment and an active stance. Multiple membership means attendance at a variety of meetings and social events and can also involve additional commitments: committee work, the preparation of items for sales, and so on. Club-going and to a lesser extent membership of fellowships and other organisations has for these reasons been described as a way of life, a dominant concern in the lives and thoughts of adherents. The concept of lifestyle is useful in differentiating between joiners and non-joiners. It is more meaningful as a basis for social differentiation in old age than social class. But we can take it further to distinguish between people within the club and fellowship population. The population of joiners has a common lifestyle viewed in terms of structure and content. Joiners play the same roles and engage in similar activities in the setting of their associations. But in terms of the meaning they attach to these processes variations occur.

For some people the primary goal seems to be to pass the time. This is a need which is recognised and articulated at all levels of the organisation, from the relatively passive member who gives this as a reason for attendance to the occasional club leader who concludes the meeting with the remark, 'Well, that's passed a couple of hours, hasn't it?' Leaders, on the whole, attach a different meaning to participation. For them it is an opportunity to help those less fortunate than themselves, and to use administrative and social skills. For other leaders in the more instrumental clubs, such as the politically active Federation branches, it is a question of changing the world, working towards a more egalitarian, less ageist social system. Fellowship members, too, find a meaning for participation in the instrumental and expressive goals of evangelism and spiritual communion respectively.

In attending to meaning rather than just the range of leisure roles and the content of leisure activities, we recognise that lifestyles are a product of personal strategies for successful ageing. The pattern of voluntary association described here is a strategy for ageing well, for accommodating change in a way which ensures continuity of self and lifestyle in the face of events which would erode them. There is a shared belief in the value (and virtue) of being active and keeping going, a process which benefits from the presence of witnesses, rivals and fellow sufferers.

In pursuit of the broad goal of an active old age, a variety of individual strategies is adopted to promote personal interests. The degree of involvement in organisational affairs is carefully arranged to match personal capacity and reflect priorities. Whether energy is spent or conserved depends on the range of commitments and on the pattern of investments over a lifetime. An important factor is the presence or absence of social pressure. In general there is room for manoeuvre in the construction of age identities and social roles but in some settings the old compete with youth on unequal terms to have their definition of the situation accepted. The age-mixed grouping of the church is one such setting. There, older people who conform to the activity model of ageing and whose service is functional in advancing the aims of the organisation are esteemed. They are rewarded with deference as embodiments of the highest values and as cultural resources in themselves. Although their performance is sometimes difficult to sustain they are under pressure to continue. Other old people whose interests are best served by abstention from involvement collude with younger people to perpetuate the status quo.

Clubs and fellowships have been treated as belonging to the same category, having similar outcomes for their members. Indeed, the similarities in experience of members of the two types of organisation seem to override the differences. They have common generational interests, adopting a similar moral stance in relation to social change and its advocates. They share a model of ageing which emphasises activity and resistance. Above all, they participate in a common lifestyle, in which voluntary association with peers in formal settings is central. But the differences are also important. Elderly men and women in the Christian fellowships enjoy an additional sense of purpose. They are part of an enterprise which does not relegate them to the margins, although it is age-mixed. In this respect the church differs from most age-mixed social worlds, which tend to be dominated by youthful adherents. Old people's presence is crucial in this enterprise. They are the repositories of cultural values, much like elders in those traditional societies which tend to be held up in the West as models of positive age relations. Within the religious community old people as a group are accepted on their own terms. Their strength rests on the congruity between the traditional moral order and the world view of Christianity. As an age-integrated social system the church offers established age roles and identities. Social mechanisms exist to ease the transition from one stage of church career to the next, and such changes are legitimated by a belief system which stresses personal service, cooperation and self-sacrifice in pursuit of instrumental goals. Issues of time and change, of continuity and the transfer of authority are dealt with in a ritual context which enables participants to confront and to some extent resolve personal dilemmas. The ontological security enjoyed by old people in the church is offset by the way in which their identification with an organisation in decline (the church in twenti-eth-century Britain, and the fellowships within it) compounds losses on different fronts. This entanglement is complex. The experience of ageing in the church highlights what for gerontologists is a critical analytical problem: that of disentangling the process of ageing from the process of history.

Whether in the church or outside it, old people in organisations – perhaps all old people – are engaged in a search for social integrity. They aspire to behave in ways which are consistent with their best images of themselves: as caring friends, as independent-minded parents, as responsi-ble association members, as old people who cope with difficulties. All aspects of behaviour are reinterpreted to preserve the integrity of the individual in those relationships which are most important to him or her. Friendship is one of the most vital in the range held by this particular set of old people. Thus the way illness is managed must conform to standards of friendship behaviour. The healthy partner should show concern and give advice; the frail should consult her friend and accept the advice she offers. The meaning of death, similarly, is sought in terms of the pattern of existing investments. When the reciprocal relationship between friends breaks down near death, friendship becomes problematic. In the presence of frailty, friendship must be offered free. The gift is acknowledged in the gratitude of the dying partner and in the surviving friend's sense of virtue mixed with grief at the loss of a valued relationship. The meaning of death lies in its capacity to express and affirm the value of friendship between friends, kinship between kin, neighbourliness among neighbours and so on.

The notion of social integrity offered here is centred on role perform-ance in an interactive setting: other people are required for its attainment. The pursuit of integrity is a constant feature of interaction among old people in groups. In the act of attaining it they find other things too: companionship, interest, a good time in the company of peers. Together they reinforce each others' prospects of a healthy old age. Friendship is a major resource and an aid to survival.

Theoretical perspectives and future needs

At the most basic level I have attempted to expose the lives and concerns of a particular group of old people, offering a mass of descriptive detail. The detailed account or ethnography of old-age organisations adds to our understanding at one level. We learn what goes on, how old people live, what symbolic systems they elaborate for themselves. At another level – the level of explanation – the study helps to account for certain features of the social structure. It offers suggestions as to why old people join formal organisations with their peers. But it raises more questions than it answers.

One suggestion was that peer grouping can be understood in terms of status: the differential between age groups, inconsistencies over a lifetime. I argued that in their associations old people engage in a competitive process of survival; that identification with peers is a way of coming to terms with status inconsistencies, with physical decline, with role ambiguity and with a change in the basis of self-evaluation. Much effort is spent in comparing their own performance with other people's in terms of a model of successful ageing. The achievement of status in the peer group is consistent with the success ethos of the wider society. I argued that the peer group is engaged in competition for social status with other age groups, partly to avoid the risk of dependency, a stigmatised state. The moral stance of the older generation in the company of their peers is in part a strategy to enhance the status of the group.

This assertion raises questions about old-age organisations not included in the study. Extending the argument to more instrumental groupings such as the Gray Panthers and the University of the Third Age (U3A), we might expect a similar strategy to uphold the status of the group. As the expressive organisations adopt a moral stance, so the instrumental organisations might develop a system which reflects their particular identities. Thus the intellectual stance of U3A might be seen as the equivalent of the moral stance of the old people's clubs. Indeed, if we look closely we might find members of the National Federation of Retirement Pensioners' Associations and U3A claiming their share of cultural resources with the intensity observed in the struggle to control values in the old people's clubs and fellowships. In the case of the former, however, the resources are not values but political and intellectual skills: power and knowledge.

To put these speculations to the test there needs to be a detailed investigation of the whole range of old-age organisations. We need to ask more questions about the role of such age-based groupings in expressing beliefs about age. In the absence of a detailed analysis we can only speculate on their significance for the experience of ageing. Pursuing the line of argument developed in the preceding chapters it seems likely that in other settings, too, old people engage in the essentially competitive process of survival. Just as the clubs and fellowships are seen to play a significant part in the social construction of old age and in the articulation of beliefs about age differences, so the other more instrumental groupings are likely to be crucial in the ageing experience of their members.

A closer study of the establishment and growth of old-age organisations might tell us something also about the emergence of age categories and the transformation of social categories into social groups – people who recognise common interests and feel the need to promote them symbolically.

There is a related question which the present study only touches upon. Britain is an age-segregated society. To what extent is the cultivation of generational distinctiveness in the elderly peer group a cause or a consequence of age segregation? Do old people associate with each other defensively in response to their marginalisation by the rest of society? Or is the pattern of segregation initiated by them in preference for association with peers?

A similar kind of intellectual problem occurs in respect of club and fellowship rituals. On the one hand we can see them as definitional rituals, ways in which old people together establish an identity and a purpose. On the other hand they can be viewed as part of the competition for scarce resources, as an aspect of community formation or the politics of age relations. But these are two sides of the same coin. The alternatives reflect merely a difference of emphasis, of theoretical orientation. We can understand social processes structurally and culturally. The cultural dimension directs attention towards beliefs and values, systems of meaning rather than the social structure or the distribution of power and wealth. The cultural approach encourages an interpretation of events in the elderly peer group in terms of a search for the meaning of ageing and death. Participants are seen to be dealing with fundamental existential problems which are highly personal but subject to ideological forces beyond the individual.

The structural dimension focuses on age relations at the level of resources. Generational interests are expressed in the battle for the control of status and privilege at the level of the group rather than the individual, though ultimately social structure is transformed or sustained by personal strategies. At the end of the day it is the individual who acknowledges and responds to social forces.

The propositions emanating from these two perspectives are not incompatible. But they rest on philosophical positions which cannot be verified or falsified by reference to empirical research. Social scientists approach the study of ageing with a particular orientation to reality. Like the objects of their study they have an idea of what ageing is all about, an idea based on their own experience, intellectual training and philosophical outlook. The enterprise of gerontology benefits from the range theoretical perspectives. They form an integrated whole which fills out our understanding of the ageing process.

In this book a number of theoretical perspectives have been combined. Both of those mentioned above – the cultural and the structural – have been brought to bear on a wide range of substantive issues: friendship and sociability, health and illness, death and dying, socialisation and social control. What started as a personal interest in friendship and its place in the ageing process has developed into a broader enquiry. The focus has shifted from the sentiment which characterises dyadic relationships to the solidarity which binds together members of a group. The study of friendship has turned into a study of social processes in the peer group and, by extension, raised questions about the structure and culture of age relations. Answers to those questions lie beyond the limits of this analysis but deserve attention in the future.

The strong face of ageing

The view of old age expressed in these pages moves away from what Gutmann called the catastrophic position. Old age is not seen as the tragic extension of an active life. It is, instead, presented as a vigorous, even robust period. Age-related hardships call for a creative response. Old people – some at least – have shown that they are capable of active engagement with each other and with the present. The keen attachment of older people to traditional ways is not a sign of detachment so much as a creative response to the demand for change.

But the view presented here, though optimistic, does not rule out the possibility of suffering and decline. It does not belong in the camp of 'the Dr Feelgoods' who, according to Gutmann, deny the tragic implications of ageing and death. The signs from this study are that members of the peer group both support one another and preserve for one another the tragic sense of life. The position taken here is that growth is compatible with an acceptance of the finiteness of existence, partly because the individual is incorporated in the life of the group which collectively transcends time.

What we see in the old-age organisation is a manifestation of the strong face of ageing. In this setting, the old are powerful and independent, confident of themselves and their importance to each other. It is an unfamiliar image. The expansive and powerful face of old age is unfamiliar and unrecorded, partly because it occurs in private. The segregation of age groups in leisure activities means that these powers are not exposed to age-mixed audiences. The audience includes gerontologists too. Private behaviour is not amenable to conventional techniques of investigation and so gets overlooked in academic constructions of old age. Another reason for its obscurity is that this new assertiveness is more typical of old women than old men. Its existence has been obscured by the masculine bias in research on ageing. For various reasons, then, students of ageing have not looked for, and have not found, evidence of a vital and creative old age. The strong face of ageing is the weak front of gerontology.

Contemporary western culture does not give much scope for the expression of powers in old age. But an awareness of their existence may shift the balance so that the weak face of ageing with which we are more familiar eventually gives way.

Bibliography

Abrams, M. (1974) 'Attitudes of the retired and elderly', Manifesto Series no. 32, (Mitcham, England: Age Concern).

Abrams, M. (1978) *Beyond Three Score and Ten, Volume One,* (Mitcham, England: Age Concern).

Abrams, M. (1980) *Beyond Three Score and Ten, Volume Two,* (Mitcham, England: Age Concern).

Abrams, M. (1985) 'Demographic correlates of values', in M. Abrams et al., eds, *Values and Social Change in Britain,* (London: Macmillan).

Abrams, M., Gerard, D. and Timms, N. eds (1985) *Values and Social Change in Britain,* (London: Macmillan).

Acker, J. Barry, K. and Esseveld, J. (1981) 'Feminism, female friends and the reconstruction of intimacy', in H. Lopata and D. Maines, eds, *Research in the Interweave of Social Roles: Friendship,* (Greenwich, Connecticut: JAI Press)

Aguilar, J. (1981) 'Insider research: an ethnography of a debate', in D.A. Messerschmidt, ed., *Anthropologists at Home in North America,* (New York: Cambridge University Press).

Allan, G. (1977) 'Class variations in friendship patterns', *British Journal of Sociology* 28: 389–93.

Allan, G. (1979) *The Sociology of Kinship and Friendship,* (London: Allen & Unwin).

Allan, G. (1986) 'Friendship and care for elderly people', *Ageing and Society* 61: 1–12.

Alonzo, A. (1979) 'Everyday illness behaviour: a situational approach to health status deviations', *Social Science and Medicine* 13.

Ariès, P. (1981) *The Hour of Our Death,* (New York: A. Knopf).

Armstrong, J. (1988) 'Friendship support patterns of older women', *International Congress of Anthropological and Ethnological Sciences,* (Zagreb).

Asiel, M. (1987) 'Does loneliness have an impact on health and health care?', Paper given at the *International Association of Gerontology Conference,* (Brighton, England).

Babchuck, N. et al. (1979) 'The voluntary associations of the aged', *Journal of Gerontology* 34: 579–84.

Bankoff, E. (1981) 'Effects of friendship support on the psychological well-being of widows', in H. Lopata and D. Maines, eds, *Research in the Interweave of Social Roles: Friendship. Volume Two,* (Greenwich, Connecticut: JAI Press: pp. 109–39).

Barker, R.G. and Barker, S.L. (1963) in R.H. Williams et al., eds, *The Processes of Aging,* (New Jersey: Prentice Hall).

Beattie, J. (1964) *Other Cultures,* (London: Routledge & Kegan Paul).

Beauvoir, S. de (1977) *Old Age,* (London: Penguin).

Beckmann, J. and Olesen, H. (1988) 'The anxiety of the unknown – dying in a psycho-existential perspective', in A. and S. Gilmore, eds, *A Safer Death,* (London: Plenum Press).

Bengston, V.L. and Cutler, N. (1976) 'Generations and intergenerational relations', in R. Binstock and E. Shanas, eds, *Handbook of Aging and the Social Sciences,* (New York: Van Nostrand Reinhold).

Bengtson, V.L. and Kuypers, J.A. (1985) 'The family support cycle: psychosocial issues in the aging family', in J. Munnichs et al., eds, *Life-span and Change in a Gerontological Perspective,* (London and New York: Academic Press).

Berger, P., Berger, B. and Kellner, H. (1974) *The Homeless Mind,* (London: Penguin).

Bernard, J. (1976) 'Homosociality and female depression, *Journal of Social Issues* 32, 4: 213–38.

Beveridge, Lord W.H. and Wells, A.F. (1949) *The Evidence for Voluntary Action – Being Memoranda by Organisations and Individuals and Raw Material Relevant to Voluntary Action,* (London: George Allen & Unwin).

Biegel, D., Shore, B. and Gordon, E. (1984) *Building Support Networks for the Elderly,* (Beverly Hills: Sage).

Blau, P. (1964) *Exchange and Power in Social Life,* (New York: Wiley).

Blau, Z.S. (1961) 'Structural constraints on friendship in old age', *American Sociological Review* 26: 429–39.

Blau, Z.S. (1973) *Old Age in a Changing Society,* (New York: Franklin Watts).

Blauner, R. (1966) 'Death and social structure', *Psychiatry* 29: 378–94.

Blaxter, M. and Paterson, E. (1982) *Mothers and Daughters,* (London: Heinemann).

Bohannan, P. (1981) 'Unseen community: the natural history of a research project', in D.A. Messerschmidt, ed., *Anthropologists at Home in North America,* (New York: Cambridge University Press).

Bois, C du (1974) 'The gratuitous act: an introduction to the comparative study of friendship patterns', in E. Leyton, ed., *The Compact: Selected Dimensions of Friendship. Newfoundland Social and Economic Research Papers No 3,* (Toronto: University of Toronto Press).

Boissevain, J.F. (1974) *Friends of Friends,* (Oxford: Blackwell).

Bott, E. (1957) *Family and Social Network* (London: Tavistock).

Bourdieu, P. (1984) *Distinction: A Social Critique of the Judgement of Taste,* (London: Routledge & Kegan Paul).

Bowling, A. (1988) 'Risk factors with mortality among the elderly bereaved', in A. and S. Gilmore, eds, *A Safer Death,* (London: Plenum).

Brain, R. (1976) *Friends and Lovers,* (London: Hart Davis/MacGibbon).

Branson, N. and Heinemann, M. (1971) *Britain in the Nineteen Thirties,* (London: Weidenfeld & Nicolson).

Brown, A.S. (1974) 'Satisfying relationships for the elderly and their patterns of disengagement', *The Gerontologist* 14, 3: 258–62.

Butler, R. (1969) 'Ageism: another form of bigotry', *The Gerontologist* 9: 243–6.

Butler, R. (1978) 'Successful aging and the role of the life review', in S.H. Zarit, ed., *Readings in Aging and Death* (New York: Harper & Row).

Cantor, M. (1979) 'Neighbours and friends', *Research on Aging* 1, 4: 434–63.

Caplan, P. and Bujra, J., eds, (1978) *Women United, Women Divided,* (London: Tavistock).

Cartwright, A. et al. (1973) *Life Before Death,* (London: Routledge & Kegan Paul).

Christiansen, D. (1981) 'Dignity in aging', in C. Lefevre and P Lefevre, eds, *Aging and the Human Spirit,* (Chicago: Exploration Press).

Clark, M. (1969) 'Cultural values and dependency in later life', in R. Kalish, ed., *The Dependency of Old People,* Ann Arbor: (University of Michigan Press).

Clark, M. and Anderson, B. (1967) *Culture and Aging,* (Illinois: C. Thomas).

Cohen, A. (1969a) *Custom and Politics in Urban Africa,* (London: Routledge & Kegan Paul).

Cohen, A. (1969b) 'Political anthropology: the analysis of the symbolism of power relations', *Man* 4, 2: 215–35.

Cohen, A. (1971) 'The politics of ritual secrecy', *Man* (NS) 6: 427–48.

Cohen, A. (1974 *Two Dimensional Man*, (London: Routledge & Kegan Paul).

Coleman, P. (1988) 'Attitudes to life and social change – points from 10-year longitudinal case studies', Paper given at *International Congress of Anthropological and Ethnological Sciences*, (Zagreb).

Coleman, P. and McCulloch, A. (1985) 'The study of psychological change in later life', in J. Munnichs, P. Mussen, E. Olbrich and P. Coleman, eds, *Lifespan and Change in a Gerontological Perspective*, (California: Academic Press).

Collett, L. J. and Lester, D. (1969) 'The fear of death and the fear of dying', *Journal of Psychology* 72: 179–81.

Coni, N.K. (1983) 'University of the Third Age', *Geriatric Medicine* March 1983: 201–4.

Copeland, J R M , Kelleher, M.J., Smith, A.M.R. and Devlin, P. (1986) 'The well, the mentally ill, the old and the old old: a community survey of elderly persons in London', *Ageing and Society* 6: 417–33.

Craney, M. (1985) 'Interpersonal support and health of older people', in W. Peterson and J. Quadagno, eds, *Social Bonds in Later Life*, (California: Sage).

Creech, J. and Babchuk, N. (1985) 'Affectivity and the interweave of social circles', in W. Peterson and J. Quadagno, eds, *Social Bonds in Later Life*, (California: Sage).

Crick, M. (1982) 'Anthropological field research, meaning creation and knowledge construction', in D. Parkin, ed., *Semantic Anthropology*, (London: Academic Press).

Cutler, S.J. (1976) 'Age differences in voluntary association membership;', *Social Focus* 55: 43–58.

Diggory, J.C. and Rothman, D.Z. (1961) 'Values destroyed by death', *Journal of Abnormal and Social Psychology* 43: 205–10.

Dixey, M. and Talbot, S. (1982) *Women, Leisure and Bingo*, (Leeds: Trinity and All Saints College).

Dono et al. (1979) 'Primary groups in old age', *Research on Aging* 1, 4: 403–33.

Dowd, J. (1975) 'Aging as exchange: a preface to theory', *Journal of Gerontology* 30, 5: 584–94.

Dowd, J. (1980) *Stratification amongst the aged*, (Monterey: Brooks/Cole)

Dowd, J. (1983) 'Social exchange and old people', in J. Sokolovsky, ed., *Growing Old in Different Cultures*, (Belmont: Wadsworth).

Dowd, J. (1984) 'Benificence and the aged', *Journal of Gerontology* 39: 102–8.

Duck, S. (1983) *Friends for Life*, (Brighton: Harvester Press).

Eckert, K. (1980) *The Unseen Elderly* (San Diego: Campanile Press).

Eisenstadt, S.N. (1956) *From Generation to Generation*, (Glencoe: Free Press).

Elias, N. (1985) *The Loneliness of the Dying*, (Oxford: Blackwell).

Equal Opportunities Commission (1980) *The Experience of Caring for Elderly and Handicapped Dependants: A Survey Report*, (London: HMSO).

Evers, H. (1983) 'Elderly women and disadvantage: perceptions of daily life and support relationships', in D. Jerrome, ed., *Ageing in Modern Society*, (London: Croom Helm).

Family Policy Studies Centre (1988) *An Ageing Population*, FPSC Fact Sheet 2.

Featherstone, M. (1987) 'Leisure, symbolic power and the life course', in J. Horne, D. Jary, and A. Tomlinson, eds, *Sport, Leisure and Social Relations*, (Keele: Sociological Review Monograph No. 33).

Fennell, V.I. (1981) 'Friendship and kinship in older women's organisations', in C. Fry et al. *Dimensions: Aging, Culture and Health*, (New York: J.F. Bergin).

Finch, J. (1984) 'It's great to have someone to talk to: the ethics and politics of interviewing women', in C. Bell and H. Roberts, eds, *Social*

Researching: Politics, Problems, Practice, (London: Routledge & Kegan Paul).

Fischer, C.S. et al. (1977) *Networks and Places: Social Relations in the Urban Setting,* (New York: Free Press).

Fiske, M. and Chiriboga, D. (1985) 'The inter-weaving of societal and personal change in adulthood', in J. Munnichs et al., *Lifespan and Change in a Gerontological Perspective,* (California: Academic Press).

Ford, G. (1985) 'Illness behaviour in old age', in K. Dean et al., eds, *Self Care and Health in Old Age,* (London: Croom Helm).

Francis, D. (1981) 'Adaptive strategies of the elderly in England and Ohio', in C. Fry et al., *Dimensions: Aging, Culture and Health,* (New York: J. F. Bergin).

Francis, D., (1984) *Will you still need me, will you still feed me, when I'm 84?* (Bloomington: Indiana University Press).

Fry, C. (1980) *Aging in Culture and Society,* (New York: Praeger).

Fry, C. and Keith, J. (1980) *New Methods for Old Age Research,* (Chicago: Loyola University Press).

Gavron, H. (1966) *The Captive Wife,* (London: Routledge & Kegan Paul).

Gay, F. (n.d.) *The Friendship Book,* 1985 (London: D.C. Thompson).

Gerard, D. (1985) 'Religious attitudes and values', in M. Abrams, D. Gerrard and N. Timms, eds, *Values and Social Change in Britain,* (London: Macmillan).

Glaser, R.G. and Strauss, A.L. (1968) *Time for Dying,* (Chicago: Aldine).

Gordon, C. Gaitz, C., and Scott, J. (1976) 'Leisure and lives: personal expressivity across the lifespan', in R. Binstock and E. Shanas, eds, *Handbook of Aging and the Social Sciences* (New York: Van Nostrand Reinhold).

Gorer, G. (1965) *Death, Grief and Mourning in Contemporary Britain,* (New York: Doubleday).

Gouldner, A.W. (1960) 'The norm of reciprocity', in *American Sociological Review,* 25: 161–78.

Gouldner, A.W. (1966) 'The norm of reciprocity', in B.J. Biddle and E. Thomas, eds, *Role Theory: concepts and Research,* (New York: Wiley).

Grant, V.J. (1986) *Day Centres for the Elderly,* (Auckland: Benton Ross).

Grant, V.J. (1988) 'Return to the community: a way back for isolated and depressed elderly people', Paper given at International Congress of Anthropological and Ethnological Sciences, (Zagreb).

Gray, M. and Wilcock, G. (1981) *Our Elders,* (Oxford: Oxford University Press).

Gubrium, J. (1975) *Living and Dying at Murray Manor,* (New York: St Martin's Press).

Gutmann, D. (1977) 'The cross-cultural perspective: Notes towards a comparative psychology of aging', in J. Birren and K. Warner Schaie, eds, *A Handbook of the Psychology of the Aging,* (New York: Van Nostrand Reinhold).

Gutmann, D. (1987) *Reclaimed Powers: Towards a New Psychology of Men and Women in later Life,* (New York: Basic Books).

Guttsman, W.L. (1963) *The British Political Elite,* (London: MacGibbon).

Hareven, T. (1982) 'The lifecourse and ageing in historical perspective', in T. Hareven and K. Adams, eds, *Ageing and Life Course Transitions,* (London: Tavistock).

Hareven, T. and Adams, K. (1982) *Ageing and Life Course Transitions,* (London: Tavistock).

Harris, C.C. (1975) 'The process of social ageing', Unpublished Ph.D. thesis, (Swansea: University of Wales).

Harris, C.C. (1983) 'Associational participation in old age', in D. Jerrome, ed., *Ageing in Modern Society,* (London: Croom Helm).

Harrison, B. (1975) 'Camden old age pensioners', in D. Jones and M.

Mayo, eds, *Community Work Two,* (London: Routledge & Kegan Paul).

Hazan, H. (1980) *The Limbo People,* (London: Routledge & Kegan Paul).

Hazan, H. (1981) 'Totality as an adaptive strategy: two case studies of the management of powerlessness', *Social Analysis* 2: 63–76.

Hazan, H. (1984) 'Religion in an old age home: symbolic adaptation as a survival strategy', *Ageing and Society* 4, 2: 137–56.

Hazan, H. (1988) '"Course" versus "cycle": on the understanding of understanding aging', *Journal of Aging Studies* 2, 1: 1–11.

Hearnden, R. and Fujishin, B. (1974) *Members of Old People's Clubs: Needs and Services, a Survey in West Bromwich,* Centre for Urban and Regional Studies, Research Memorandum 35, University of Birmingham.

Hellebrandt, F A (1980) 'Aging among the advantaged', *The Gerontologist* 20, 4: 404–17.

Hendricks, J. and Hendricks, C.D. (1977) *Aging in Mass Society,* (Cambridge, Mass: Winthrop).

Hepworth, M. and Featherstone, M. (1986) 'Distinction, life style and the ageing body', *British Sociological Association Conference,* (Loughborough, England. Unpublished).

Herzlich, C. (1973) *Health and Illness,* (London: Academic Press).

Hess, B. (1972) 'Friendship', in M.W. Riley, M. Johnson and A. Foner, eds, *Ageing and Society, Volume Three: A Sociology of Age Stratification,* (New York · Russell Sage Foundation).

Hess, B. (1979) 'Sex roles, friendship and the life course', *Research on Aging* 1: 494–515.

Hinton, J. (1974) 'The organisational and social implications of death and dying', *Fourth International Conference on Social Science and Medicine,* (Denmark, Unpublished).

Hochschild, A.R. (1973) *The Unexpected Community,* (New Jersey: Prentice Hall).

Hockey, J. (1983) 'Just a song at twilight: residents' coping strategies expressed in musical form', in D. Jerrome, ed., *Ageing in Modern Society,* (London: Croom Helm).

Hockey, J. (1985) 'Cultural and social interpretations of dying and death in a residential home for elderly people in the north east of England', *Curare,* 4/85: 35–43.

Hockey, J. (1989) 'Residential care and the maintenance of social identity', in M. Jefferys, ed., *Growing Old in the Twentieth Century,* (London: Routledge).

Hockey, J. (1991) *Experiences of Death,* (Edinburgh: Edinburgh University Press).

Holy, L. (1984) 'Theory, methodology and the research process', in R.F. Ellen, ed., *Ethnographic Research,* (London: Academic Press).

Hornum, B. (1983) 'The elderly in British new towns', in J. Sokolovsky, ed., *Growing Old in Different Cultures,* (Belmont: Wadsworth).

Hornum, B. (1987) 'Depressing fears, negative referencing and social distance among the elderly at Summer Hill, a life care community in the United States', Paper given at the *International Association of Gerontology Conference,* (Brighton, England).

Hornum, B. (1988) 'Elderly women in an age segregated community: gender issues', Paper given at the *International Congress of Anthropological and Ethnological Sciences,* (Zagreb).

Huyck, M.H. (1974) *Growing older,* (Spectrum: USA).

Itzin, C. (1986) 'Ageism awareness training', in C. Phillipson, ed., *Dependency and Interdependency in Old Age,* (London: Croom Helm).

Jacoby, A. (1966) 'Personal influence and primary relationships: their effect on associational membership', *Sociological Quarterly* 7: 76–84.

Jefferys, M. (1987) 'Prospects for a healthy old age', Unpublished paper given at the *International Association of Gerontology Conference*, (Brighton: England).

Jerrome, D. (1973) *Continuity and Change in the Social Organisation of the Ibos in London*, (Unpublished Ph.D. thesis, University of London).

Jerrome, D. (1974) 'Ibos in London: a case study in social accommodation', *New Community* 3, 1–2: 175–97.

Jerrome, D. (1979) 'Conflict and collusion in a Nigerian community abroad', *Women's Studies International Quarterly* 2: 421–37

Jerrome, D. (1981) 'The significance of friendship for women in later life', *Ageing and Society* 1, 2: 175-97

Jerrome, D. (1983) 'Lonely women in a friendship club', *British Journal of Guidance and Counselling 11 1:* 10–20.

Jerrome, D. (1984) 'Good Company: the sociological implications of friendship', *Sociological Review* 32, 4: 696-718.

Jerrome, D. (1986) 'Me Darby, you Joan', in C. Phillipson, ed., *Dependency and Interdependency in Old Age*, (London: Croom Helm).

Jerrome, D. (1989) 'Virtue and vicissitude: the role of old people's clubs', in M. Jefferys, ed., *Growing Old in the Twentieth Century*, (London: Routledge).

Jerrome, D. (1990) 'Intimate relationships', in J. Bond and P. Coleman, eds, *Ageing in Britain: an Introduction to Social Gerontology*, (London: Sage).

Johnson, F. and Aries, A. (1983) 'The talk of women friends', *Women's Studies International Forum* 6 4: 351–61.

Jones, D. (1980) 'Gossip' *Women's Studies International Forum* 3: 139–98.

Jones, D., Victor, C. and Vetter, N. (1985) 'The problem of loneliness in the elderly in the community', *Journal of the Royal College of General Practitioners* 35 272: 136–9.

Jones, S. (1980) 'Education for the second half of life', in N. Dickson, ed., *Living in the Eighties*, (Mitcham, England: Age Concern).

Jones, S. (1986) 'The elders: a new generation', in *Ageing and Society* 6, 3: 313–31.

Kalish, R. (1976) 'Death and dying in a social context', in R. Binstock and E. Shanas, eds, *Handbook of Aging and the Social Sciences*, (New York: Van Nostrand Reinhold).

Kart, C. and Longino, C.F. (1987) 'The support systems of older people', *Journal of Aging Studies* 1, 3: 239-52.

Keith, J. (1980a) 'Old age and community creation', in C. Fry ed., *Aging in Culture and Society*, (New York: Praeger).

Keith J. (1980b) 'Participant observation', in C. Fry and J. Keith, eds, *New Methods for Old Age Research*, (Chicago: Center for Urban Policy, Loyola University).

Keith, J. (1982) *Old People as People*, (Boston and Toronto: Little & Brown).

Keith, J. (1983) 'Age and informal interaction', in J. Sokolvsky, ed., *Growing Old in Different Cultures*, (Belmont: Wadsworth).

Keith-Ross, J. (1977) *Old People, New Lives*, (Chicago: Chicago University Press).

Kertzer, D.I. (1983) 'Generation as a sociological problem', *Annual Review of Sociology* 9: 125–49.

Kuypers, J.A. and Bengtson, V.L. (1976) 'Social breakdown and competence: a normal model of aging', in B.D. Bell, ed., *Contemporary Social Gerontology*, (Illinois: C. Thomas).

Lake, T. (1980) *Loneliness*, (London: Sheldon Press)

Lakoff, R. (1975) *Language and Women's Place*, (New York: Harper & Row).

Lambeck, M. (1988) 'Exchange cycles and the experience of aging in the constitution and decline of the civic arena in Mayothe', Paper given at the *International*

Congress of Anthropological and Ethnological Sciences, (Zagreb)

Lasch, C. (1978) The Culture of Narcissism: American Life in an Age of Diminishing Expectations, (New York: Norton Press).

Laslett, P. (1984) 'The education of the elderly in Britain', in E. Midwinter, ed., *Mutual Aid Universities*, (London: Croom Helm).

Legesse, A. (1979) 'Age sets and retirement communities', in *Anthropological Quarterly* 52, 1: 61–9.

Lehr, U. (1987) 'Psychophysical well-being and patterns of social participation in old age', *International Association of Gerontology Conference*, (Brighton, England).

Lemon, B., Bengtson, V. and Peterson, J. (1976) 'An explanation of the activity theory of aging: activity types and life satisfaction among in-movers to a retirement community', in B. Bell, ed., *Contemporary Social Gerontology*, (Springfield: C. Thomas).

Leninger, M. (1988) 'The concept of care', Paper given at the *International Congress of Anthropological and Ethnological Sciences*, (Zagreb).

Littlejohn, J. (1963) *Westrigg*, (London: Routledge & Kegan Paul).

Litwak, E. and Szelenyi, I. (1969) 'Primary group structures and their functions: kin, neighbours and friends', *American Sociological Review* 34, 4: 465–72.

Lopata, H. (1975) 'Couple companionate relations in marriage and widowhood', in N. Glazer-Malbin, ed., *Old Family / New Family*, (New York: Van Nostrand Reinhold).

Lopata, H. and Maines, D. (1981) *Research in the Interweave of Social Roles: Friendship, Volume Two*, (Greenwich, Connecticut: JAI Press)

Lowenthal, M. and Haven, C. (1968) 'Interaction and adaptation: intimacy as a critical variable', *American Sociological Review* 33: 20–30.

Lowenthal, M. and Robinson B. (1976) 'Social networks and isolation', in R. Binstock and E. Shanas, eds, *Handbook of Aging and the Social Sciences*, (New York: Van Nostrand Reinhold)

Lupton, T. and Wilson, C.S. (1959) 'The social background and connections of top decision makers', *The Manchester School* 27: 30–51.

Malinowski, B. (1922) *Argonauts of the Western Pacific*, (London: Routledge & Kegan Paul).

Mannheim, K. (1952) 'The problem of generations', in K. Mannheim, ed., *Essays on the Sociology of Knowledge*, (New York: Oxford University Press).

Marshall, V. ed. (1986) *Later Life*, (London: Sage).

Matthews, S. (1979) *The Social World of Old Women*, (California: Sage).

Matthews, S. (1983) 'Definitions of friendship and their consequences in old age', *Ageing and Society* 3, 2: 141–56.

Matthews, S. (1986) 'Friendship in old age: biography and circumstance', in V. Marshall, ed., *Later Life*, (London: Sage).

Maxwell, E. (1986) 'Finding out: resource control and cross-cultural patterns of deference', *Journal of Cross-cultural Gerontology* 1, 1: 73–89.

McCall, G.T. and Simmons, S.L. (1969) *Issues in Participant Observation*, (Cambridge, Mass: Addison-Wesley).

McCulloch, A. (1986) 'Social change and elderly people', *Generations* 3.

Mogey, J.M. (1956) *Family and Neighbourhood: Two Studies in Oxford*, (Oxford: Oxford University Press).

Munnichs, J.M.A., Mussen, P., Olbrich, E. and Coleman, P., eds, (1985) *Lifespan and Change in a Gerontological Perspective*, (California: Academic Press).

Murphy, E. (1982) 'Social origins of depression in old age', *British Journal of Psychiatry* 141: 135–42.

Murphy, E. (1987) 'Excess mortality in late-life depression', Paper given at the

International Association of Gerontology Conference, (Brighton, England).

Musgrove, C. (1974) *Ecstasy and Holiness: Counterculture and the Open Society,* (London: Methuen).

Myerhoff, B. (1978) *Number Our Days,* (New York: Simon & Schuster).

Myerhoff, B. (1984) 'Rites and signs of ripening: the intertwining of ritual time and growing older', in D. Kertzer and J. Keith, eds, *Age and Anthropological Theory,* (London: Cornell University Press).

Myerhoff, B. and Simic, A. (1978) *Life's Career: Aging,* (California: Sage).

Neugarten, B. and Hagestad, G. (1976) 'Age and life course', in R. Binstock and E. Shanas, eds, *Handbook of Aging and the Social Sciences* (New York: Van Nostrand Reinhold).

Nydegger, C. (1980) 'Age and life-course transitions', in C. Fry and J. Keith, eds, *New Methods for Old Age Research,* (Chicago: Loyola University Press).

Nydegger, C. and Mitteness, L. (1983) 'Experiencing social generations', *Research on Aging* 5, 4: 527–46.

O'Laughlin, K. (1983) 'The final challenge: facing death', in E. Markson, ed., *Older Women,* (Lexington, Kentucky: Lexington Books).

Olsen, T. (1980) *Tell me a Riddle,* (London: Virago Press).

Packard, V. (1959) *The Status Seekers,* (New York: MacKay).

Pahl, R.E. (1971) 'A sociological portrait: friends and associates', *New Society* 18: 980–2.

Paine, R. (1970) 'Anthropological approaches to friendship', *Humanitas* 6: 139–59.

Paine, R. (1974) 'Anthropological approaches to friendship', in E. Leyton, ed., *The Compact: Selected Dimensions of Friendship* Newfoundland Social and Economic Papers No. 3, (Toronto: Toronto University Press).

Pelto, P.J. and Pelto, G.H. (1978) *Anthropological Research: the Structure of Enquiry,* (Cambridge: Cambridge University Press).

Phillipson, C. (1982) *Capitalism and the Construction of Old Age,* (London: Macmillan).

Pifer, A. (1987) Lecture to the *Royal Society of Arts,* (London: 4 February 1987).

Plath, D.W. (1982) 'Resistance at forty eight: old age brinkmanship and Japanese life course pathways', in T. Hareven and K. Adams, eds, *Ageing and Life-Course Transitions,* (London: Tavistock).

Pleck, J. (1975) 'Man to man: is brotherhood possible?' in N. Glazer-Malbin, ed., *Old Family / New Family,* (New York: Van Nostrand Reinhold).

Pohjolainen, P. (1987) 'Social participation among retired people', Unpublished paper given at European Section of the *International Association of Gerontology,* (Brighton, England).

Powers, E. and Bultena, G. (1976) 'Sex differences in intimate friendships in old age', *Journal of Marriage and the Family* 38, 4: 739–47.

Robinson, D. (1971) *The Process of Becoming Ill,* (London: Routledge & Kegan Paul).

Rose, A.M. (1960) 'The impact of aging on voluntary associations', in C. Tibbitts, ed., *Handbook of Social Gerontology,* (Chicago: Chicago University Press).

Rose, A.M. (1965) 'Group consciousness among the aging', in A.M. Rose and W.A. Paterson, eds, *Older People and their Social World,* Philadelphia.

Rosow, I. (1967) *The Social Integration of the Aged,* (New York: Free Press).

Rosow, I. (1970) 'Old people: their friends and neighbours', *American Behavioural Scientist* 14: 569.

Rosow, I. (1975) *Socialization to Old Age,* (California University Press).

Rosow, I. (1976) 'Status and role change through the life span', in R. Binstock and E. Shanas, eds, *Handbook of Aging and the Social Sciences,* (New York: Van

Nostrand Reinhold).

Saifullah-Kahn, V. (1976) 'Purdah in the British situation', in D.L. Barker and S. Allen, eds, *Dependence and Exploitation in Work and Marriage*, (London: Longman).

Salmond, A. (1982) 'Theoretical landscapes: on cross-cultural conceptions of knowledge', in D. Parkin, ed., *Semantic Anthropology*, (London: Academic Press).

Sarsby J. (1984) 'Special problems of fieldwork in familiar settings', in R. Ellen, ed., *Ethnographic Research*, (London: Academic Press).

Seiden, A. and Bart, P. (1975) 'Woman to woman', in N. Glazer-Malbin, ed., *Old Family / New Family* (New York: Van Nostrand Reinhold).

Simenon, G. (1972) *The Cat. Ninth Omnibus Edition*, (London: Penguin).

Smith, D. (1977) 'Some implications of a sociology for women', in N. Glazer and H. Wacher, eds, *Women in a Man-Made World*, (Chicago: Rand McNally).

Sokolovsky, J. (1980) 'Network methodologies in the study of aging', in C. Fry and J. Keith, eds, *New Methods for Old Age Research*, (Chicago: Loyola University Press).

Sokolovsky, J. and Cohen, C. (1978) 'The cultural meaning of personal networks for the inner city elderly', *Urban Anthropology* 7: 323–42.

Spencer, P. (1987) 'Anthropology and theories of age in society', (University of London, School of African and Oriental Studies, mimeo).

Spender, D. (1980) *Man Made Language*, (London: Routledge & Kegan Paul).

Spradley, J. (1980) *Participant Observation*, (New York: Holt, Reinhart and Winston).

Stephens, J.B. (1976) *Loners, Losers and Lovers*, (Seattle: University of Washington Press).

Stevenson, J. (1984) *British Society 1914–45*, (London: Allen Lane).

Streib, G. (1976) 'Social stratification and aging', in R. Binstock and E. Shanas, eds, *Handbook of aging and the Social Sciences*, (New York: Van Nostrand Reinhold).

Svanorg, A. (1987) 'Prospects for a healthy old age', Plenary paper presented at the *International Association of Gerontology Conference*, (Brighton, England).

Taietz, P. (1976) 'Two conceptual models of the senior center', *Journal of Gerontology* 31: 219–22.

Taylor, H. (1983) 'The hospice concept and the National Health Service', in D. Jerrome, ed., *Ageing in Modern Society*, (London: Croom Helm).

Taylor, R. and Ford, G. (1981) 'Lifestyle and ageing', in *Ageing and Society* 1, 3: 329–46.

Taylor, R. and Ford, G. (1983) 'Inequalities in old age', in *Ageing and Society* 3, 2: 183–208.

Thane, P. (1987) 'Economic burden or benefit? A positive view of old age', *London Centre for Economic Policy*, (Research Discussion Paper).

Timaeus, I.M. (1986) 'Family and households of the elderly population: prospects for those approaching old age', *Ageing and Society* 6, 3.

Tomlinson, A. (1979) *Leisure and the Role of Clubs and Voluntary Groups*, (Brighton: Brighton Polytechnic).

Townsend, P. (1963) *The Family Life of Old People*, (London: Penguin).

Trela, J.E. (1976) 'Social class and association membership: an analysis of age-graded and non-age-graded voluntary association participation', *Journal of Gerontology* 31: 198–203.

Troll, L. and Smith, J. (1976) 'Attachment through the lifespan', *Human Development* 19: 156–70.

Unruh, D. (1983) *Invisible Lives*, (California: Sage).

Van Der Veen, K.W. (1988) 'Social support for the aged in cross-cultural perspective: a comparison of the Indian and Dutch case', Paper given at the *International Congress of Anthropological and Ethnological Sciences*, (Zagreb).

Veblen, T. (1962) *The Theory of the Leisure Class*, (New York: Mentor) (first published 1899).

Verbrugge, L.M. (1977) 'The structure of adult friendship choices', *Social Forces* 56: 576–97.

Vesperi, M. (1985) *City of Green Benches*, (Ithaca: Cornell University Press).

Victor, C. (1987) *Old Age in Modern Society*, (London: Croom Helm).

Ward, R.A. (1979) 'The meaning of voluntary association participation to older people' *Journal of Gerontology* 34: 438–45.

Wenger, C. (1983) 'Loneliness: a problem of measurement', in D. Jerrome, ed., *Ageing in Modern Society*, (London: Croom Helm).

Wenger, G. C. (1984) *The Supportive Network*, (London: Allen & Unwin).

Wenger, G.C. (1987) 'The special role of friends and neighbours' Paper given to the *International Association of Gerontology*, (Brighton, England).

Wentowski, G. (1981) 'Reciprocity and the coping strategies of older people', *The Gerontologist* 21, 6: 600–9.

White, E.G.(1965) *Clubs for the Elderly*, (London: National Old People's Welfare Council).

White, E.G. (n.d.) *The Over-Sixties Club and the Community*, (London: National Council of Social Services).

Whyte, W.F. (1955) *Street Corner-Society*, (Chicago: Chicago University Press).

Williams, I. (1979) *The Care of the Elderly in the Community*, (London: Croom Helm).

Williams, R. (1980) 'Illness in old age: a new approach', in M. Johnson, ed., *Transitions in Middle and Later Life*, (London: British Society of Gerontology).

Williams, R. (1986) 'Images of age and generation', Unpublished paper given to *British Sociological Association Conference*, (Loughborough).

Willmott, P. (1987) *Friendship Networks and Social Support*, (London: Policy Studies Institute).

Willmott, P. and Young, M. (1960) *Family and Class in a London Suburb*, (London: Routledge & Kegan Paul).

Wilson, E. (1980) *Only Half Way to Paradise: Women in Post War Britain 1945–68*, (London: Tavistock).

Wolf, E. (1966) 'Kinship, friendship and patron-client relations in complex societies', in M. Barton, ed., *The Social Anthropology of Complex Societies*, (London: Tavistock).

Yates, P. (1985) 'Science and sensibility', (University of Sussex, mimeo).

Index

activity
    principle, 11, 132, 135–6, 139–41, 143, 144–5, 191–4
    theory, 13–14
age categories, 5, 135, 147
Age Concern
    clubs, 35–6, 43, 49, 173–80, 186–7
    Research Department, 17–18
ageism, 31, 176
Aguilar, 31
alienation, 153, 158–9
    see also anomie
Allan, 107–9
anomie, 100
    see also alienation
Ariès, 122
attachment, 58, 191–3, 198

Babchuk, 14
Bates, 14
bereavement, 9, 123–6, 127, 184
    see also death; loss
bingo, 36, 44, 47, 80, 81, 95–6, 168
biographical approach, 7, 21–2, 144
Boissevain, 73, 74, 85
Bourdieu, 157
British Association of Social
    Anthropologists in Policy and
    Practice, 188

Cartwright, 126
Cohen, 156–7
Coleman, 23, 159
courtship, vii
    see also marriage

death, 9, 16, 43, 46, 54, 69–70, 90, 106, 108–9, 111–29, 171, 186, 190, 195
dependency, 16, 78, 92, 98, 109–10, 144, 148, 157
depression, see mental health
disability, 49, 93–4, 95–7, 103
    see also ill-health
Dowd, 77, 136

Elias, 112–13
ethnicity, 45, 51, 126–9
exchange, 16, 40–1, 44, 56–7, 59, 76–7, 81–2, 136, 157, 177–8

family relationships, 20, 42, 44, 48, 55, 57, 66, 98, 120, 122, 125, 138, 147, 150–1, 167, 168
    metaphorical, 54, 67, 175, 186–7
    see also kinship
Featherstone, 157
Ford, 20
frailty, see ill-health
Francis, 24–5
friendship, xii, 2, 8–9, 45, 49, 53, 55–6, 64–5, 72–92, 93, 97, 98–101, 104–5, 106–10, 111, 120–1, 122, 125–6, 146, 156, 167, 168, 169, 174–5, 178, 180–6, 195
    networks, 16, 22, 39–40, 88, 146, 174, 185
    rituals, 50
    study of, xii, 21–2, 73–6

gender, 4, 6, 18, 21, 44–5, 60–3, 65–6, 68–9, 77–9, 83, 135, 152, 198
generations, 10, 50, 58; 61–2, 70, 135, 147–60, 166-7, 168, 190–1, 194, 196
generativity, 158
Glaser, 113
Gorer, 122, 123
Grant, 184–6
Gray Panthers, 17, 143, 196
Gubrium, 93, 127
Gutmann, 3, 11, 21, 64–5, 197–8

Harris, 15–16, 21
Hazan, 126–7
health, 17, 41, 82, 93, 96, 103, 106–7, 137, 144, 168, 189
    see also ill-health
Hepworth, 157
Herzlich, 103–4
Hess, 74–5, 78
Hinton, 113, 124
Hochschild, 6, 81, 127, 146
Hockey, 24, 50–1, 102, 127–8
hospice, 115, 125, 159
humour, 45, 48, 81, 91, 94–5, 177

identity, 23, 51, 53, 80, 87, 92, 104, 123, 128, 142–3, 146–7, 149, 181, 189, 190–1, 194, 196
ill-health, 9, 12, 20 53, 57, 61, 83, 93, 110, 130, 140, 144, 153, 182–3, 184, 190, 192